A History of East Africa

A History of East Africa

E. S. Atieno Odhiambo
T. I. Ouso
J. F. M. Williams

Longman

LONGMAN GROUP UK LIMITED
LONDON
Associated companies, branches and
representatives throughout the world

First published 1977
Tenth impression 1994

ISBN 0 582 60886 4

Filmset by Keyspools Ltd, Golborne, Lancs
Printed in Hong Kong
CPP/10

Acknowledgements

The publishers are indebted to the following for their help and permission to reproduce photographs:

British Institute in East Africa: figs 1.4, 3.2(a); British Library: figs 17.3, 20.4, 20.6; British Museum: fig. 10.6; Camera & Pen International: fig. 6.1; Camera Press Ltd: figs 6.3, 6.4; Church Missionary Society: figs 7.1, 7.3(b), 11.5(a), 12.2, 12.6, 14.3; N. Chittick: fig. 3.2(b); Bruce Coleman Ltd: figs 3.5(a), 8.1, 10.3; Dept. of Antiquities, Lagos: fig. 14.5; East African Railways Board: figs 14.1, 15.5, 16.6; Elliott and Fry: fig. 14.4; Mary Evans Picture Library: figs 3.6, 5.3, 11.2; Werner Forman Archive: figs 3.3, 3.4, 10.2, 10.4; Historical Picture Service: fig. 9.3; Illustrated London News: fig. 11.4; Kenya Information Services: fig. 6.2; R. E. Leakey: figs 1.2, 1.3, 1.5; The Mansell Collection: figs 2.1, 11.5(b), 12.4, 13.2, 14.2, 15.3(b);

Paul Popper Ltd: figs 7.6, 14.6, 15.1, 15.2, 15.3(a), 15.4, 15.6, 15.7, 16.1, 16.3, 16.4, 16.5, 17.1, 17.2, 19.1, 19.3, 19.4, 19.5, 19.6, 19.7, 20.2, 20.3, 20.5; Radio Times Hulton Picture Library: figs 1.1, 10.1, 10.5, 11.1, 11.3, 12.5, 12.8, 13.1, 16.2(b), 17.4, 19.2; Royal Commonwealth Society: fig. 7.2; Tanzania Information Services: figs 9.1, 9.5, 21.1; Professor Fergus B. Wilson: figs 4.1, 6.5, 8.4, 10.8, 21.2, 21.3; Zambia Information Services: figs 9.1, 9.5, 12.3, 21.1.

Cover Photograph was kindly supplied by Werner Forman Archive.

The publishers regret that they have been unable to trace the copyright owners of the following photographs, and would like to apologise for any infringement of copyright caused: 3.1, 3.5(a), 5.1, 5.2, 7.4, 9.4, 13.3, 16.2(a), 10.7, 12.1, 12.9.

Contents

Preface

One of the chords that bind us together in Eastern Africa is that of history. We do share a common heritage. Our present communities have been forged out of the migrations of various groups of people. The striking phenomenon over the last two thousand years is that of people from different directions—east, west, north and south, coming together to make Eastern Africa their new home. In this process of emergence, neighbours have learnt to live together, to borrow ideas from one another, to accommodate new styles and new ways of doing things. In short, the people living in this part of Africa have demonstrated that they are part and parcel of mankind struggling against their environment. This theme of struggle, experimentation, of triumph, also of failure, is one of the salient ones we seek to bring out in this book.

Secondly, and related to the first, we want to suggest the *newness* of the respective ethnic communities, more popularly known as tribes, in this region. Human history stretches over thousands of years. Many East African 'tribes' are only two to three hundred years old in their present forms. And even in their present forms, they are an amalgam of past histories. Therefore, there is in fact a need to emphasize, in our present stage of development, the fact that we are new peoples who should therefore open up to embrace new experiences. That way, we may speed up the cultural, spiritual unity that is such a desirable goal for the future.

The colonial situation brought with it new challenges to our societies. African initiative played a major role in the process of fighting colonialism. That initiative was not new. It was the heritage of our two thousand years of history. It must continue to assert itself in the struggle to face the challenges of the future. Initiative is therefore a necessary weapon in facing up to the challenges of environment.

The writing of history represents an aspect of this initiative. For the writing of history involves a deliberate selection of issues which were important in the making of societies. A book of this nature is an attempt to present a careful, thoughtful, considered interpretation. It draws from the opinions, researches, and writings of others. It therefore aims at providing the reader with an up-to-date assessment of East African History. We have kept the story simple, and sought to emphasize the major ideas that have been advanced by practising historians of this area. It should thus provide a sound introduction to East African history.

This book is primarily intended for the student. It is however not a short-cut to success. It is hoped that it will inspire the reader to further study and discussion, in class and outside. Only in this way can a clear picture of our history emerge. We therefore urge both the students and the teachers to participate in the learning process. Without this participation history cannot be lively. And one of the justifications for the teaching and learning of history in Africa is that it provides an opportunity for lively reflection and comment.

Dr Atieno Odhiambo

Nairobi,
April, 1976.

List of Maps

Chapter 1
The sources of East African History and the evolution of Man

Introduction

Our subject is the history of man in East Africa from his origins to the present. But since this covers a period of several million years we can only concentrate on the major developments in the growth of societies and cultures; of how men came to live together in communities and evolved their own political and social institutions. We shall also attempt to show how and why changes in these societies have taken place. Before doing so, we shall look briefly in this first chapter at the way in which man first developed as a species, distinct from the apes and other primates, and then at the principal sources for East African history.

The origins of Man in Africa

Man is a primate, as are gorillas and chimpanzees. The fossil remains of primates dating back thirty million years have been found in East Africa. It is now generally accepted that East Africa is a most important area in the study of the evolution of Man: the long and gradual process by which Man developed into an erect being, capable of thinking and of transmitting his ideas to his fellow human beings through the medium first of speech and later in the form of print and art. All of this took millions of years, as is indicated in the chart on page 5.

First, Man developed an erect posture by adapting his feet and legs to enable him to stand and walk upright. This two-legged, or bipedal position, enabled him to see further, to look over tall grass and vegetation, and this in turn gave him earlier warning of enemies as well as the advantage in spotting his prey. At the same time his hands were freed for the manipulation of tools and weapons.

Man thus became a bipedal creature; the first of these that we know of were the Australop-ithecines. The best known of such fossils to be unearthed was Zinjanthropus, discovered by Dr and Mrs Leakey at Olduvai Gorge in 1959. These creatures differed from modern Man in a number of ways. They had smaller brains, only one third the size of modern human brains. They were also very short, the tallest being only 1·2 metres (4 ft.) high. The remains found at Olduvai are believed to be between $1\frac{1}{2}$ to $1\frac{3}{4}$ million years old. A contemporary of the Australopithecines in East Africa was a creature named Homo Habilis; six such skeletons have been found at Olduvai. They had larger brains and were apparently able to make and use tools. This ability is significant as it helps to distinguish them from the other primates. They fed on small animals, such as young pigs, frogs and birds.

It used to be held that the principal distinction between Early Man and apes was that the former could make and use tools to a set and regular pattern. This definition has had to be modified since it was found, as a result of Jane van Lawick Goodall's research into the behaviour of chimpanzees, that they too can make tools. The tendency now is to use a combination of terms to define Man: his ability to make tools, including *cutting* tools; as well as his ability to walk, stand and run on two legs. In addition Man has developed in further ways; his brain grew larger, he became taller, and so better able to think and to hunt for his food. He developed the power of speech and hence the growth of languages with the ability to transmit ideas. Man became more settled, less of a wanderer. He relied more and more upon his skill in making and using tools, from the simplest form of hand-axe to the finest stone implements.

During this period Man was a hunter and food-gatherer and tended to live near lakes or rivers. He learnt to fish, dig up roots and eat fruit and nuts from trees. Although scattered right across Africa it is estimated that there were perhaps 100 000 men in

Fig. 1.1 Stone tools made by Early Man.

Fig. 1.3 Dr Leakey making a hand axe in the same way as Early Man.

Fig. 1.2 Rock painting at Fock's Farm, Laikipia District.

Fig. 1.4 An excavation in Kyuga Cave, South Pare Hills.

Africa half a million years ago, while others had already moved to Asia and parts of Europe. Sites in East Africa where Stone Age Man lived have been found at Olorgesailie, Nsongezi, Isimilia and Olduvai. The discovery of fire about 50 000 years ago was a great step forward for Man. With it he was able to drive out dangerous animals from rock shelters and caves, clear away forest and bush, and cook food.

The inhabitants of East Africa at this time consisted mainly of Bushmen-type people. Then, about 12 000 years ago Caucasoid people from Asia began to enter East Africa, settling in the Rift Valley area of Kenya and on the central plains of Tanzania. They brought with them smaller, sharper weapons, and the custom of burying their dead. Skeletons of these people have been found at Gamble's Cave in Kenya. From these two groups all the present day Negro people of Africa are descended. By about 6000 B.C. the Stone Age inhabitants of East Africa seem to have developed a fairly settled way of life. Those living around the lakes had become fishermen, and it is possible that a form of boat was in use. Others left evidence of their activities in the form of rock paintings on the walls of caves. These can still be seen at sites near Endebess on Mount Elgon and in Turkana and Maasailand and Karamoja, but the largest number of all are in the Kondoa, Singida and Eyasi areas of Tanzania.

During the Stone Age period the population remained sparse and thinly scattered over a wide area. Man had little time for anything other than seeking his food. It was to be the coming of agriculture and the knowledge of iron-working that brought the biggest changes of all, and these came in with the Bantu and Nilotic migrants in the first millenium B.C. This we shall come to in the following chapter. Before doing so, however, mention must be made of the chief sources of our knowledge of East African history. The time chart, fig. 1.5, will help you to put history in perspective.

Sources of East African History

The historian relies mainly upon written records for his principal source. But the absence of written records for most of the period in East Africa has led historians to make use of other sources. These include the following.

1. Archaeology

This is the study of the material remains of Man's past.

This highly specialised work is carried out by archaeologists. Through their excavations at sites such as Olduvai, Olorgesailie and Biggo (see figs 1.3

3

and 1.4) they have been able to tell us a great deal about the life and culture of the people of that time. Some, like Dr Leakey, have concentrated on the period of Early Man, others like Dr Posnansky have worked on sites relating to the Chwezi Empire in the fourteenth and fifteenth centuries, while Chittick and Kirkman have excavated coastal sites of the twelfth to sixteenth centuries. What they have found has been of immense value in attempting to piece together the past in East Africa.

Perhaps you wonder how archaeologists know where to start their excavations. In many cases they will look for a place where erosion or some geological fault has exposed a stratum of rock and soil well below the surface. Sometimes they may be guided by local tradition or even by partly visible remains, as at Gedi. Excavation is a long and laborious process, each piece of material found has to be carefully examined and recorded so that the archaeologist can give as complete a reconstruction as possible of what he has found. In the process of excavating buildings or burial sites he will often find the remains of pottery, household implements, ironware, weapons and even coins. All these help us to learn more about the past (see Map 2, p. 11).

2. Anthropology

The study of existing social institutions and relationships.

Although anthropologists are concerned with the societies of their own day and age, much of what they discover can be used in interpreting the past, especially where we have good reason to believe that societies in certain areas have not altered very much in recent times. By means of a detailed examination of cultural systems—the ideas, beliefs and institutions of a given society—anthropologists can tell us much about the settlement and growth of people in East Africa. For example, important work has been done by anthropologists such as John Beattie on the Banyoro, Allan Jacobs on the Maasai and Aidan Southall on the Alur. Of equal interest is the work of Professor Mbiti on African religions, in which he has attempted to explain African ideas about God, time and destiny.

3. Linguistics

The study and analysis of languages, their sound, structure and formation, and also the relationship between various language groups.

In this way linguists can suggest approximately when and how the languages now spoken in East Africa came into existence. This in turn can lead to some indication of the movement and settlement of people in East Africa, and to how and when they merged with or separated from each other. It is important to remember that languages are never static, but constantly changing and adapting. Some survive while others die out, just as those who speak them may conquer or be vanquished. The names by which the major groups are known—Nilotic, Bantu—are linguistic rather than physical or geographical descriptions. In fact we depend upon the work done by linguists for our principal method of classifying and grouping the peoples of East Africa.

4. Oral tradition

The study of our past as revealed by what has been handed down by word of mouth from one generation to another.

The source here is the spoken, rather than the written word. By recording and then carefully checking the words of informants the trained historian or anthropologist can attempt to reconstruct the past. The information may take a variety of forms—legends and myths, poems, songs, proverbs or lists of kings or rulers. In this last example the material is obviously historical, but even in the others the historian will be able to identify and relate events and personalities to the history of that particular community or region. He will learn from experience to make allowances for bias or exaggeration, and to distinguish what was real from what was imaginary. He has one important advantage over the historian working with written records, namely that he is in a better position to assess the value and reliability of his sources, because he is working with living people. Thus the importance of myths and legends should never be under-rated when studying the history of a community. They are closely bound up with their social customs, their religious beliefs and their systems of government. Among the pioneers in the study and evaluation of oral tradition in East Africa are Professor Ogot and Professor Were.

5. Written records

The study of written records is a principal source of material for the historian. In the case of East Africa, however, they are only available for the past 200 years or less; except for the coastal area where written records exist which go back to the time of early Greek, Egyptian and Moslem traders. Perhaps the earliest example is the commercial guide

Years	Approximate geological period	Human and Pre-human types	Important sites	Remarks
1500 AD	IRON AGE		NYERO, Uganda	Latest use of stone tools
500				Rock paintings
AD			NSONGEZI rock–shelter	Bantu agriculturalists
BC				
1500	....	....	HYRAX HILL, Nakuru	
			MAGOSI	First spread of pastor–alism
10,000 BC		Development of present day African races	ISHANGO GAMBLE'S CAVE	
	LATE STONE AGE	HOMO SAPIENS		First systematic burials
50,000 BC			GILGIL RIVER NSONGEZI SANGO BAY	Fire making and new tools make man more adaptable
	MID STONE AGE			
300,000 BC		(Pithecanthropus) HOMO ERECTUS	NSONGEZI OLORGESAILIE ISIMILIA	Hand axe industry becoming fully developed Man now a tool maker and user
750,000	EARLY STONE AGE		OLDUVAI	First spread of man into Europe and Asia
1,500,000 BC		HOMO HABILIS (Australopithecines)	OLDUVAI	
3,000,000 BC			OMO EAST RUDOLF	
	PLIOCENE	RAMAPITHECUS (KENYAPITHECUS)	OMO FORT TERNAN	Period when bipedal primates probably developed
15,000,000 BC	MIOCENE			
30,000,000 BC		PROCONSUL (Dryopethecus)	RUSINGA Is. HOMA Mt. NAPAK MOROTO	Partially bipedal primates developing

Adapted from: Zamani (New Edn.) p. 58—59

Fig. 1.5 A time chart of Early Man and the Stone Age.

written in the first century A.D., known as *'The Periplus of the Erythraean Sea'*. From about 1800 written records in the form of diaries, reports and letters from visiting European missionaries, explorers, traders and administrators provide much additional source materal for the historian. By studying these objectively the professional historian is able to build up a picture of what happened in the past, and to make his suggestions as to how and why these things occurred.

It is important to distinguish these two facets of the historian's work. In the first he is primarily concerned with the search for the truth, with what actually happened. This will involve, as with the study of oral tradition, a process of evaluation and assessment. In the second he attempts to explain what happened, to pick out what he thinks is most significant, and to relate it to the mainstream of history.

Historians cannot always be expected to come to the same conclusions; they represent the opinions and background of their times and peoples. Thus history is constantly being rewritten and revised, as attitudes change and as fresh evidence comes to light.

Questions

1. How do historians collect the data from which they write history?
2. How useful and reliable is oral tradition as a source of history?
3. With the aid of a sketch-map indicate the major archaeological sites in East Africa.
4. Describe how Man first became a distinct and separate being from the other primates.
5. What contribution has linguistics made to our knowledge of East African history?

Activities

1. Visit (where possible) a nearby archaeological site, or a museum with an archaeological display (Nairobi, Kampala and Dar es Salaam all have National Museums).
2. Arrange a class discussion on the use and value of oral tradition, with examples from local experience.
3. Set the class a holiday task involving the use of oral tradition methods (Family History; Legends, Tribal Customs).

Chapter 2
The peopling of East Africa

Introduction

Perhaps the most important stage in the evolution of modern Man came when he learned to grow his own food and to keep domestic animals. He thus became a producer of food as opposed to a food gatherer or hunter. This was to have far reaching effects on human life and civilisation. Man was no longer forced to lead a nomadic way of life, he was able to settle down and had time to spare for other interests and occupations. When combined with the knowledge of iron-working, this enabled him to become much more independent and to control his environment rather than let it control him. So far as East Africa was concerned these two great innovations were introduced by Negro peoples moving in from the north, west and south, as well as by a semi-Caucasoid group, the Cushites, from the Ethiopian highlands. It was the Cushites who were the first food producers in East Africa. But before describing the movement of these peoples in greater detail something must be said about food production and iron-working.

Fig. 2.1 An Egyptian mural found at Thebes. Notice the various agricultural occupations including the cultivation of corn.

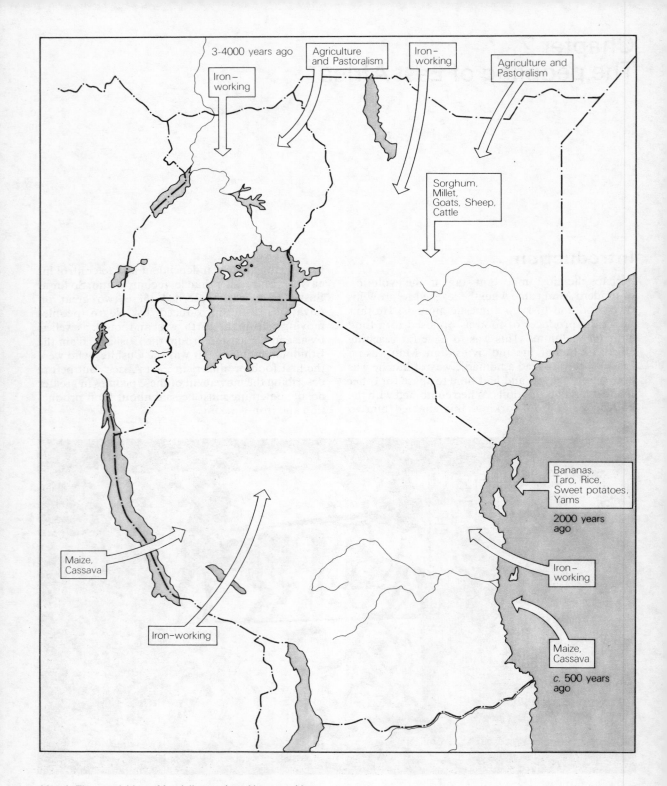

Map 1 The acquisition of food, livestock and iron-working

Within the map:

3-4000 years ago

Iron-working

Agriculture and Pastoralism

Iron-working

Agriculture and Pastoralism

Sorghum, Millet, Goats, Sheep, Cattle

Bananas, Taro, Rice, Sweet potatoes, Yams

2000 years ago

Iron-working

Maize, Cassava

c. 500 years ago

Maize, Cassava

Iron-working

Food production and iron-working

Food production

The earliest evidence of food production comes from the Middle East, from Shanidar in Northern Iraq. By a process known as radio carbon dating archaeologists have been able to determine its date as approximately 9000 B.C. Further evidence of cultivation has been unearthed at Tell es Sultan, the site of Jericho, which has been dated at about 8000 B.C. From here the knowledge of pastoralism and agriculture spread to the north-west and south into Egypt. At Fayum in the Nile Delta conditions were ideal for the cultivation of wheat and flax, the keeping of sheep, goats and cattle, as well as fishing. This site probably dates back to 6000 B.C. From this and similar places grew the great Egyptian civilisation. It was also from this area that the techniques of food production spread southwards into the rest of Africa, following the valley of the Nile. By about 1500 B.C. this knowledge was beginning to enter East Africa, but until approximately A.D. 500 its influence was slight, confined to the region of the Eastern Rift Valley as far south as Lake Eyasi.

The skills needed to produce food, together with the crops and animals involved, were carried from one region to the next by means of trade, migration or simply contact between neighbouring people. Cultivators and herdsmen had to learn by trial and error what would adapt best to new climates and soils. Of the grain crops, wheat and barley flourished in North Africa, while sorghum, millet and eleusine were better suited to the hotter, more tropical conditions south of the Sahara. In the heavily forested, wet regions around the lakes planted crops such as bananas did well. Nearly all these staple crops were introduced into East Africa from outside: millet and sorghum from the Ethiopian highlands about three to four thousand years ago; bananas, rice, certain yams and possibly sweet potatoes from the Indian Ocean trade routes about two thousand years ago; while maize and cassava came from the Americas in the last five hundred years. East African cultivators have shown much skill in adapting crops to suit local conditions and in developing special varieties. Similarly with livestock, the first domesticated cattle, sheep and goats were brought into North Eastern Africa from Western Asia, and thence into East Africa. By a process of selective breeding pastoralists have been able to improve the number and quality of their animals. In certain pastoral societies cattle have played an important part not only for their economic value but because of their social and cultural significance.

As people became more skilled and specialised in different forms of food production so they tended to look for and settle in the areas best suited to their needs; the banana cultivators to the fertile, well watered shores of the lakes and the herdsmen to the open grassland plains. But many groups relied upon both crops and cattle, while trade between agriculturalists and pastoralists enabled many to benefit from both types of economy. The quality and quantity of food produced depended not only on the climate and variations in weather but also upon land use. Both agriculture and grazing tend to exhaust the land, and long before the use of modern fertilisers East Africans had learned the need to practice shifting cultivation, and moving their livestock from pasture to pasture. In order to do so they required a much wider area of land than would be possible with today's heavily populated countryside. The efficiency of crop production also depended a great deal upon the kind of tools used. At first the cultivators had to rely upon stone tools, hence the term 'Neolithic' that is sometimes used to refer to these Late Stone Age food producers. But with the introduction of iron-working great advances were made possible. You can see how this happened in Map 1.

Iron-working

This was the second great technical innovation that revolutionised the life and culture of men. The knowledge of how to smelt iron and other minerals from sand or rock with the use of fire, and then to fashion it into knives, arrows, hoes and other implements was a highly specialised and valued skill. It is not yet known for certain when the knowledge of iron-working entered East Africa. The old idea that it came from Meroe on the River Nile is now considered unlikely; instead a variety of sources have been put forward—the Congo, the Indian Ocean and Ethiopia—all at some time during the first millenium A.D. In the northern parts of East Africa it may have been the Highland Nilotes who were the first to use it; elsewhere it would appear to have come in with various Bantu-speaking migrants. Nor did its use spread quickly throughout the region. Many, particularly the hunters and gatherers of food, continued to use stone tools. However, by about A.D. 1000 the majority of the inhabitants of East Africa had moved from the Stone to the Iron Age.

The use of iron tools and weapons had many important effects. It was now possible to clear and cultivate land where once it had been impossible to settle. Iron hoes could dig much deeper, iron knives and axes could cut faster and better. Greater food production led to larger and more settled populations, and the rise of systems of government and highly organised societies. It is interesting to note that the smiths, or workers in iron, acquired great influence and prestige, particularly among the agricultural communities. The frequency in Bantu languages of the stem word 'uma' is a further indication of the important role played by iron. Quite apart from its economic value, iron weapons made a considerable difference to the fighting forces of this period, giving them an overwhelming advantage over those armed only with stone weapons.

We have mentioned in the previous chapter a number of well-known Stone Age sites in East Africa. For the Iron Age a place of particular significance is Engaruka in Northern Tanzania, an agricultural settlement dating back to some time between the fifteenth and eighteenth centuries A.D. It was probably built and occupied by a group of Southern Cushites, and consists of dry-stone walled homes and animal pens together with a system of fields and irrigation channels (see Map 2).

Migration and settlement

The movement into East Africa of peoples of Negro and Cushitic stock (see Map 3), with their knowledge of food production and iron working, was a long drawn out process, but it marks the beginning of the permanent settlement of the region. There is still a great deal to be learned about the movements of individual groups, and one cannot expect to find definite answers or fixed dates for every stage in the period of migration and settlement. But thanks to the research completed by linguists, anthropologists and others we can now see the broad picture of the way in which this happened.

It is important to remember that we are dealing with a time span of many hundreds of years and that the people whom we are considering did not all enter East Africa at once but over a period of two thousand years. It was a slow process; people moved in small groups, as clans or families rather than as tribes, moving from one settlement to the next. Perhaps the pastoralists tended to move faster and further than the cultivators, in search of fresh grazing for their cattle. Movements could be backwards as well as forwards; they could also be seasonal, as shown by 'transhumance' practised by the Luo people in search of water and grass in the dry season, returning to cultivate their land when the rains came. During the course of migration there would be frequent meeting and mixing with other groups, not necessarily of the same stock. This could lead to the adoption of new ideas and customs, and in some cases even to the absorbing of one group by another.

Contacts between groups of migrants were more often peaceful than hostile, due to their mutual interdependence. Pastoralists needed food crops, while the agriculturalists were often anxious to acquire cattle. There were, of course, rivalries and clashes from time to time but these should not disguise the less obvious but more enduring process of assimilation that continued throughout the period. The motives for migration varied considerably. Famine and drought frequently forced a community to move. The pressure of population growth was another cause, leading to dispersal in search of fresh land. Yet another reason was political oppression which frequently led to refugees escaping to neighbouring territories. Nor must we forget the occasions when military invasion, often in search of plunder, led to the occupation of land.

Prominent physical features, such as mountains, often played a significant role in the movement and dispersal of these early settlers. We see this in the traditional histories and legends of many tribes which often refer to such places as their homelands or places of origin—Mt Kilimanjaro for the Chagga, Pare and some Coastal tribes; Mt Elgon for the Kalenjin group; Mt Kenya for the Kikuyu and Meru; Mt Moroto for the Teso group.

In the chapters which follow will be found a more detailed account of how individual groups of settlers established themselves and assumed their own languages, customs and forms of government. Before we turn to them it would be useful to get a general impression of who they were and where they came from. Nor must we forget the fate of the original inhabitants, the Bushmen-type people. Because of their very simple form of life they were unable to offer much resistance to the newcomers. They were either absorbed into the new communities or else retreated to the drier and less hospitable areas where they declined in numbers and importance. Their only direct descendants today are the Sandawe and possibly the Hadza in North Tanzania, who still retain the 'click' form of language used by the Bushmen of the Kalahari.

The Cushites

These stem from a branch of the Caucasoid race, which includes the Western Asians, Arabs and

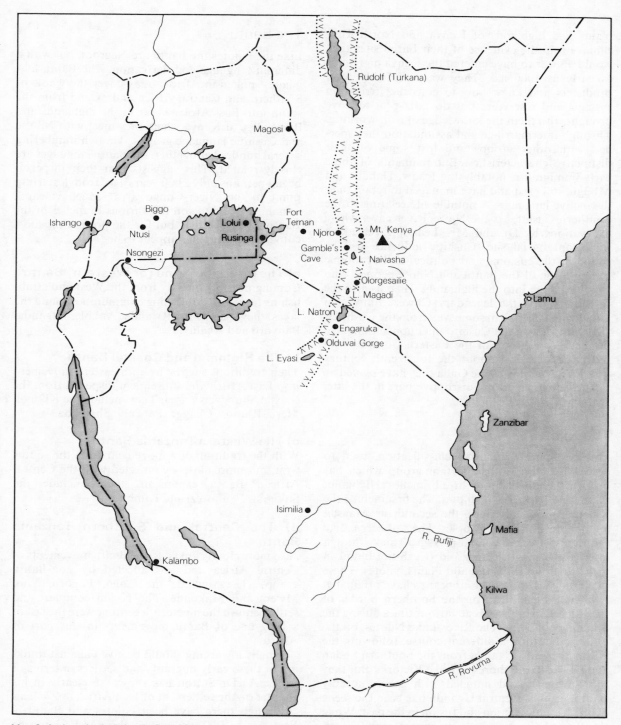

Map 2 Archaeological sites in East Africa

Europeans. The term Cushite does not refer to the ancient kingdom of Cush, although the Cushites did come from the Ethiopian highlands. From here they spread out to occupy most of North Eastern Africa. Those that moved south into East Africa have been called the Southern Cushites, who occupied the

11

plains and highlands of Kenya and North Tanzania. From the evidence of their burial sites they would appear to have entered the Kenya highlands as early as 1000 B.C. They were probably food producers and knew how to construct irrigation systems and reservoirs but do not seem to have brought with them the knowledge of iron-working. Through intermarriage and assimilation they merged with other groups and lost some of their distinctive characteristics. But remnants of these early immigrants, notably the Iraqw, Dahalo and Mbugu, still exist and have managed to retain their distinctive language. A notable site relating to the Southern Cushites is the Njoro River cave, where excavations by Dr and Mrs Leakey revealed an important burial site. Cushitic influence will be found in the customs and political and economic organisation of the Bantu and Nilote peoples who followed them into the highlands. There is also the possibility that the legendary Chwezi Empire in Uganda may derive in some way from the Cushites.

Before leaving the Cushites mention should also be made of a group of the Eastern Cushites who moved into Kenya about the fourteenth century A.D. Known today as the Galla they have played an active, some would say disruptive part in the later history of that area.

The Nilotes

This is a purely linguistic classification, used to describe a large and important group which has been further divided into three branches: Highland, Plains and River-Lake Nilotes. The first include the Kalenjin group of tribes, the second the Maasai, and the third the Lwo peoples. They all derive, like the Bantu, from a common Negro stock, though intermingling with Caucasoid (Cushitic) blood in the case of the Highland and Plains Nilotes. These two branches, moreover, appear to have originated in their present form on the Southern border of the Ethiopian highlands at various times during the first millenium A.D. The River-Lake Nilotes, on the other hand, took a different course, following the Nile Valley into Uganda from the Southern Sudan and thence to the shores of Lake Victoria. But they too have met and mingled with other, notably Bantu, groups. Central Uganda has been the scene of much ethnic friction and fusion in the past. While the River-Lake Nilotes have been a mainly agricultural people, with their cattle and fishing as additional activities, the Plains Nilotes became predominantly pastoral as they moved south across the grasslands of the Rift Valley.

The Bantu

Like the Nilotes the Bantu are Negroes, but with a different language and derivation. The Bantu languages spoken in Africa today cover the whole of Southern and Central Africa and extend from the south into East Africa as far as the highlands and Rift Valley of Kenya where they meet with Nilotic and Cushitic language groups. Though numbering several hundred altogether, the Bantu languages are closely related. This suggests that their dispersal began perhaps only 2 000 years ago, from a starting point in the Niger-Congo area. Much research remains to be done on the various branches of the Bantu in East Africa, but for the present the most convenient groupings appear to be:

a) The Interlacustrine (or Western) Bantu

Coming possibly directly from the West and establishing large and flourishing communities round the lakes, they include the Rwanda, Ankole, Baganda, Banyoro and Abaluyia.

b) The Highland and Coastal Bantu

Their traditions suggest a south-eastern movement into East Africa and subsequent dispersal from the coastal Shungwaya area. They include the Kikuyu, Meru, Kamba, Chagga, Pare and Shambaa.

c) The Western Tanzania Bantu

With the tradition of a movement from the south-west, but more closely connected with the Central African Bantu expansion, these include the Sukuma, Nyamwezi and Kimbu.

d) The Central and Southern Tanzania Bantu

Also more closely linked to the Bantu movements of Central Africa and less affected by non-Bantu groups. They include the Gogo, Pogoro, Yao, Mwera and Makonde. The Ngoni conquest and settlements in the nineteenth century were the last of a long line of Bantu movements in this part of Africa.

Finally a warning should be given against thinking of these early migrants and settlers in terms of tribes. As Dr Sutton has shown so clearly in his chapter on the settlement of East Africa in *Zamani*: 'Although there have been Nilotes and Bantu in East Africa for one or two thousand years, the traditional histories of individual Nilotic and Bantu tribes usually go back only one, two or three hundred years, and never more than six hundred years.' He also goes on to point out the danger of

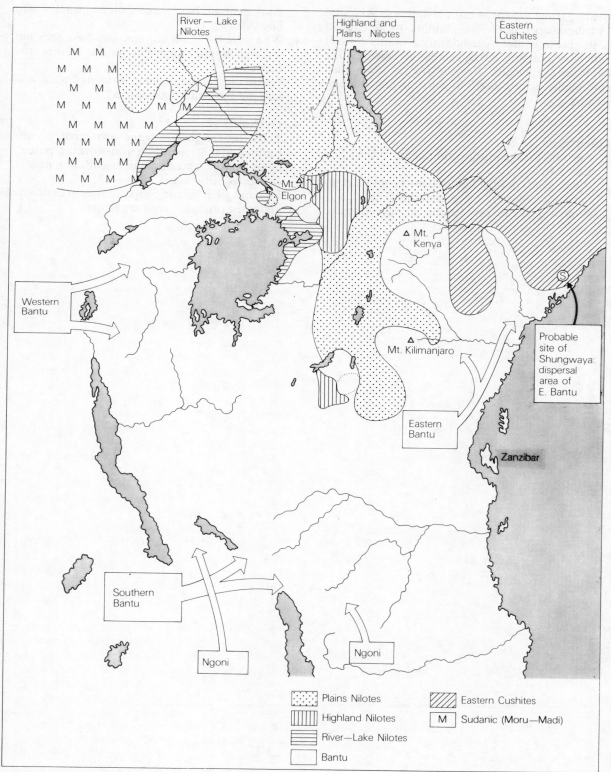

Map 3 The peoples of East Africa: major language groups and movements

Within the map, the following labels appear:

River — Lake Nilotes

Highland and Plains Nilotes

Eastern Cushites

M M
M M M
M M M
M M
M M M M
M M M
M M M M
M M M
M M M

Mt. Elgon

△ Mt. Kenya

△ Mt. Kilimanjaro

Western Bantu

Eastern Bantu

Probable site of Shungwaya: dispersal area of E. Bantu

Zanzibar

Southern Bantu

Ngoni

Ngoni

Legend:

⸱⸱⸱ Plains Nilotes

||| Highland Nilotes

≡ River—Lake Nilotes

☐ Bantu

/// Eastern Cushites

M Sudanic (Moru—Madi)

treating tribal groups as distinct and isolated units: 'A tribe emerges not by maintaining the pure blood of its ancestors, not by sedulously avoiding contact with its neighbours, but by successfully assimilating its diverse elements. To survive, a tribe must continually adjust itself to surrounding circumstances.'

Questions
1. Account for the introduction of agriculture into East Africa.
2. What effects did the knowledge of iron-working have upon those who acquired this skill?
3. What were the reasons behind the migration and movement of Bantu and Nilotic peoples into East Africa?
4. Who were the Cushites, and why have they not survived in the same way as the Nilotes and Bantu?
5. Where did the Bantu come from, and when and how did they enter East Africa?

Activities
1. Trace the origins in your own area of any traditional skills such as in iron-working, pottery or agriculture, and stories or legends that may be connected with them.
2. Find out what the old people in your area believe about the origins of their ancestors.

Chapter 3
The coast until 1500

Fig. 3.1 An old engraving of Kilwa, about 1590.

Map 4 The East African Coast showing principal towns and settlements

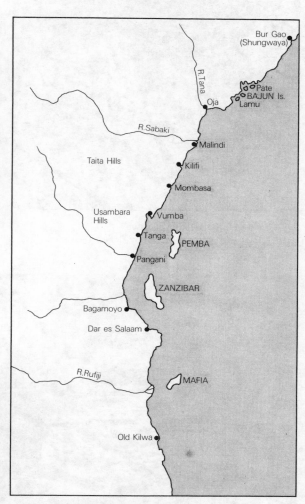

Introduction

The East African Coast is distinct from the interior in a number of ways both historically and geographically. It has had contact with the outside world for the last 2 000 years through its links with the Indian Ocean trading system. Most important of all has been the influence of the Moslem religion and civilisation which, since the tenth century has had a profound effect on the peoples of the East African Coast, making them a distinct and separate community, looking more to the sea than the hinterland for their livelihood and culture.

Because of this early contact with other lands and peoples we find that there are written records referring to the Coast which go back to the first century A.D.

Sources of history for the Coast

a) Written records

These are of two types, those written by visitors to

East Africa and those written by inhabitants. The former include Pliny, the Roman geographer, who mentioned the Gulf of Aden in his *Natural History* written in A.D. 75, and a Greek merchant from Alexandria who wrote a guide book for traders, *The Periplus of the Erythraean Sea* in the first century A.D. This is important because it contains the first direct, though often rather vague, re-ferences to people and places on the East African Coast. It is primarily concerned with articles of trade and deals also with the other land bordering the Indian Ocean which was known to the Greeks and Romans as the Erythraean Sea. Ptolemy's *Geography* contains references to Eastern Africa, and dates from the fifth century. These early writers refer to the East African Coast as 'Azania', while to the Arabs it was known as the land of 'Zenj'. Much clearer and more detailed accounts are given by Arab travellers who visited the Coast later on: Al Masudi in the tenth century, Al Idrisi in the twelfth century and Ibn Battuta in the fourteenth century. They are able to give first-hand impressions of the places they visited and the people they met.

Then there are the written records of people living on the Coast, usually in the form of chronicles, of which the 'Kilwa Chronicle' is perhaps the most famous. Written in Arabic they recount the names of rulers, their exploits and achievements. Although often recorded long after the events they describe (the oldest dating from 1530), and frequently biased or mythical, they have a great deal to say about the pre-Portuguese period.

b) Archaeology

This is the other major source of information. In recent years a great deal of work has been done at

Fig. 3.2a Careful excavation at Kilwa.

Fig. 3.2b The Great Mosque of Kilwa from the air after excavation was completed.

coastal sites such as Gedi and Kilwa by archaeologists such as Dr Kirkman and Mr Chittick. Not only have the remains of entire buildings and towns been excavated, but the remains of pottery and porcelain, coins, beads, and inscriptions on tombs have added considerably to our knowledge of this period.

The Coast before and after the coming of Islam

The pre-Islamic period

Originally the Coast of East Africa, like its interior, was inhabited by hunters and food-gatherers, Stone Age people similar to the Bushmen. These were then replaced by, or merged with, Cushitic speaking people from the North, who may well have been the tall, piratical men referred to in *The Periplus*. But we cannot be sure from these early written accounts of the exact origin of the Coastal people. The Greek term for the inhabitants of Africa was 'Ethiopian', a word often used very loosely to refer to the whole of Africa south of the Sahara. It is fairly certain that in the early centuries of the first millenium A.D. Bantu-speaking Negroes started to move northwards along the Coast as far as the area known as Shungwaya (see Map 5), on the southern borders of Somalia. Although little trace of it can be found today (it is believed to have been in the vicinity of Port Durnford) this became an important settlement area for these early Bantu migrants, and it was from here that they later dispersed and scattered southwards after coming into contact with the Galla.

Along the coast they came into contact with traders from overseas and would have started that process of trade, settlement and intermarriage that led to the formation of a distinct coastal people and culture. North of Shungwaya, along what came to be known as the Benadir Coast, there is little evidence of Bantu occupation. This was occupied by Eastern Cushitic groups, notably the Somali, with the Galla further south.

Of those who came to East Africa by sea, the early Greeks, Egyptians and Arabs were traders and did not settle permanently. The first evidence of permanent settlement on any scale dates from the eleventh century as we shall see in the next section on the Islamic period. There was, however, another group of immigrants who travelled by sea across the Indian Ocean—the Indonesians. We know that some time in the first millenium A.D. a large number settled in Madagascar, and it is quite probable that

some stayed on the East African Coast. They brought with them various food crops, the most important being the banana which they introduced into Africa. They also appear to have brought the outrigger canoe, sewn-plank boats used by fishermen, and the xylophone. The Malagache language spoken on the island of Madagascar is certainly of Malayo-Polynesian origin.

The culture of this pre-Islamic period on the East African Coast is not as fully documented or recorded as the later period. We gather from Al Masudi that the people had their own kings or chiefs, and that each state had its own army. Described as 'pagan' by the Arabs this does not mean that they had no religions of their own; on the contrary they were well able to provide for their spiritual needs, and would appear also to have been very fond of oratory.

According to Al Masudi they knew how to harness and make use of oxen for transport and

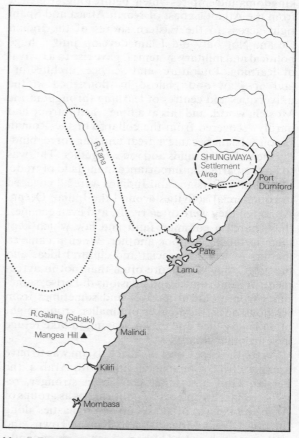

Map 5 The Shungwaya settlement and dispersal area, and extent of East Bantu settlement

17

for war. They cultivated bananas, millet and coconuts. Some were said to be cannibals with the practice of sharpening their teeth. Trade in ivory and gold was carried on, chiefly with the ports of Oman and Siraf. Imported articles included glass and iron tools, with wine and wheat often used as gifts. Little is known of the towns and settlements of this period; at Kilwa, for instance, archaeological evidence has shown that between A.D. 800 and 1200 the site was occupied by a fishing community whose buildings were of wattle and daub. The existence of fish hooks and smelting implements suggests that the people had acquired the knowledge of iron-working.

The coming of Islam

As a result of the life and teaching of the Prophet Mohamed (A.D. 570–632) a great new religion and civilisation grew up in the Middle East. Inspired by this new faith its followers set up a series of kingdoms and empires which, before long, stretched from the Atlantic coast of North Africa and Spain right across to the Eastern shores of the Indian Ocean. Not only did Islam develop into a huge political and military system; it gave rise to a revival of learning. Literature and science, architecture and art, law and philosophy flourished in the universities and centres of learning throughout the Moslem world, and this at a time when Europe had hardly recovered from the collapse of the Roman Empire. Islam became a great unifying force, binding men of many lands and races together. This was to have a particular importance in the field of trade, since Arabs, Persians and Indians were all engaged in commercial activities around the Indian Ocean. Although they were often rivals, and even enemies, they shared a common faith and law which kept them in touch with one another. When it came to matters of worship, social and cultural ideas and practices, they were more often than not in agreement. When disputes and divisions did arise, sometimes from political motives and sometimes from religious ones, the weaker or smaller group might often be expelled and exiled, leaving to take refuge in some other country.

As for the East Coast of Africa, Islam was to have a major effect. Commercial links with Arabia, the Persian Gulf and India grew even stronger, reinforced in many places by political ties as groups of Arab and Persian origin set up new dynasties along the coast from Mogadishu to Kilwa. Towns and settlements which had hitherto been predominantly Negro in culture and rule became centres of Moslem Arab and Persian influence. New towns of permanent stone buildings grew up, governed by sheikhs and sultans following the principles laid down in the Koran. Customs, clothing, food and architecture all followed Moslem ideas and beliefs. This does not mean that African traditional systems were entirely removed. As we shall see, the typical civilisation that developed on the East African Coast blended both African and Moslem cultures.

Traders and settlers

From about the eleventh century the pace of emigration and settlement on the East African Coast seems to have increased. These were no longer travelling merchants, prepared to stay for a season or two before returning home, but whole clans and families coming to put their roots down and establish new homes for themselves. From the Benadir Coast, where they made Mogadishu their

Fig. 3.3 This Lamu style door from Fort Jesus shows Arab influence.

18

most important centre, they gradually moved further south, intermarrying and scattering to different settlements. Some were almost certainly religious refugees, such as the followers of the Shia leader, Zaid, who may have come as early as the eighth or ninth century A.D. However, there is a good deal of uncertainty about some of the earlier leaders and their followers who are said to have settled along the Coast. A group of refugees from Al Ahsa near Bahrein are said to have founded Mogadishu and Barawa in the eleventh century, and it is certainly from this century that we obtain archaeological evidence of the establishment of permanent towns and settlements.

One group which deserves particular mention were the Shirazi, named after the capital of Fars province in Persia which controlled part of the Persian Gulf trade. One family at least settled in Mogadishu, while the rest moved further down the Coast to Shungwaya. Through inter-marriage and assimilation they became gradually more African in character though still proud and conscious of their Shirazi blood. Later in the twelfth century they migrated still further south, to the Lamu Islands, the Tanga area, Pemba, Mafia, the Comoro Islands and Kilwa. It was in the last of these places that they established what was to become their most famous and powerful dynasty, whose fame and glory was to be preserved in the Kilwa Chronicle. But by far the greatest and most lasting influence brought by these people, reinforced by their political and economic links with Persia and Arabia, was that of Islam.

Traders

Apart from those who came to settle permanently in East Africa there remained a large number of traders and sailors who travelled seasonally up and down the Coast. They included not only Arabs from the great trading ports of the Yemen, the Hadramaut and Oman, but Persians from Siraf, Qais and Hormuz as well as Indians from Gujerat and the Malabar Coast. Trade with China and Malaya was probably conducted indirectly through the merchants of Oman and the Persian Gulf. So far as we know these traders did not go into the interior themselves to obtain gold, ivory and leopard skins which they came for.

Goods may well have come from tribe to tribe towards the Coast through a gradual process of barter. Commodities such as cloth and iron goods were the common articles of barter, though at Kilwa cowrie shells were used and later on, in some of the larger towns, coins were minted.

Trade and industry

The rulers of the Coastal settlements took an active part in developing and encouraging trade through their own towns. Of all the occupations of the inhabitants that of merchant was the most prominent and prosperous. Not only were they involved in the purchase and sale of goods, but they had the responsibility for their ships and sailors. The building and repairing of dhows was a major occupation in the ports. These sailing vessels were built for the conditions and winds of the Indian Ocean. They varied considerably in size but all carried the triangular shaped sails (lateen sails) that the Portuguese were later to copy.

Each year they would come south with the N.E. Monsoons, which blow from November to April, returning to Arabia and the Persian Gulf with the S.W. Monsoon between May to October. This cycle of trade has continued for over 2 000 years, and still exists today though on a much reduced scale. To get a clearer picture of the extent of Indian Ocean trade look at Map 6.

The list of articles imported and exported which is given below varied considerably in volume and value with time and place.

Imports

Glass	Beads	Axes	Ghee
Pottery	Cloth	Swords	Wheat
Porcelain	Copper	Spear-heads	Wine

Fig. 3.4 A Celadon plate with lotus flower pattern brought from China via the silk routes. It was found near Fort Jesus.

Fig. 3.5a A large dhow used for trading.

Fig. 3.5b Smaller coastal dhows in Lamu today.

Exports

Ivory	Leopard skins	Turtle shells
Gold	Ambergris	Aromatic gums
Palm Oil	Slaves	Rhinoceros horn

Of all the items exported ivory was probably the most important. Apparently the quality and size of the ivory obtained from African elephants was finer than any other, and it was particularly prized in India and China. Gold became increasingly valuable as an export later on, after the tenth century. It came almost exclusively from the interior of Central Africa, known to the Arabs as Waq Waq and to the Portuguese later as the kingdom of Monomotapa. It was exported through Sofala and along the East African Coast to Arabia and India. The control of this particular trade first gave Mogadishu and then Kilwa their power and wealth. Slaves do not appear to have played a major part in East African trade at

this time, though there was a steady supply from the Horn of Africa to Arabia and states bordering the Persian Gulf. There are also references in Chinese manuscripts to slaves from Zenj and Madagascar. Gums and spices were also shipped from this northern region of the coast.

Most imports consisted of goods that were necessary or decorative in the coastal towns, although some, such as cloth and iron-ware must have had a wider use as barter with the tribes of the hinterland. Although some knowledge of iron smelting did exist on the coast it is apparent that manufactured iron tools and weapons from abroad were still valued. The lances were specially made at Mouza for this trade. As the townspeople grew more prosperous so the demand for articles of luxury such as carpets, glazed-ware from Persia, porcelain from China, silks and other fine materials increased.

Apart from trading and shipping there were several other occupations in the coastal settlements, of which the biggest was probably that of cloth making. Other crafts included metal-working, including the minting of coins, carving in bone and ivory, stone-masonry, and the making of jewellery. Agriculture and fishing also occupied a good many people, the former often on the mainland close to the island settlements on which many towns were based.

The coastal towns and their rulers

It is noticeable that most of the towns were sited on islands or peninsulas, giving them added natural protection from the mainland. This suggests a division between the townspeople of the coast and the tribes of the hinterland, or at least a lack of trust and confidence. The relationship cannot have been made any easier by the obvious wealth and comfort enjoyed by those in the towns, in contrast to the hard and simple life of the mainland people.

Each town had its own ruler, whether sheikh or sultan, usually chosen from the leading local family, many of which claimed descent from Arab or Persian ruling families. These rulers would govern with the advice of a small council, with specific tasks for certain officials. The Kadhi was in charge of the courts and the Koranic system of law; the Muhtasib was in charge of the police force and the Amir or Wazir supervised the administrative affairs of the state. The rulers followed the principles and directives laid down by the Islamic faith, as embodied in the Koran.

There were frequent wars and struggles between these coastal states. At no time were they subjected to the domination of a single ruler. Occasionally the more powerful settlements would gain control over the smaller towns nearby, and would even lay claim to other areas, but this rarely lasted for long. Mogadishu and Kilwa were, perhaps, the two outstanding settlements during this period, the former in the thirteenth century, the latter in the fourteenth–fifteenth centuries. Later their places were to be challenged by others, such as Pate and Mombasa, before finally they fell to the Portuguese.

Of the towns on the Benadir Coast, Mogadishu was by far the largest, and the first to rise to prominence, due no doubt to its proximity to the northern trade routes. It would have been the first major port of call for traders coming south along the coast. Founded in the eleventh century it had become the leading town on the coast by the thirteenth century. It was visited by Ibn Battuta in the fourteenth century. He described it as being large and prosperous, with a sheikh who lived in great luxury. But by this time it had lost control of the gold trade from Sofala and started to decline in importance.

Mombasa was visited by Al Idrisi in the twelfth century, and by Ibn Battuta in 1331, when the inhabitants impressed him as being both pious and honourable. However, the people of Mombasa were to become better known for their war-like spirit. They were fortunate in possessing one of the best natural harbours on the coast. Mombasa became steadily more powerful and important in the fifteenth century, offering the most stubborn resistance of all to the Portuguese forces.

Kilwa came to prominence in the thirteenth century with a new dynasty of rulers, the Shirazi. Under their rule, and that of their successors, the Ahadali or Abu'l-Mawahib family, it became the largest and most prosperous of all the coastal towns, with magnificent buildings such as the Husuni Kubwa, the largest building in Africa south of the Sahara at that time. Kilwa had by this time a monopoly of the gold trade from Sofala and it was from the profits of this trade that its rulers and citizens built such fine palaces, mosques and houses.

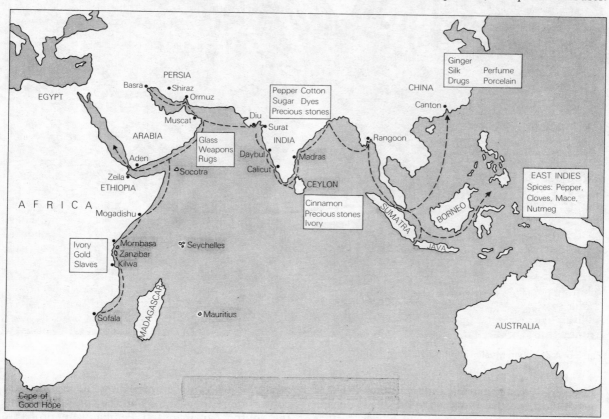

Map 6 Indian Ocean trade, 1000–1500 A.D.

21

Fig. 3.6 A Zanzibari Muslim and his son, circa 1880.

However, dynastic quarrels and rivalries in the later part of the fifteenth century led to the steady decline of this settlement, a process which was further hastened by the coming of the Portuguese. But even at the height of its power Kilwa did not directly control more than Mafia and the coastal towns to the south. Zanzibar and Pemba were probably under its influence for a period, but not for long, as we know that in the fifteenth century Zanzibar was minting its own coins, a sure sign of independence. Pemba became the granary of Mombasa, a safer and more reliable supplier of food than the mainland in times of war or danger.

There were of course many other flourishing settlements along the coast, each with its mosque and principal buildings in stone, each with its own rulers and local dignitaries but all linked to each other by common bonds of interest in trade and with a common religious and cultural heritage.

The society and culture of the coastal settlements

By the fourteenth century the coastal towns had acquired a distinctive character and life of their own. While this derived a great deal from Moslem religious and cultural ideas from Arabia and the Persian Gulf, it also owed a good deal to local African traditions and ways of life. Through inter-marriage over a period of centuries a people of mixed blood had emerged, brown in colour, speaking the Swahili language which, while Bantu in construction, was also strongly influenced by Arabic. They still relied upon Arabic for writing and since so much of their life was moulded on the Koran their society was primarily Islamic.

This was immediately noticeable in the social structure within the larger towns. This was headed by the ruling family, often of mixed African and Arab ancestry but always zealous Moslems; then would come the principal landowners, merchants and religious leaders, also of mixed blood; and finally the labourers, sailors, and unskilled workers, many of whom were treated as slaves.

The towns consisted of tightly packed groups of buildings, some of stone, others of temporary materials; usually flat roofed, those of the wealthier citizens being of more than one storey in height. Houses were usually built around a sunken court-yard, often with impressively carved and decorated entrances. Walls were thick and windows faced into the courtyard, so that rooms were dark but cool. Roofs were of stone laid over mangrove poles, which meant that they had to be long and narrow, except (as in the case of Husuni Kubwa at Kilwa) where stone vaults and domes were used. The nearest we can get to imagining what these old towns and buildings looked like is by looking at pictures of Lamu today. Inscriptions on walls and tombstones were in Arabic script of various styles.

Wells were built of stone, and water was often stored in cisterns within the houses. The pillar tombs found at certain points along the coast appear to be unique to this area.

From remains of pottery and other articles found, as well as descriptions of visitors such as Ibn Battuta, we gather that the rich lived in considerable luxury, eating off Chinese porcelain or glazed-ware, dressing in silks and fine materials and decorating their walls with carpets. The merchants of Pate were said to have had their doors studded with gold and silver! And it was quite common to find porcelain bowls fitted into niches on walls and tombs.

The daily pattern of life would be much like that of any other seaport in the Islamic world of that time: regular prayers offered at the mosques, Moslem festivals observed, the coming and going of ships and traders, occasional military operations on the mainland, the tending of fields and plantations, the weaving of cloth and the construction of new buildings. It was a flourishing and active society, but one which was confined to the coastal towns and settlements and had little influence on the hinterland. Practically the only link between them was that based on trade. As Neville Chittick has written: 'To people who have ships, the sea is a road, not a barrier; it is the land, especially waterless land and thick forest, which divides.'

Questions

1. What are the chief sources for the study of the history of the East African Coast before 1500?
2. Imagine that you are a sailor going from Egypt to 'Azania' in the first century A.D. Write a letter to your parents in Alexandria explaining where you have been and what you have seen.
3. What form of political organisation did the coastal towns have by the fifteenth century, and how closely were they linked with each other?
4. What was the extent of Arab influence on the East African Coast before 1500?
5. Describe the pattern of trade around the shores of the Indian Ocean in the thirteenth to fifteenth centuries, and show the part played by the East African sea ports.

Activities

1. At some time try to visit the East African Coast and see something of the early civilisations there: Lamu, Gedi, Mombasa (Fort Jesus), Bagamoyo and Kilwa are some of the places that have interesting relics of the past.

Chapter 4
The Bunyoro-Kitara Empire and the interlacustrine area until 1500

Introduction

The word 'interlacustrine' is generally used to refer to the region between and around the Great Lakes of East Africa, and more particularly in this chapter to the areas occupied by the Bachwezi and Babito Empires in Uganda. We know that by A.D. 1000 Bantu-speaking groups had been settled here long enough to have evolved their own political and social systems. But for much of this early period they appear to have been dominated by others who were not Bantu in origin. According to oral tradition these were the Abatembuzi, the Bachwezi and the Babito. Of these the first would appear to have been purely mythical and in all probability never existed at all. They were regarded as gods, the founders and originators of the later kingdoms. Of the Bachwezi we can be more certain, although even their origins are shrouded in mystery. But they certainly existed and established an empire which was later taken over by the Babito, a Luo group of Nilotic origin who, in turn, were to be the founders of many of the later kingdoms in this area.

Early interlacustrine rulers

The Abatembuzi

Our information about the Abatembuzi is derived entirely from myths and legends handed down from one generation to the next by the people of Western Uganda. They represent an attempt to explain the origins of their people and although not an accurate record of events or personalities they nevertheless deserve careful consideration. All human societies have their ancestral accounts of how and when they were founded, often told in the form of stories, poems, songs and pictures. We know that much in them is imaginary and not to be taken literally,

and yet they may contain elements of truth. What is perhaps more important is that they have become part of the culture and identity of their particular society. So the historian can still learn something from such sources, both about the legends and about the people who recounted them.

Stories of the legendary kingdom of Bunyoro-Kitara are to be found in the traditions of the Banyoro, Batoro and Banyankole people. All agree that it was founded by the Abatembuzi who, they believe, were gods. They start with the God Ruhinda (the Creator) who lived with his brother Nkya. The latter had four sons: Kintu, Kairu, Kahuma and Kakama. Kairu became the ancestor of the cultivators, Kahuma of the herdsmen, and Kakama of the rulers. Each ruler bore the title of 'Omukama'. Ruhinda and Kintu then went to live in heaven, leaving Kakama to rule the earth. He in turn disappeared and was succeeded by his son Baba. During Baba's reign the population increased, as did the number of livestock. The first death also occurred at this time. Baba was followed by Mukonko, and he by Ngonzaki. Then Isaza succeeded to the throne, and divided Kitara into separate states one of which was known as Tsaza. Isaza married Nyamata, the daughter of Nyaminyonga, god of the underworld. She gave birth to a son, Isimbwa. Isaza was the last of the Abatembuzi gods and, like his forerunners, disappeared.

From these myths, which were intended to explain the origin of man in that region, we learn that there were both cultivators and pastoralists in Kitara at that time.

When Isaza disappeared, his gate-keeper, Bukuku, proclaimed himself Omukama instead of Isimbwa. But the chiefs refused to recognise him and instead divided the kingdom among themselves. Bukuku had been told by the prophets that if his daughter Nyinamwiru gave birth to a son the young man would one day kill Bukuku. So he

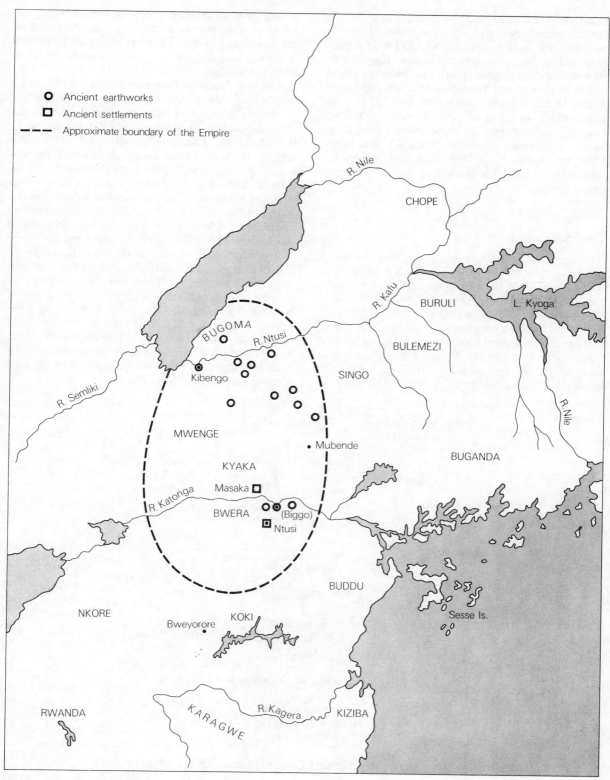

Map 7 The Kitara Empire of the Bachwezi

imprisoned his daughter and mutilated her by cutting out an eye, an ear and a breast. However Isimbwa managed to find his way to her and made love to her. She gave birth to a son, Karubumbi, who in due course grew up and speared his grandfather to death, and then reconquered the former Kitara lands in Nkore, Buganda, Bulega, Busoga, Toro, Madi and Bukedi—in effect, the whole of modern Uganda. Having done so he changed his name to Ndahura, the first of the Chwezi kings. Thus the legends establish a link between the Abatembuzi and the Bachwezi, as the diagram below shows.

The Bachwezi

Although much has been learned about the Bachwezi and their culture, there is still a good deal of uncertainty as to their origins. Some writers have concluded that they were of Caucasoid stock, possibly Egyptian; another theory is that they may have been Cushitic immigrants from the direction of Ethiopia. This second idea is the more likely, since it fits in with other possible Cushitic movements into East Africa. What is certainly true, and supported by the traditional histories, is that they came as strangers and that they were pastoralists, with great herds of long-horned cattle. Like the Abatembuzi they are supposed to have possessed supernatural qualities, and imposed themselves upon the local Bantu as a ruling aristocracy.

The new rulers of Bunyoro-Kitara introduced a number of administrative changes; a centralised monarchy with a hierarchy of officials both in the royal palace and in the provinces, all appointed by the Mukama. The latter maintained a standing army, and constructed large earthworks for defensive purposes, such as the one at Biggo in Bwera district (see Map 8). Excavation at this site has revealed a system of ditches over $10\frac{1}{2}$ kilometres ($6\frac{1}{2}$ miles) in extent, sufficient to protect large herds of cattle, and evidence of a royal enclosure (orirembo) similar to those in Karagwe, Rwanda and Ankole.

Biggo lies on a tributary of the River Katonga, so must have been built partly to defend the southern marches of the empire. There are other earthworks nearby, and in Mubende District, as well as one in Bunyoro. They must have been built some time between about A.D. 1350 and 1500 the approximate time of the Bachwezi culture. The Bachwezi power was centred on the area of western Buganda, eastern Toro and southern Bunyoro, between the Kafu and Katonga Rivers (see Map 7).

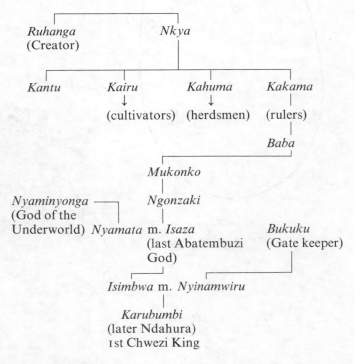

Family tree to show descent of Chwezi from Abatembuzi rulers

26

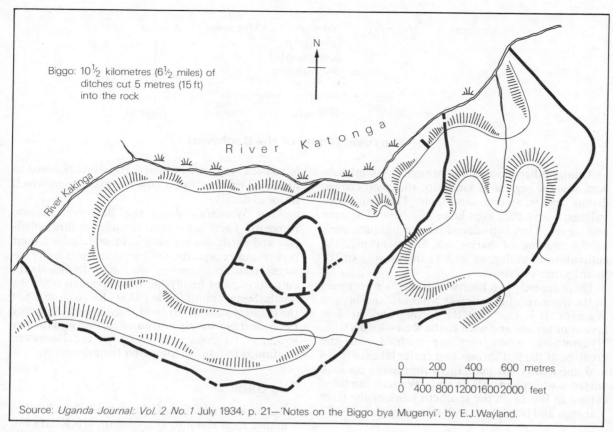

Biggo: 10½ kilometres (6½ miles) of
ditches cut 5 metres (15 ft)
into the rock

N

River Katonga

River Kakinga

| 0 | | 200 | 400 | | 600 metres |
| 0 | 400 | 800 1200 | 1600 | 2000 | feet |

Source: *Uganda Journal: Vol. 2 No. 1* July 1934, p. 21–'Notes on the Biggo bya Mugenyi', by E.J.Wayland.

Map 8 Plan of trenches at Biggo

Fig. 4.1 Long horned Ankole cattle with herdsman.

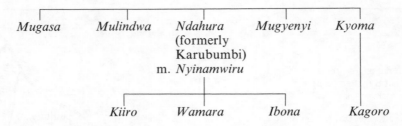

The royal family of the Bachwezi

Among other innovations brought by the Bachwezi was the regalia of kingship; the royal crown, drums, spears, arrows, stools, etc. They built reed palaces, where they kept large numbers of women and slaves. They introduced new techniques, such as the making of bark-cloth, iron-working, the cultivation of coffee, as well as the playing of the board game 'omweso'.

There are only two Bachwezi Bakama mentioned in the more reliable sources; Ndahura and his son Wamara. It is said that the former abdicated in favour of his son and went to the west with his wife, Nyinamwiru, where they are credited with the creation of the hot springs and crater lakes of Toro and apparently left permanent footmarks on rock surfaces which can still be seen. Wamara built his capital in Bwera on the southern bank of the river Katonga and lived there with his relatives.

The royal family of the Bachwezi

The Bachwezi, especially Mugyenyi, are said to have been very fond of their cattle. He is believed to have had one particular cow named Bihogo which he loved dearly.

After Wamara's death the Bachwezi Empire broke up. There are several reasons for this: small-pox and cattle disease may have undermined their power and prosperity, civil wars in outlying provinces, resistance among the subordinate Bantu cultivators, and finally the Lwo invasion from the north. Some traditions say that the Bachwezi left the country voluntarily, and legend has it that they never died but simply moved on further and further south. A religious cult, based on the Bachwezi, continued to flourish long after their departure.

The Babito

Like the Bachwezi before them, the Babito tried to enhance their claim to rule in Bunyoro-Kitara not only by conquest but by proving their connection with the former ruling dynasty and through them

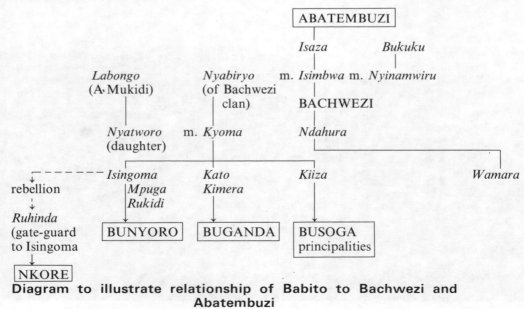

Diagram to illustrate relationship of Babito to Bachwezi and Abatembuzi

the Abatembuzi gods. This was a practice common to many new dynasties in other parts of the world as well as Africa.

The Babito were part of the Lwo migration of the River-Lake Nilotes which will be dealt with in the next chapter. How far the Bito dynasty established itself in other parts of Uganda, notably Buganda, may be open to question. But they certainly took over in Bunyoro in the fourteenth century, and their rule lasted for six centuries. Tradition suggests that they came in peacefully, and this is supported by the diagram opposite which shows a family connection through marriage. A number of related dynasties were also set up in other parts of the interlacustrine area, notably Busoga (Bukoli, Bugwere, Bulamogi, Bugabula) and Bukoba (Kiziba). Some authorities claim that Kimera, founder of the Buganda dynasty, belonged to the Bachwezi period, before the Babito influx. It was not long before these dynasties and sub-dynasties broke away from the old empire of Bunyoro-Kitara to form new states.

The Babito found the Bachwezi culture superior to their own in a number of ways. Rukidi himself had to be trained in the rituals of kingship and affairs of state as the first of the Bito kings. He copied the styles of the Bachwezi in building palaces and took over some of the royal drums, notably the two known as 'Kajumba' and 'Nyaleba'. The Babito also introduced certain cultural elements themselves, for instance 'empako' or pet names, such as 'Amoti' and 'Okali', the latter used only in referring to the Omukama. New items of regalia included the throne (Nyamyawo), the royal drums known as 'Tibamulinde' and 'Nyakangubi', spears, a shield, a horn, sandals, a rake, the royal fire, and the bag of millet. They initiated the system of granting land to clans, the origin of the 'bataka'

system, by which each clan became landowner of a specific area of the country. The practice of royal burial, involving separate burial sites for the jaw bones and bodies of the Abakama, led to the development of these places as shrines, many of which can still be located to this day.

It will be noted that little has been said of the earlier inhabitants of the region, the Bantu. Nor do they figure very prominently in the traditional histories of this period. It must be assumed that they submitted to the Bachwezi and Babito rule, and with their society and economy based on cultivation they probably complemented the pastoral culture of their overlords. Their role in this process of assimilation may well have been much more than passive acceptance of new ideas and techniques. More will be said about this in Chapter 7.

Questions

1. Write a story about the creation of man on earth such as was imagined in the traditions of Bunyoro-Kitara.
2. What are the Bachwezi chiefly remembered for?
3. Was the Kingdom of Bunyoro-Kitara a myth?
4. What is known of the origins of the Abatembuzi and Bachwezi?
5. How do myths and legends contribute to our understanding of the past in Africa?

Activities

1. Having read about the Bachwezi and Abatembuzi legends of their gods find out what you can about traditional ideas of god(s) in your own area.
2. Write an imaginary account of the birth of an African kingdom in East Africa about 1000 years ago; illustrate it with maps or drawings.

Chapter 5
The River–Lake Nilotes

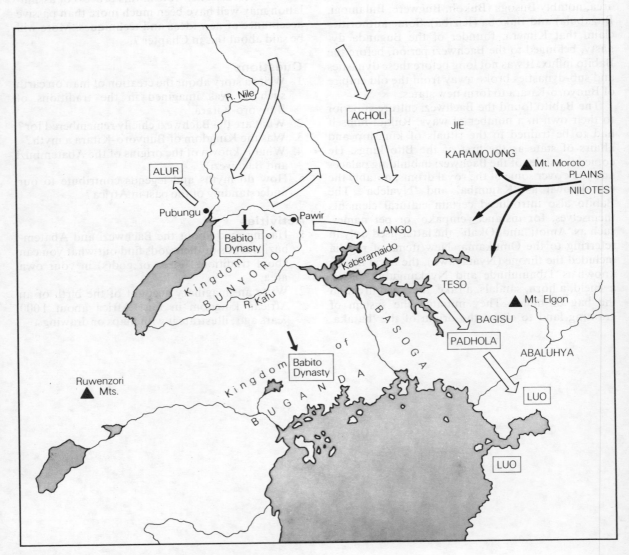

Map 9 River–Lake Nilotes: movement and settlement in East Africa

Introduction

The migration and expansion of the Lwo-speaking peoples has received a great deal of attention in recent years. As shown in Chapter 2 they have been classified as Nilotes for linguistic reasons, although the subsequent history and movement of the Highland, Plains and River-Lake Nilotes show wide differences and divergences. It is with the last of these groups that we are concerned in this chapter. The term 'River-Lake' indicates one feature common to most if not all of those belonging to this section—their pattern of migration south from the cradleland in the southern Sudan, along the Nile and its tributaries and around the lakes of Uganda. A second characteristic is the survival and persistence of the Lwo languages which, as we shall see, were often adopted and accepted by people of different ethnic origin. The term 'Lwo' is used here in a linguistic sense and should not be confused with the 'Luo', those Lwo-speaking people who finally settled in Kenya and Tanzania.

The River-Lake Nilotes include the Dinka, Shilluk, Bor, Anuak, Alur, Acholi, Jonam, Jopaluo, Padhola and Luo (see Map 10). Their history can be traced back to about A.D. 1000, largely by means of oral tradition and linguistic research. At this time they were living in the Equatoria and Bahr el Ghazal provinces of the Sudan, the area shown on Map 10 as 'Cradleland'.

They were pastoralists and fishermen, living in isolated communities along the banks of the Nile, their lives governed by the seasonal pattern of rains and drought. For a variety of reasons they started to migrate from this area; overpopulation, overstocking, or some external pressures may have been among them. The Dinka and Nuer were the first to move, going north. Then the ancestors of the Lwo-speakers started to move south, towards the Juba-Nimule area. It was from this area that the Shilluk and Anuak returned north, while the rest continued southwards, settling at Pubungu, near Pakwach. At this point in their migration a number of important divisions took place:

a. A group led by Nyipir moved west across the Nile, colonised the Lendu, Okebu and Madi groups, and founded small chiefdoms. These followers of Nyipir came to be known as the Alur.

b. A second group, led by Labongo, moved south, crossing the Nile at Pawir and invaded Bunyoro-Kitara. They founded the Babito dynasty together with other sub-dynasties elsewhere in Uganda. Reference has been made to these in the previous chapter. Some of Labongo's group, however, returned north and moved into Acholi, Lango, and parts of Alur, Busoga and Padhola.

c. A third group remained at Pubungu, then gradually moved into the country of the Acholi, Lango, Padhola and so into Kenya.

e. A fourth group entered Acholi from the direction of Lafon Hill, having broken away from the Anuak. They occupied Acholi, Padhola and Nyanza.

These movements are shown on Map 10.

Fig. 5.1 A traditional Shilluk, one of the ethnic groups of the Southern Sudan.

31

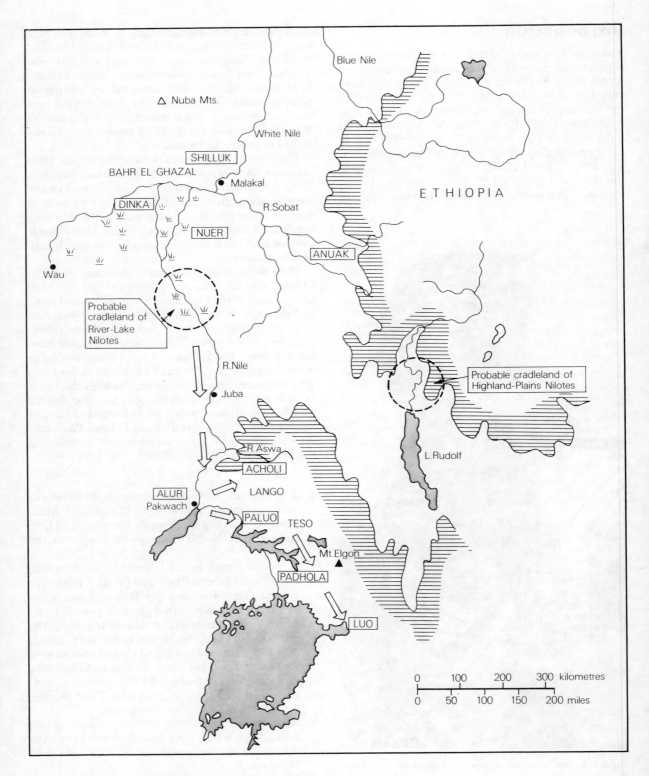

Map 10 The Nilotes: showing cradlelands and movements into Uganda

Characteristics of Lwo migration

Before examining some of these Lwo-speaking groups in more detail something should be said about the general features of this movement and mixing of people across the north and east of Uganda. In many ways this region became a meeting point of languages and cultures during the sixteenth to nineteenth centuries. The remarkable thing about the Lwo-speakers was the way in which they adjusted to new situations; adapting to suit conditions of environment or climate, absorbing and incorporating alien traditions and cultures. The most recent research on Lwo history stresses this characteristic as common to them all. 'Their flexibility among new peoples, their ability to adapt and absorb.' (D. W. Cohen: *Zamani* p. 136.) It was, as we have seen with the Babito in Bunyoro, a two-way process; the Lwo-speakers retaining many of the ideas and techniques they found, while at the same time transmitting something of their own culture, notably their language.

It used to be pointed out that two basic features of Lwo culture were their 'cattle complex' and the institution of divine kingship. However, historians do not appear to attach the same importance to these aspects today. While it is true that the tradition of 'rethship' or 'rwotship' (chiefs or kings) often added prestige to Lwo-speaking groups and attracted others to them, it does not appear to have led to the same rigid hierarchical structure of society as was found in the Bunyoro-Kitara Empire and later in the Kingdom of Buganda. Similarly with the 'cattle complex', where great importance is attached to the possession of cattle for economic, social and emotional reasons, this was by no means universal to all Lwo-speaking groups. Where conditions were unsuitable they did without cattle.

It is also important to emphasise that throughout this period of movement and settlement, which spanned the fifteenth to the nineteenth centuries, migration took the form of small groups travelling independently of each other, sometimes settling down together and then moving on, not always moving in the same direction and, often coming into contact or conflict with non-Lwo groups. Yet throughout this time they retained their common traditions and identity, although always prepared to cooperate with others.

The Alur

The former inhabitants of this area, such as the Kebu, Lendu, Lugbara and Kakwa were of Sudanic stock. When, by the mid-fifteenth century Lwo-speaking groups were beginning to disperse from Pubungu, two leaders, Nyipir and Tifool, moved west with their people and established themselves as chiefs over the area known as Alur today. The non-Lwo of this area gradually gave up their language for that of the Lwo and the two groups merged into one, though the Lwo still retained their status as royal clans, each with its rwot, while the non-Lwo Alur remained the 'common clans' or 'Jukal'. Early in the eighteenth century a new group of Lwo-speakers which had earlier moved into Bunyoro-Kitara came and settled in the lowland area of Alur country. By the nineteenth century the Ukuru had become the dominant chiefdom among the highland Alur, while the KocRagem chiefdom was the most important among the lowland Alur.

The Acholi

The Lwo-speaking group which moved from Pubungu to the north-east, into present-day Acholiland, were known as the Patiko. They met Ateker-speaking cultivators who had come from the east and north-east, and also Sudanic-speaking cultivators coming in from the west. They would appear to have merged with each other without too much friction, on the basis of small clans. Despite a great deal of movement, the coming and going of different ethnic groups, over many years, the Acholi were beginning to emerge as a distinct people by the seventeenth century. Helped by their growing numbers and their ability to absorb and adapt, the Lwo-speaking element had come to dominate this area through the formation of small centralised states. Each was formed out of a group of clans linked by a common loyalty to a rwot and his family. Many of these had their own ritual and regalia, while the rwot appointed village chiefs or 'jago', who were responsible for the raising of taxes and tribute all of which went to support the rwot and maintain the security of the state. Although independent of each other, these states were so similar in structure and style of government that one can trace the influence of Lwo culture and ideas here, just as much as in Alur and other parts of Uganda.

The Langi

The Langi were not part of the main-stream of River-Lake Nilotic migration. They represent, in fact, an interesting example of the fusion of two separate peoples and cultures leading to the for-

Fig. 5.2 Batchelor quarters in Lango, Northern Uganda.

mation of a new society. When the Lwo-speaking migrants came into this area from the north they met, as in Acholi, Ateker-speaking cultivators. The latter gradually lost their own language and started speaking Lwo, though retaining their own characteristic dialect. They also gave up their cyclical age-system. The Langi society that developed out of this was a real fusion of the two cultures. The basic unit was the clan, or 'ateker' as they called it. The clan name was retained however scattered or separate they might become. Thus an Atek group living among the Oki clan would describe themselves as 'Atek me Oki' which means the Atek living among the Oki. It is not therefore difficult to identify clans in Lango. The clan leaders were often referred to as rwot or 'rwodi' in the plural. However, unless they combined this with skill in military leadership they were not particularly powerful figures.

War became a crucial feature of Langi society. It was a source of wealth and prestige. From the north-west, fighting against the Madi, the Langi could return with women, weapons, cattle and goats. From the Kumam in the east they could obtain captives. The Langi acquired a great reputation as fighters. They fought for the Banyoro princes, Kabigumire, Mupina and Kabalega, and

brought back with them as their reward sweet potato vines, copper and iron bracelets. In 1872 they were strong enough to prevent an armed force from Egypt from harrying their country and killed 250 of the invaders. War called for special organisation, so that by the nineteenth century an overall war-leader, or 'Witong', (meaning 'the tip of a spear') had emerged whose task was to coordinate all military activity. Among famous holders of this office were Ogwal Abura of Bar, Akedi of Moroto and Agoro Abwango of Bar. So intense was the rivalry to succeed the latter, following his death in 1886, that civil war broke out in Lango. The Langi also distinguished themselves serving with Kabalega's 'abarusura'. When the British entered Uganda they met with stiff resistance in Lango, so that it took their representative, Semei Kakungulu, a long time to subdue the district.

The Padhola

The people known as Jopadhola are descended from two strands of Lwo migration, one from the third group mentioned above, that had remained at Pubungu for a time before continuing through Acholi and Lango to the east, and the other from

34

Fig. 5.3 An early view of Victoria Nyanza from Murchison Bay.

that part of the second group (Labongo's) above, some of whom had returned from Bunyoro-Kitara and moved north and east.

Migrating as clans, both groups had passed through Port Atura, east of the present Murchison Falls bridge on the Kampala-Gulu road. When they moved into the Kaberamaido Peninsula they found it uninhabited so settled there for a time. They then appear to have moved east to northern Teso, on to Bugwere, and through Mbale and Tororo to West Budama, Bunyole and Budola. This last movement covered about 100 years, from the late sixteenth to the late seventeenth centuries. Traditions speak of their having to fight off cattle-raiding Maasai from the east and it may have been this that forced them to the western part of the area, where they had to clear away thick forest before they could settle. By about 1700 they had settled down.

The common bond that linked these people and others who later joined them was the relationship with Adhola, the leader of one of the early groups. As the population grew, a unified Padhola society began to develop, bringing together people of many different backgrounds, some Lwo-speaking, some Bantu, but all united by the common need to survive in the face of attacks and natural obstacles within their country. It was probably the experience of previous hardships and dangers that enabled the Lwo-speaking group in this community to survive and to dominate.

The Luo of Kenya and Tanzania

The movement of Lwo-speaking people into Kenya and Tanzania marks the furthest and final stage in the migration of the River-Lake Nilotes. Although the Luo of these areas claim descent from a common ancestor, Ramogi, this is probably no more than a mythical attempt to show that they are one people. The clan traditions give, instead, accounts of four quite distinct waves of migration into the Nyanza province of Kenya. As with Lwo migration elsewhere, these would have been widely separated in time and distance. They are:

1. Joka Jok—the Jok group
2. Joka Owiny—the Owiny group

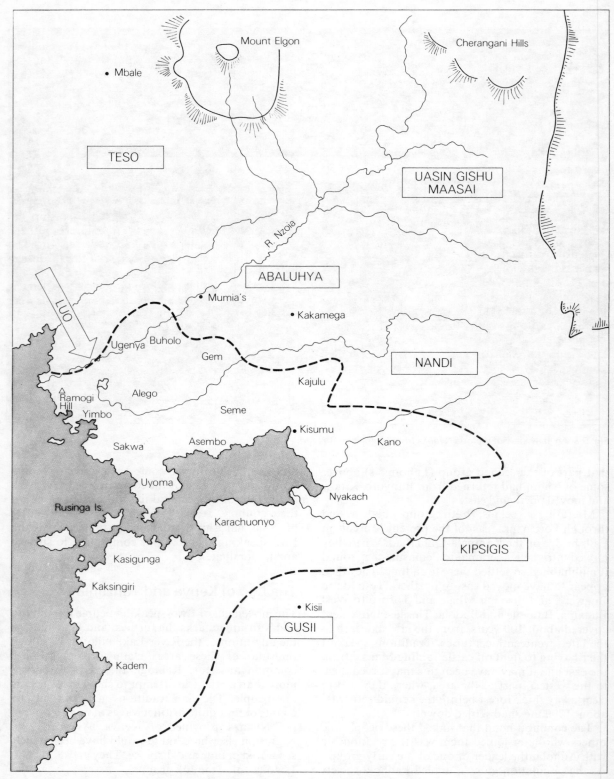

Map 11 Movement and settlements of the Luo and their neighbours in West Kenya

3. Joka Omolo—the Omolo group
4. The Abasuba—a mixed group

It will be clearer and easier to understand if we take each of these in turn.

The Jok group

Unlike the others, this group had no connection with Pubungu or Pawir, having apparently migrated directly from the Sudan into northern Uganda, settling around Lamogi in Acholi, south of the Agoro Hills. From here they moved via Gulu, Soroti and Mbale into Nyanza. Their most famous settlement was at Ramogi Hill in Kadimo, Siaya District, where Joka Jok are said to have arrived in the sixteenth century.

The Jokowiny group

Normally associated with the Padhola in Uganda, this group apparently decided to move from there into Kenya. Their major settlement was at Sigoma in Alego, and their most famous leader was Owiny Sigoma, a ruthless man and a hard fighter. These people were also known as the Jokaruoth, the people of the chief or king, for they were great conquerors. Their arrival in Nyanza has been dated to the early seventeenth century.

The Jokomolo group

They migrated from Pawir in North Bunyoro, and travelled through North Busoga, settling at Ibanda and Bukoli. Then they moved east into Kenya and are now represented by two major groups, the Jo-Gem and the Jo-Ugenya. They appeared in Nyanza about the start of the seventeenth century.

The 'Abasuba' group

This group is made up of a very mixed variety of people, many of whom were refugees from Buganda and Busoga or migrants from the shores of Lake Victoria. Although non-Lwo on arrival they became Lwo-speaking in due course as they merged with the Luo of Nyanza and settled in the southern part of the province, and on the off-shore islands, as you can see in Map 11.

The settlement of these groups around the lake shore and in Nyanza was accompanied by a good deal of inter-clan warfare, quite apart from wars with the Maasai, Nandi and Abaluhya to the east and north. The latter tended, in fact, to consolidate the Luo and gave them a sense of unity that they had hitherto not been conscious of. The increase in population during the eighteenth and nineteenth centuries caused many clans to break apart and disperse, seeking fresh land. At the same time the increasing importance attached to land forged new ties and loyalties, increasing the influence of certain prominent families at the expense of the old clan system. Gradually the pattern of political and economic organisation among the Luo changed, based on the larger unit of the tribe rather than the clan. With this a new form of chieftainship developed in northern, central and later southern Nyanza, in response to these local conditions. The Luo continued to expand and extend their frontiers until the end of the nineteenth century. But as wars became less frequent and the process of settlement completed, so the links between the Luo people were strengthened and their sense of identity hardened. They were now conscious of being a 'nation'.

Questions

1. How far is it true to speak of the Langi as a Lwo people?
2. Describe the evolution of the Acholi as a people and state.
3. Give an account of the way in which migration among the Lwo-speaking peoples took place.
4. What was the effect of the Lwo-speaking migrants upon the rest of the inhabitants of Uganda?
5. Trace the movement of the Luo of Kenya from the original 'Cradleland' of the River-Lake Nilotes to Nyanza.

Activities

1. Draw a sketch map to show the migration of the Luo and Padhola and their ancestors from their original cradleland in the Sudan to the shores of Lake Victoria. Show the people with whom they came into contact.
2. Discuss in class the stages and process by which a small family group could grow and develop eventually into a recognised and established tribe.

Chapter 6
The Highland and Plains Nilotes

Introduction

Recent research has shown that the Nilotes, River-Lake, Plains and Highland, all shared a common homeland on the south-western fringe of the Ethiopian Highlands. It was from here that the River-Lake Nilotes were the first to move, dispersing west to the Nile and thus losing contact with the

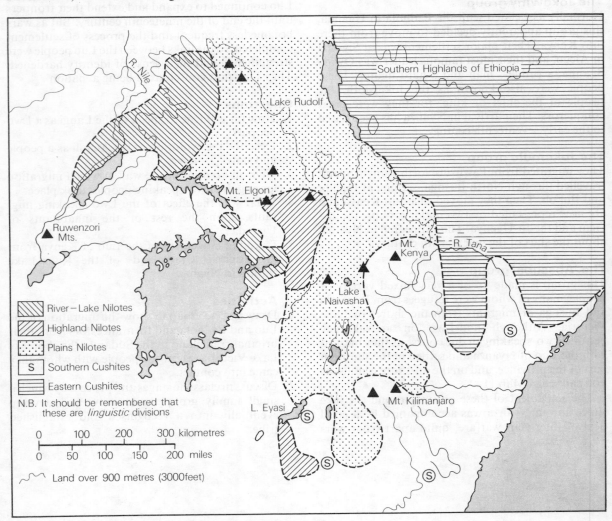

Map 12 The spread of Cushitic and Nilotic peoples into East Africa

Key:
- River–Lake Nilotes
- Highland Nilotes
- Plains Nilotes
- S Southern Cushites
- Eastern Cushites

N.B. It should be remembered that these are *linguistic* divisions

0 100 200 300 kilometres
0 50 100 150 200 miles

Land over 900 metres (3000feet)

Labels on map: R. Nile, Southern Highlands of Ethiopia, Lake Rudolf, Mt. Elgon, Ruwenzori Mts., Mt. Kenya, R. Tana, Mt. Naivasha, Lake Naivasha, L. Eyasi, Mt. Kilimanjaro

others and with many of the influences that were to affect them. But common to all three were certain Nilotic characteristics, such as the keeping of cattle, and possibly the bleeding and milking of cattle as well, linear age-sets and the removal of the lower incisor teeth. These characteristics were modified as a result of contacts with different cultures later. In the case of the Highland Nilotes, and to a lesser extent the Plains Nilotes, the strongest influence came from the Cushites.

We need to remember that our knowledge of the early Nilotes, as with most of the first migrants and settlers in East Africa, is still very limited. Our present information, in the case of the Highland and Plains Nilotes, has come largely from research carried out by linguists. This has helped to clarify the movements and links between the various groups who came in from the north. There is obviously a great need for additional and alternative material and it is hoped that archaeology in particular will have a contribution to make as it has done for the coastal civilisation. Oral tradition is yet another valuable tool for the historians working on this problem but cannot contribute much beyond the last few centuries.

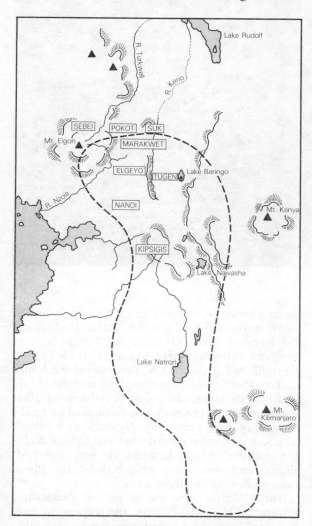

Map 13 The Highlands Nilotes: showing settlement areas of Kalenjin groups and the former extent of Highland Nilote influence c.1500

The influence of the Cushites

Brief reference has been made to the Cushites in the first chapter. Since they played such an important part in moulding the culture of the Highland and Plains Nilotes we ought to say a little more about them in this chapter. Formerly the term 'Nilo-Hamite' was used to describe the ancestors of the inhabitants of northern Kenya and parts of Uganda. It was thought that the Hamites were a particular group coming from north-east Africa bringing with them a superior civilisation which they imposed upon Nilotes and Bantu alike. This theory has been abandoned, as it has been proved that no such single group could have existed. Instead there was a much more complex and subtle pattern of relationships and contacts between Nilotes and the Cushitic-speaking people from the Ethiopian Highlands, and this was a two-way process. Moreover, there was more than one group of Cushites. It was the Southern Cushites who were the first to settle in East Africa, the earliest cultivators in that area, establishing their own Cushitic culture over a wide area of northern and western Kenya, extending as far as the south-western shores of Lake Victoria (see Map 12). While this was taking place, possibly as early as three or four thousand years ago, the ancestors of the Highland Nilotes were coming into contact with another group, the Eastern Cushites, in the area mentioned above as being the Nilotic homeland. They adopted many Cushitic practices such as the initiation ceremony of circumcision and the habit of not eating fish. Also, they absorbed many Cushitic words into their language. In their turn the Eastern Cushites may have borrowed the idea of age-sets and intensive cattle keeping from the Nilotes. All this took place over a long period of time and certainly before the Highland Nilotes started to move south into East Africa, where they were to come into contact with the

Fig. 6.1 Mount Elgon.

Southern Cushites. The Plains Nilotes evolved later and so do not appear in this early process of cultural growth.

The Highland Nilotes

The ancestors of the present-day Kalenjin people of Kenya would appear to have started migrating into East Africa during the last millenium B.C. They spread over a wide area covering much of north and western Kenya and the Rift Valley, gradually absorbing the Southern Cushites and displacing them as the dominant culture, except where the latter held out in a few remote and isolated pockets (see Map 13). But many of these Highland-Nilote communities of the extreme south and west were later to be absorbed by Bantu migrants from the south and west during the first millenium A.D. Three

groups, however, retained their distinctive language and culture—the Kalenjin, the Tatoga (Dadog) and the Kenya-Kadam. Of these the Tatoga were in northern Tanzania where they co-existed with hunters and food-gatherers (the ancestors of the Aramanik and the Sonjo), expanding later into the Mbulu and Singida areas, absorbing or influencing other communities and finally being swallowed up by the advancing Bantu-speaking Nyaturu and others. The Kenya-Kadam spread from east to west across the low, dry country between Mt Kenya and Mt Elgon, and were later absorbed by the Plains Nilotes moving into these parts.

The Kalenjin were the largest of these three groups of Highland-Nilotes and appear to have benefited from their situation in the western highlands of Kenya, where they were able to consolidate and then to expand unhindered by other groups.

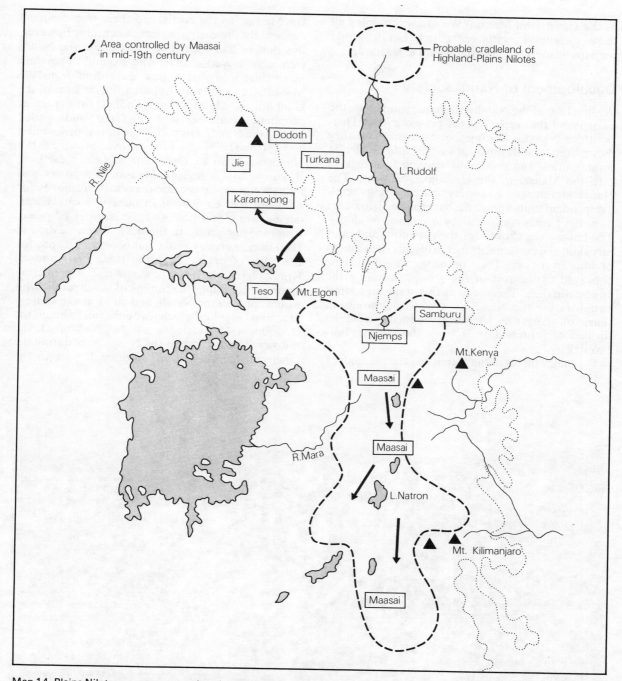

Map 14 Plains Nilotes: movements and settlement in East Africa

Within the map:

Area controlled by Maasai in mid-19th century

Probable cradleland of Highland-Plains Nilotes

R. Nile

Dodoth

Jie

Turkana

L. Rudolf

Karamojong

Teso

Mt. Elgon

Samburu

Njemps

Mt. Kenya

Maasai

Maasai

R. Mara

L. Natron

Mt. Kilimanjaro

Maasai

These were the ancestors of the modern Pokot, Sebei, Marakwet, Elgeyo, Tugen, Nandi and Kipsigis. Their evolution as a distinct group dates from the early part of the second millenium A.D. As they expanded and moved out, they came into contact with different people and so began the process of adaptation and absorption again. The Pokot, to the north, became heavily involved with the Karamojong-Teso group, while the Nandi to the south acquired a distinct way of life that owed much

41

to the Uasingishu Maasai. We cannot examine all these societies in sufficient detail, but it would perhaps be useful to take the Nandi as a sample.

Development of Nandi society

We first hear of the Nandi as a small group along the escarpment that separates the present Nandi District from Nyanza. During the seventeenth century they moved steadily north, absorbing other Kalenjin communities, and eventually coming face to face with the Maasai of the Uasingishu Plateau. The Nandi developed a society based upon semi-independent units known as 'bororoisiek' (singular: 'bororiet') each controlled by a council of elders. The latter were chosen for their wisdom and military skill, and customarily met to discuss their affairs of state over beer. Their decisions would then be conveyed to the rest of the group, including the young warriors. There was at this stage no central authority for the Nandi as a whole, although in times of danger a territorial council would be formed of representatives from the various bororoisiek.

The major threat to the Nandi was the presence of the Maasai, to the north, and there were frequent clashes. By the early nineteenth century, however, this danger had started to decline and the Nandi were able to settle down and expand. They had meanwhile inherited a new institution from the Maasai, the 'orkoiyot'. Apparently a member of the Oloiboni, a Maasai family noted for its great prophetic qualities, had migrated and settled among the Nandi. His name was Barsabotwo and it was not long before his advice proved of value to the Nandi who won a series of battles against the Luo, Bukusu and Uasingishu Maasai. His power and influence grew, he became the central authority for each bororiet to consult in matters such as war, circumcision, sacrifices and the transfer of power from one age group to the next. When he died in 1860 intense rivalry broke out between his sons for the office of orkoiyot. In the 1880s his grandson Kimnyolei emerged as a powerful leader, predicting among other things the coming of white people who would conquer the Nandi, and also a snake spitting fire and smoke which would run along the escarpment—a reference to the coming of the railway. The strength of the Nandi grew during the nineteenth century, due in no small part to the

Fig. 6.2 Maasai and their homes.

42

unifying influence of the orkoiyot. They harrassed their neighbours to the north and west, and were only stopped from further expansion by the arrival of the British at the end of the century.

The Plains Nilotes

During the second millenium A.D. (i.e. from about A.D. 1000) the Plains Nilotes emerged as a new and powerful force in East Africa. Traditions speak of a dispersal point somewhere in the Lake Rudolf area. One group, the Bari-speakers, moved into the Sudan; the other, the Teso-Maasai group split into three sections—the Lotuko, the Karamojong-Teso and the Maasai. Of these the Maasai became by far the most far-reaching and influential. The Lotuko eventually settled in the Sudan, the Karamojong-Teso moved west towards Mt Elgon, while the Maasai spread south-east towards Mt Kenya and then throughout most of central Kenya and northern Tanzania.

The Plains Nilotes were to have a profound effect on the later settlement and development of the peoples of East Africa. Being primarily pastoralists they preferred the open grasslands of the Rift Valley and the highlands for their cattle, while the need for water and fresh pasture meant that they were frequently on the move. They acquired a reputation, as pastoralists often do, for fierce and aggressive behaviour, not always justified. However, in the case of the Maasai particularly, they established a military predominance over large parts of Kenya and Tanzania that remained unchallenged until the nineteenth century.

Fig. 6.3 Rendille women of Northern Kenya.

The Maasai

From their original dispersal point the ancestors of the Maasai moved southwards, settling first to the east of the Rift Valley, in the area between Mt Kenya, Mt Kilimanjaro and the Taita hills (see Map 14). Some of the habits adopted from the Eastern Cushites they passed on to Bantu people, such as the early Chagga and Kikuyu, among whom they lived. The Maasai were also influenced by the Highland Nilotes, in whose steps they followed as they expanded south down the Rift Valley. This process had begun by the start of the seventeenth century and by the end of the eighteenth century the Maasai were approaching the height of their power, ranging from the Uasingishu Plateau in the north-west to the Laikipia and Samburu Uplands, and south into Tanzania as far as the country of the Gogo. By trading, raiding and intermarriage they affected

Fig. 6.4 A Turkana family.

43

nearly every major group in Kenya and northern Tanzania. Their movements were like a stone thrown into a pool, causing ripples that flow out right across its surface. And yet their influence was out of all proportion to their numbers, which remained relatively small.

We have seen that a number of Maasai-speaking groups developed. The Samburu fought and traded with the Galla and Rendille (Eastern Cushites) to the east and with the Turkana and Pokot to the west. The Laikipia Maasai, further south, alternately attacked and exchanged goods with the Bantu-speaking people of the Mt Kenya region. The Uasingishu Maasai, as we have seen, fought with the Kalenjin in general and the Nandi in particular, but also left their influence in more permanent ways. The great Maasai expansion southwards along the Rift Valley had led to the emergence of two distinct groups—the Iloikop, or Wakwavi, who were both agriculturalists and pastoralists, and the IlMaasai who remained pastoralists. Civil wars and struggles between and within these groups indicate that the Maasai were never a single united people; in fact they never had a stable, centralised form of government.

Leadership was exercised through the system of age-sets, the 'moran' or warriors providing the fighting forces while the administration of each group was the responsibility of the elders.

Among the IlMaasai there existed the system of ritual leadership based on the Oloiboni, copied by the Nandi. Supet was the first known such leader, born about 1778, succeeded by Mbatian in the mid-nineteenth century, and on his death the authority was claimed by Sendeyo and Lenana. The latter, supported by the British, was recognised as paramount chief in 1901. But the significance and influence of these leaders, or 'laibons' as they were called, as overall leaders of the Maasai people did not grow until the nineteenth century.

How then can we account for the dominance of the Maasai during much of the seventeenth to nineteenth centuries over large areas of East Africa? Foremost among the reasons is their ability as warriors. With their long spears, shields of hide, clubs and war-paint and ostrich feather plumes they must have presented a formidable spectacle. They were trained from youth to show extreme courage in the face of danger, whether against man or beast. Secondly, not only did they fight for themselves, but often as allies to other communities, such as the rulers of Wanga and Chief Rindi of the Chagga, thus gaining influence and prestige further afield. Thirdly, they controlled a number of important caravan routes, so that traders wishing to cross their territory were forced to pay for the privilege. Finally, in their relationships with close neighbours, such as the Kikuyu, they often built up ties of kinship and common interest, based on intermarriage and trade, which benefited both sides. The Kikuyu sold ochre, honey, pots, calabashes, weapons, and foodstuffs to the Maasai in return for skins, leather and livestock, and later on (through the caravans from the Coast) beads, salt, cowrie shells, brass and iron-ware which the Maasai received as tribute. There were local trade routes called by the Kikuyu 'njira cia agendi' that ran from their country to Naivasha, Narok and Nanyuki which remained open even in times of war. Frequent marriages arranged between the Maasai and Kikuyu helped to reduce tension between them. Thus when the Purko Maasai defeated the Laikipia Maasai in a war between 1870 and 1875 the latter fled and hid among their Kikuyu relatives. There were other signs of cultural interchange, the Kikuyu adopting Maasai military techniques and styles.

Reasons for the decline in Maasai influence are varied. Their own civil wars, becoming more frequent in the nineteenth century, provide a major explanation. Then a series of calamities hit the Maasai in the latter part of the nineteenth century; small-pox, cholera and rinderpest, which killed off large numbers of cattle as well as people. They were more vulnerable to periods of famine and drought than the agricultural Bantu with their settled communities. Maasai society was probably less adaptable to changed circumstances than others, making it harder for them to seize the opportunities brought by Arab and then British intervention in the final years of the nineteenth century.

The Karamojong-Teso

Though perhaps less famous than the Maasai the other branch of the Plains Nilotes that settled in East Africa, the Karamojong-Teso people, were no less active in their way. Their period of active expansion and movement was also the seventeenth to eighteenth centuries, in the area of north-west Kenya and north-east Uganda. Also pastoralists by origin, they preferred the dry open country north of the Kenya Highlands. They displaced or absorbed smaller groups as they moved, the Karamojong eventually settling to the north, while the Teso moved to the area between Mt Napak and Lake Bisina where they were settled by the early years of the nineteenth century, then round the slopes of Mt

Fig. 6.5 The fertile land of Bugisu, Mount Elgon, of the sort that attracted the Teso.

Elgon to their present homeland.

Teso traditions refer to descent from a people called Itunga, one of whose clans was known as Ateker. This bears a strong resemblance to the ancestral Langi history, and confirms the impression that there was a strong movement of non Lwo-speaking people from the Karamoja region into Uganda at this time.

As the Teso moved into fertile land around Mt Elgon and not far from the lake, they gradually adapted to the life and ways of agriculturalists. New crops were introduced by a group known as the Iworopom. Banyoro and Basoga traders brought iron implements, so that the Iteso were able to develop more intensive cultivation. With the growth in food supplies their numbers rapidly increased and a more highly organised form of society developed. This was based upon clans, the clan meeting being called the 'etem'. There were smaller groups as well, 'eitela', each with its functionaries. The most important of these was probably the 'emuron', who possessed divine powers such as rain-making, predicting the outcome of wars and blessing the warriors. The 'ekareban' was the village ambassador, and the arbiter and settler of disputes, while the 'aruwon' was primarily a military leader, chosen for his bravery and skill in battle. When a common enemy confronted them the various aruwon would bring their forces together, having first consulted the emuron.

Questions

1. What role did the orkoiyot play in Nandi society?
2. How true is it that the Maasai were purely a warrior race?
3. How was Teso society organised?
4. What effect did the Cushites have upon the Highland and Plains Nilotes?
5. What was the relationship between the Kikuyu and the Maasai?

Activities

1. Discuss in class the different qualities needed among pastoral and agricultural communities—comparing, say, the Maasai and the Chagga.
   How did these affect their
   a) government,
   b) religion,
   c) social life.
2. Find out more about the Early Cushites (see Chapter 8 in *Zamani*) and the evidence that may link them with the archaeological site of Engaruka in northern Tanzania.
3. Make a list of the similarities and differences between Highland and Plains Nilotes, using the Maasai and Kalenjin peoples as examples.

Chapter 7
The Western Bantu peoples, 1500–1900

Introduction

We concluded Chapter 4 with an account of the Bunyoro-Kitara Empire under the Babito dynasty who first established themselves as rulers in the fourteenth century. They continued to rule for the next six centuries. Similar Babito dynasties were set up in neighbouring territories, so that we see the emergence of the kingdoms of Buganda, Toro, Nkore, Haya and Wanga, with smaller principalities in Busoga (see Map 15). Linked in varying degrees by common traditions of descent from Babito founders they form a striking contrast, with their centralised government and royal traditions, to the more loosely united, less compact societies in other parts of East Africa at this time. The people of these kingdoms were predominantly Bantu, and as agriculturalists they occupied some of the most fertile land in East Africa, well watered and close to the lakes. Equipped with iron tools and the knowledge of the cultivation of bananas and yams, it is not surprising that they flourished, economically as well as politically. Despite the large amount of material collected on the history of these kingdoms, largely in the form of oral traditions relating to the rulers and their achievements, there is still much that is incomplete about our knowledge.

The lake kingdoms

Bunyoro

Bunyoro traditions have been recorded in two important documents, *Bukya Nibwira* by Prince Karubanga and *Abakama ba Bunyoro-Kitara* by John Nyakatura. These give the royal histories of the kingdom as handed down from generation to generation. They tell us how the Bachwezi Empire was inherited by the first of the Babito rulers, Ising-oma Mpuga Rukidi, and describe the fortunes of the dynasty through twenty-six successive Abakama from the fourteenth to the twentieth centuries.

Although notable warriors, the Babito lacked any great cultural heritage and adopted much of the Bachwezi system, including the rituals and customs of kingship. For a further two hundred years they kept Bunyoro all powerful, raiding east and south without hindrance, though never able to restore the kingdom to its former strength and size under Bachwezi rule. In the course of time some of the outlying provinces broke away, including the important grain producing and iron manufacturing province of Buddu.

Bunyoro was governed as a loose federation of provinces, or 'saza', each under a chief appointed by the Omukama, and responsible directly to him. However, owing to the extent and size of the kingdom these saza chiefs were often semi-independent, especially those on the borders. It was in such areas as Koki, Buddu and Toro that they could and did break away. Many of these chiefs came from the royal dynasty, the Babito, from which the Omukama was chosen. Frequently disputes arose between the princes as to who should succeed. This usually took the form of a struggle to acquire the jawbone of the dead Omukama, since whoever buried it acquired the legitimate right to succeed. Rebellions often broke out, and during the long reign of Kyebambe Nyamutukura III four of his sons turned against him. One of them, Kaboyo Omuhanwa, broke away and set up the kingdom of Toro for himself. The fact that the saza chiefs could raise their own provincial armies or 'obwesengeze' did not always make matters any easier for the Omukama. However, a powerful ruler could unite and defend the kingdom most effectively.

Such a man was Omukama Kabalega, in the late nineteenth century. He created a standing army of

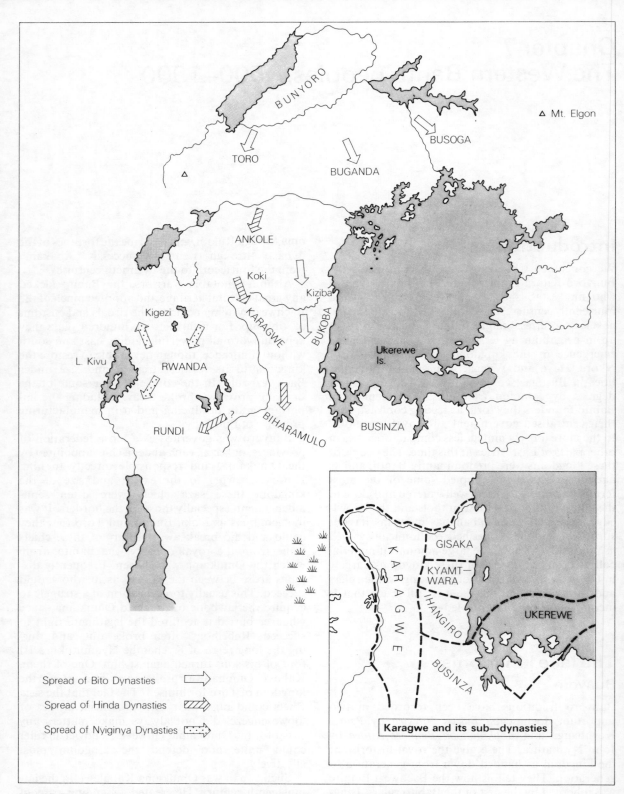

Map 15 The Kingdoms of the interlacustrine area, including Karagwe and its sub-dynasties

Labels within map:

BUNYORO

△ Mt. Elgon

TORO

BUSOGA

BUGANDA

ANKOLE

Koki

Kiziba

Kigezi

KARAGWE

BUKOBA

Ukerewe Is.

L. Kivu

RWANDA

RUNDI

BIHARAMULO

BUSINZA

Spread of Bito Dynasties

Spread of Hinda Dynasties

Spread of Nyiginya Dynasties

Inset:

KARAGWE

GISAKA

KYAMT—WARA

IHANGIRO

UKEREWE

BUSINZA

Karagwe and its sub—dynasties

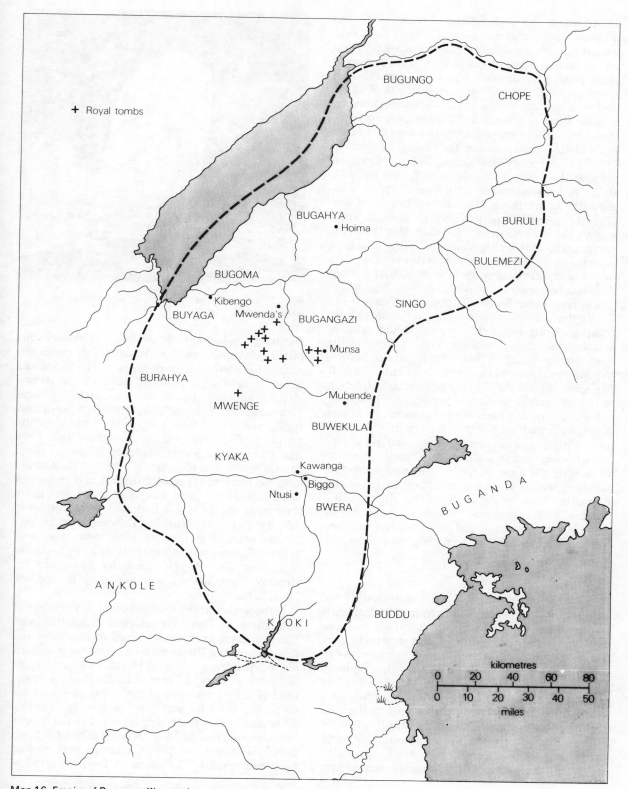

+ Royal tombs

BUGUNGO

CHOPE

BURULI

BUGAHYA

• Hoima

BULEMEZI

BUGOMA

SINGO

• Kibengo

BUYAGA

Mwenda's

BUGANGAZI

+ + +
+ + +
+ +
+ +   + + • Munsa

BURAHYA

+

MWENGE

• Mubende

BUWEKULA

KYAKA

• Kawanga

BUGANDA

• Biggo

Ntusi •

BWERA

ANKOLE

BUDDU

KOOKI

kilometres

| 0 | 20 | 40 | 60 | 80 |

| 0 | 10 | 20 | 30 | 40 | 50 |

miles

Map 16 Empire of Bunyoro–Kitara at its greatest extent in the sixteenth century

49

20 000 men, the 'Abarusura', divided into ten divisions, each under a commander. These were posted to outlying areas to guard against invasion and to act as a check on the powers of the princes in these parts. One division was at the capital, Masindi, under Kabalega's greatest general, Rwabudongo, while that to the south was commanded by another famous general, Kikukuule. Not only was this army used to maintain internal law and order but Kabalega used it to raid Toro and Busongora in 1876. He defeated Sir Samuel Baker's Egyptian force at the battle called Baligota Isansa in 1872. Baker had attempted to set up an Egyptian protectorate in northern Uganda on behalf of the Khedive Ismail. Finally Kabalega led his army against the British in a guerilla war which lasted for seven years. But by this time Bunyoro had long since lost its supremacy. As early as the closing years of the seventeenth century a more powerful kingdom was emerging to the south, namely Buganda.

The reasons for Bunyoro's decline are not hard to see. In the first place it was not an easy state to hold together, being too widely scattered and open to attack from many directions. The economy of the kingdom was based on pastoralism and agriculture, the latter practised by the Babito's Bairu subjects. It has been said that they did not pay enough attention to the interests or welfare of the Bairu. The loss of some of the richest parts of the kingdom, Koki and Kyaggwe important for their iron, north Bulemezi and north Singo for their grazing, and Buddu as already mentioned, further weakened Bunyoro while strengthening its rivals. It was probably the steady growth of these neighbours, especially Buganda, that brought Bunyoro down. This process was continued by the intervention of outside forces, such as the Arab traders and the European imperialists in the nineteenth century.

Toro

It was the Babito prince, Kaboyo, mentioned above, who set up the kingdom of Toro in the nineteenth century (see Map 17). There are two possible explanations as to the name of this state: one, that Tooro was the name of a hill in the Ruwenzori range and that the people living around it, originally known as Banyakanziga, came to be called the Batooro; the other is that the Chwezi king Ndahura found the people so friendly on a visit to the area that he called the place Tooro, meaning 'festival'.

Toro itself comprised Burahya county, around the present town of Fort Portal. But Kaboyo also controlled the areas of Bunyangabu, Busongora,

Fig. 7.1 The Omukama of Toro being 'crowned' by his mother in 1933.

Bwamba and probably Kibale. Although his father's favourite son, Kaboyo had become impatient for power and responsibility. His father had named him 'Okwiri', official head of the Babito clan, but with this title went the rule that he could not succeed as Omukama of Bunyoro. When the opportunity arose he broke away and found that the people of Toro were willing to support him. They had their own reasons: distance from the royal capital meant that they hardly ever saw the Omukama. Secondly they resented the fact that princesses were sent as chiefs to rule over them, but more important the Toro felt that they were not being adequately protected against their enemies. Helped by the men of Busongora with their bows and arrows, Kaboyo was able to resist the army his father sent after him. Besides the latter had given instructions that his son was not to be pursued or killed in the fighting.

Kaboyo therefore became the first of a new line of Omukama in Toro. He adopted much the same form of government as was used in Bunyoro, and relied upon the Busongora bowmen to safeguard his independence. He died in the 1850s and there followed a period of civil wars for twenty years, until Nyaika I emerged as the victor by killing his own brother. It was his action in stealing Kabalega's cattle in Mwenge that led to the latter's invasion of Toro in 1876. Nyaika died of a heart attack, although his people claimed that he had been bewitched by Kabalega. A further period of

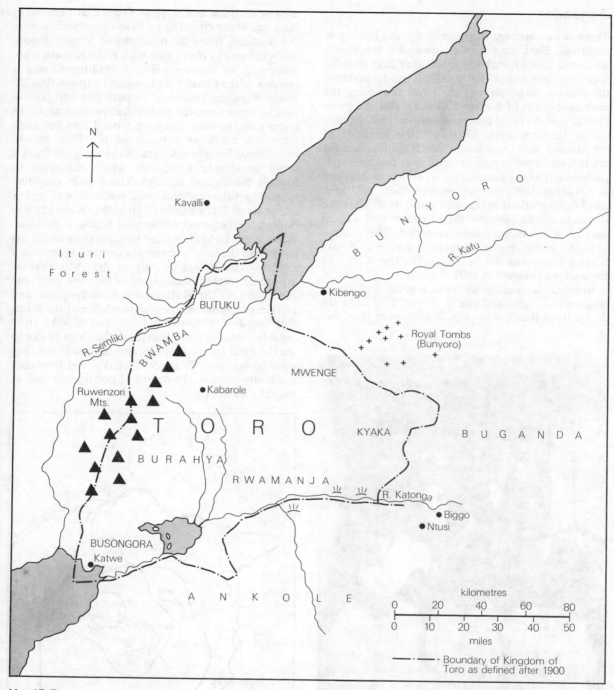

Map 17 Toro

confusion followed with Kabalega's forces attempting to retain power. Eventually it was the British forces that restored Toro to independence by overthrowing Kabalega and installing Kasagama as their puppet. He signed the Toro Agreement with the British in 1901.

51

Buganda

There is no shortage of material for the history of Buganda. Each clan kept its own oral traditions, while the court historians made sure that nothing was forgotten about the royal family. In addition the custom of preserving the royal jawbones, the umbilical cords of former Kabakas, and the guardianship of the royal tombs all ensured that the past would be kept alive. Moreover the methods of inheritance and succession in Buganda society made it easier for people to recall their predecessors, particularly as the population was more stable than in neighbouring pastoral communities. All these conditions made it easier and more likely that the Baganda would preserve their history, and a good deal of this has now been recorded. The earliest written record by a Muganda was Sir Apolo Kagwa's *Basekabaka be Buganda* (The Kings of Buganda) published in 1901.

From these sources we learn a great deal about Buganda's origins and rise to power. The Baganda derive from Bantu clans which were already in this area as far back as A.D. 1000. Other clans moved in later on, some claiming to have come with Kintu, the founder, from the direction of Mount Elgon, while others say they came with Kato Kimera who, according to Bunyoro-Kitara traditions, was a brother of the Omukama Isingoma Mpuga Rukidi. Some Buganda historians dispute this and believe that he came from the earlier Bachwezi dynasty. In either case, he may well have moved into Buganda from the north as a result of the Lwo Babito invasion of Bunyoro-Kitara. Buganda grew from a small nucleus in Kyadondo which expanded to include Busiro and Busujjo. This was in the fourteenth to fifteenth centuries, while it was still a minor state. The authority of the early Kabakas was limited by the power of the clan heads or Batakas. When Kabaka Mutebi tried to bring them under his control in the mid seventeenth century there was a mutiny. The Kabaka's role at first was that of arbitrator rather than ruler. Disputes over the succession to the Kabakaship were frequent and further strengthened the independence of the clans. But faced with constant raids and attacks from outside, notably from Bunyoro, the clans began to see the need for closer links and more unity if they were to survive. Thus the Kabaka and his court gradually became the centre of political as well as military authority.

Fig. 7.2 Kabaka Mutesa and Apolo Kagwa (right).

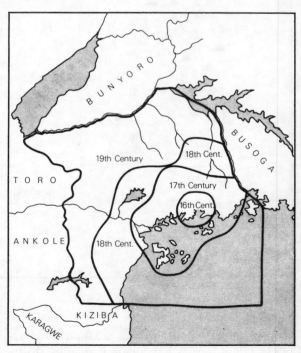

Map 18 The expansion of Buganda

52

During the eighteenth century the tide began to turn against Bunyoro, as the Baganda captured the rich province of Buddu in Kabaka Junju's reign, then Bwera, followed by Buwekula early in the nineteenth century. As Bunyoro's power shrank so the Baganda moved in to the bordering lands such as Ssingo, Buruli, Bugerere and Bulemezi. We can see from Map 19 that Buganda possessed certain natural and strategic advantages: it was small and compact, with the shores of Lake Victoria as its southern boundary, it was well watered and possessed fertile soil giving ideal conditions for intensive cultivation, especially bananas. Food was therefore plentiful and the banana became the staple diet, available throughout the year. Consequently Buganda's population grew rapidly and may well have reached half a million by the early nineteenth century. When one adds to this a highly organised and centralised system of government, centred round the Kabaka, it is not difficult to explain the main reasons for Buganda's rise to power, helped of course by the weakness of her chief rivals, and by the influence of new forces from outside—Arab and European—to which we shall turn later.

The way in which Buganda developed such a highly centralised and efficient structure of government deserves closer attention (see Map 19). Much was due to the tradition of monarchy established by the Kabakas, many of whom were great leaders; this gave a sense of continuity and prestige that kept

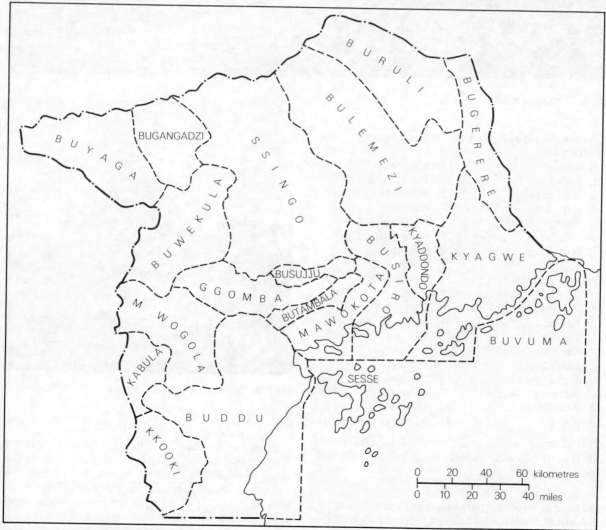

Map 19 Buganda: Ssaza areas (as in 1948)

53

Fig. 7.3a Rubaga, Mutesa I's capital.

Chronological list of the Kabakas of Buganda

1. Kintu
2. Chwa
3. Kalimera
4. Kimera
5. Lumansi
6. Tembo
7. Kigala
8. Kiimba
9. Wampamba
10. Kaima
11. Nakibinge
12. Mulondo
13. Jemba
14. Suna I
15. Sekemanya
16. Kimbugwe
17. Katerega
18. Mutebi
19. Juko

20. Kayemba
21. Tebandeke
22. Ndawula
23. Kagulu
24. Kikulwe
25. Mawanda
26. Musanje
27. Mwanga I
28. Namugala
29. Kyabagu
30. Junju
31. Semakokiro
32. Wasanje
33. Kamanya
34. Suna II
35. Mutesa
36. Mwanga II
37. Daudi Chwa
38. Mutesa II

(Based upon information supplied to Dallington Muftaa by Mutesa: quoted in *Uganda Journal* Vol. 26, p. 95)

Fig. 7.3b The exterior of Mutesa's tomb.

alive the loyalty and patriotism of their subjects.

Around the Kabaka himself there grew up all the rituals and ceremonies of royalty, so that he was regarded as a semi-divine being, whose every word must be obeyed and every wish supplied. During the reign of Mulondo, ninth Kabaka, the coronation throne or 'Namulondo' was first used. Other symbols of royalty, for example the drums, spears and stools, were also to be found. A hierarchy of officials, each with his particular title and functions,

Fig. 7.4 Kabaka Mwanga in 1894.

was appointed by the Kabaka. Some had cere-monial duties at court, while others were res-ponsible for state departments. The Katikiro was chief minister, the Omulamuzi was chief justice and the Omuwanika was treasurer. By a skilful practice of marrying a wife from each of the principal clans the Kabakas strengthened the links of loyalty, giving the clans a closer interest in the monarchy. Important posts at court would be awarded to specific clans. Also, the leading families from each clan were encouraged to send their sons to the court as pages or 'bagalagala' where they would be educated and obtain office and profit. Promotion at court came through military or civil service to the Kabaka, and in this way a compact system of authority was built up. By the appoint-ment of chiefs of his own choosing the Kabaka was gradually able to weaken the power of the Bataka in the provinces. This process, started under Kabaka

Mawanda early in the eighteenth century, meant that by the end of that century seven of the ten county chiefs owed their position directly to the Kabaka, and only three remained hereditary. In the nineteenth century the process of centralisation was continued under Kabakas Suna and Mutesa I. Although they had a council or 'lukiko' to advise them, the Kabakas were absolute in their power and authority. One weakness in such a highly centra-lised structure could be the personality and charac-ter of the Kabaka. Under a wise, far-sighted ruler all would be well. But it only needed a weak, hesitant king to bring the whole kingdom to chaos and disorder. Another danger was to appear with the growth of Islam and Christianity in Buganda in the second half of the nineteenth century; loyalty to Kabakas such as Mutesa and Mwanga could not be reconciled with conversion to such religions.

The accounts of the first European and Arab

visitors to Buganda in the nineteenth century present an impression of a prosperous and flourishing society. Stanley described it as 'a garden of Eden', full of well tended gardens and plantations, a network of roads, peaceful and well organised people going about their business.

Although proud of their own achievements and culture the Baganda were quick to try out new ideas and techniques. This was to be of great importance to them with the coming of Arab traders and European missionaries, travellers and administrators. Notable among their own skills were the manufacture of bark-cloth, the construction of elaborate reed palaces and fences, iron-working and the building of canoes using a special method of sewing wooden planks together with strong fibre. These canoes, some of which were of considerable size, were used for both peaceful and warlike purposes. The Baganda controlled the northern shores of the Lake as well as the neighbouring islands.

Nkore

Following the disappearance of the Bachwezi a power vacuum was created in the area of Eastern Ankole. Into this moved the Bahinda clan under their leader Ruhinda who established the kingdom of Nkore (see Map 20). These people were Bahima who had moved from the south-west into western

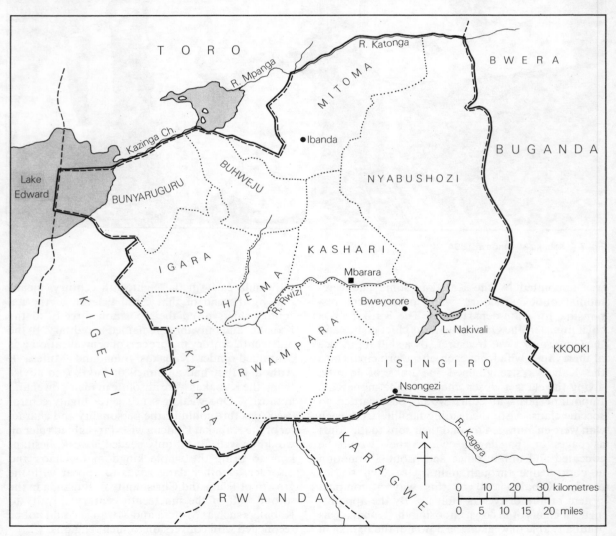

Map 20 Ankole, the kingdom of Nkore

Uganda by about A.D. 1350. A new dynasty, with Ruhinda as its first ruler, or Omugabe, began to settle in Isingiro, the nucleus of the kingdom. The Bahinda claimed to be descended from the Bachwezi whom they, like others, regarded as gods. It was said that Omuchwezi Wamara had married Njunaki, a slave girl, at Mbarara, the Nkore capital, and that Ruhinda was her son. The kingdom of Nkore consisted of two quite distinct groups, the ruling Bahima who were pastoralists, and the agricultural Bairu.

The open plains of Nkore, with their herds of cattle, were a tempting target for the rulers of Bunyoro who frequently invaded and raided the state. At the beginning of the eighteenth century Omukama Cwamali invaded them, and went on to raid Rwanda, where he was killed. His retreating army was routed by the Banyankole under their Omugabe, Ntare IV. For this exploit he earned the title Kiitabanyoro or killer of the Banyoro. It was during his reign that Nkore's rise to power began. He extended his northern border as far as the River Katonga. Then the counties of Shema and Rwampara were inherited from Mpororo, a neighbouring state. In the mid-eighteenth century Omugabe Rwebishengye seized the pasture lands of Kabula from Bunyoro. Perhaps the greatest Omugabe was Mutambuka who conquered Igara and Buhweju in the nineteenth century and raided into Toro, Busongora and Karagwe. By the time of Ntare V's accession in 1875 Nkore was at the height of its power. However in a matter of years the kingdom appeared to be on the verge of disintegration. A series of epidemics of rinderpest, jiggers, tetanus

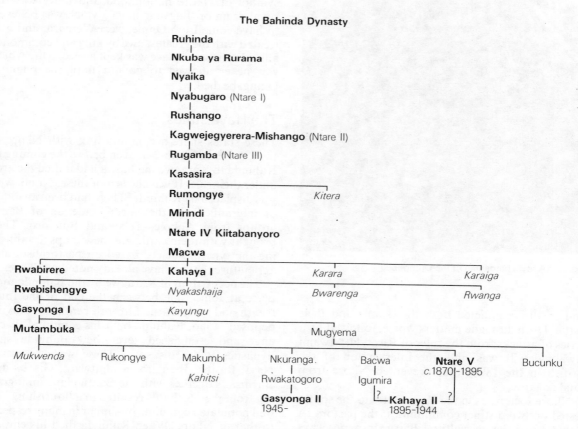

Source: Katate and Kamugungunu: 'Abagabe b' Ankole, Ekitabo I and II (Eagle Press, Kampala, 1955)
As printed in: H.F. Morris: 'A History of Ankole' (E.A.L.B., Nairobi, 1962)

Note: True ABAGABE lettered in bold; usurpers in italics.
Opinion differs as to whether Kahaya II was son of Ntare V or Igumira.

Fig. 7.5 The Bahinda Dynasty.

Fig. 7.6 A royal herdsman of the Omugabe.

supply without which the population could not have increased as steadily as it did. The Bahima provided the fighting forces to protect and extend their common interests. To the Bahima cattle were everything, their whole life being centred round them. Not only were cattle valuable in themselves but they added social status and prestige to their owners, and were an invaluable means of rewarding faithful followers. This tended to give the Bahima the position of a ruling class into which the Bairu could rarely ascend. The Omugabe ruled over them all, appointing his own chiefs 'Bakungu' to organise and lead the military units or 'Emitwe' in each region. He could not take his authority for granted, however, and needed to prove to his followers that he had the necessary qualities of leadership. He was the final arbiter in all legal disputes, so he needed to show mental as well as physical ability. The greatest symbol of Nkore nationhood and unity was the royal drum or 'Bagyendanwa', which was believed to have come from Omuchwezi Wamara, and was treated with the greatest awe by king and commoner alike. In the same place was kept a special fire which was never allowed to go out until the reigning Omugabe died.

The Haya states

These states share a common link with Nkore in their Bahinda rulers. But even before the coming of Ruhinda to Karagwe the Basita had united the area under their rule. It was the last of these, Nono, who was displaced by Ruhinda. There had been an influx of migrants from the north made up of Bantu groups from Ankole, Toro and Bunyoro. They brought with them cattle and new crops, establishing the type of society based on pastoralism and agriculture that we have already noted in Nkore.

The occupation of Karagwe by the Bahinda took place at some time between the end of the fourteenth and early in the fifteenth centuries. Having deposed Nono, Ruhinda built his capital at Bwehange and established seven new Bahinda sub-dynasties under his sons. These were Ukerewe, Nasa, Busiba, Ihangiro, Kyamtwara, Gisaka and Buzinza. Together with the Bantu clans immigrating from the north this resulted in a flourishing and well populated community, similar in many respects to that of Nkore. When Ruhinda died his empire broke up into independent states, each retaining its Bahinda rulers. The latter had brought with them the Chwezi cult of divine royalty, with all the attendant symbols such as drums and spear, so that their authority was not easily challenged.

and smallpox afflicted both the people and their cattle. Drought made matters worse, followed by a series of attacks from the ruler of Rwanda, Mwami Rwabugiri. It was only the intervention of the British in the 1890s that prevented Nkore from total collapse.

Nkore society, as in the Haya states to the south, rested on two distinct communities; the pastoralist Bahima and the agricultural Bairu. In many ways they complemented each other, the Bahima supplying the meat, milk, hides and produce of a cattle-owning community, while the Bairu provided the grain, yams and iron goods such as spears needed by the Bahima. The cultivators ensured the steady food

The Bahinda were accepted as rulers because of their fair minded judgments in local disputes, and for their proven ability as military leaders. Loyalty and unity was maintained by the practice, similar in some ways to that in Buganda, of gathering together the boys of a particular age group at the residence of the local chief where they would be trained to respect their elders, learn about the hierarchy of the state and acquire military experience. The most outstanding would be sent on to the Mukama's court.

The characteristic pattern of two classes, that of Bahima pastoralists and Bairu cultivators was maintained, and since so much prestige and status was given to the ownership of cattle it was inevitable that the Bahima remained the dominant group. Yet the two classes were essential to each other and to the state. The Bairu introduced new crops such as the plantain and coffee, the latter under strict control as it was regarded as something of a status symbol. Coffee berries were used on certain ceremonial occasions to establish blood-brotherhood between individuals or groups. Coffee was also exported to the northern kingdoms of Bunyoro, Nkore and Buganda in the nineteenth century, in return for cattle and barkcloth.

By the nineteenth century contacts were being made with the coastal trade that led to the introduction of a whole new range of goods. But more important still was the fact that Karagwe became a staging post along the trade route from the coast into Buganda. These new commercial activities started with the Nyamwezi and Usumbwa traders even before the Arabs appeared on the scene.

Rwanda and Burundi
The formation of the Kingdoms of Rwanda and Rundi

It is surprising that the area covered by the present states of Rwanda and Burundi, formerly Rundi, has so often been left out of books concerning the peoples and history of East Africa. Not only is it part of the physical region comprising the East African Highlands and Rift Valleys but its people have had more to do with their neighbours to the north and east than with those to the west. It is probably the fact that for the last forty years of the colonial period Rwanda-Rundi was administered by the Belgian Government as part of the Belgian Congo which accounts for this omission. These two states of Rwanda and Rundi occupy some of the

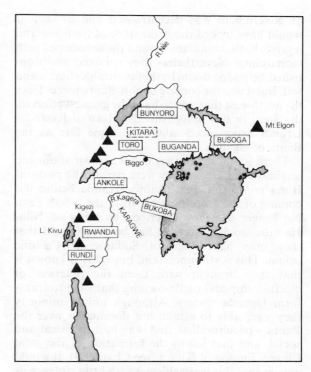

Map 21 Kingdoms of the Lakes Region

most spectacular country in East Africa, traversed from north to south by the western arm of the great Rift Valley and ranging from volcanic mountains to steep valleys and lakes. It is hardly surprising that early German travellers referred to it as the Switzerland of Africa. With its even rainfall and fertile soil it has been able to sustain a greater density of population than many of the drier regions of East Africa. Its people derive from three main groups; the Batwa, the Bahutu and the Batutsi.

The Batwa are of pygmy origin, short in stature and limited in their range of skills and development. Although the oldest inhabitants of the area they are the smallest in numbers and were easily subdued by the later immigrants. They were regarded with a mixture of fear and contempt by the Hutu and Tutsi who often referred to them as 'the ancient people', unable to adapt and therefore condemned to stagnate. By far the largest group were the Bahutu who, as Bantu agriculturalists, had moved into the area during the general Bantu movement during the first millenium A.D. Although little evidence remains it would appear likely that the Hutu along with other Bantu communities in the interlacustrine region established their own political and social systems. These would have been based on the typical unit of Bantu society, the clan. This meant that their system of government was decentralised and as such it would have lacked the great store of tradition and legend that accumulated round those societies with monarchies. Nevertheless they survived and flourished, helped no doubt by the favourable climate and soil. But it was the coming of non-Bantu forces from the north-east that was to have the greatest effect on the area. In this movement the Hutu of Rwanda-Urundi experienced much the same fate as the Bantu of Uganda.

There is still much that is not known about the origins of the Tutsi. They were part of the pastoral Hima group that moved into Uganda before the coming of the Lwo, possibly from the North East. No longer are they described as being of Nilo-Hamitic stock; instead it has been suggested that they may have been of Sudanic or Cushitic origin. This is still uncertain, but what is known is that they brought with them the practices of chieftainship and cattle-owning that were to transform Uganda society. Although only a minority they were able to establish a dominance over the Bantu agriculturalists that was both political and social, and that led to the formation of the great Chwezi Empire of Kitara (see Chapter 4). It would appear that this was achieved with little violence or resistance, due largely no doubt to the prestige and status that accompanied the Hima tradition of semi-divine monarchy.

From the evidence of traditional history, supported more recently by the archaeological research on the ancient earthworks in Western Uganda, Karagwe and Rwanda, it seems clear that the Tutsi shared in the inheritance of the great Chwezi dynasty. Thus the origins of the Kingdom of Rwanda can be traced back to a period prior to the sixteenth century, along with other principalities in the region, all of which claimed descent from the Bachwezi. The founders of Rwanda were the Nyiginya of Buganza and the impetus behind their rise to power came in a series of attacks made by the Babito of Bunyoro during the sixteenth century. In meeting this challenge the Nyiginya united and led their neighbours and so gradually extended their authority over a much wider area—the Kingdom of Rwanda. The initiative and leadership shown by the Nyiginya owed much to their pride and assurance in themselves. Who else could claim, as they did, to be the descendants of Imana, the supreme being and ancestral figure in Bachwezi mythology, who had with his followers 'left the sky with their cattle and after walking for a long time arrived at Mubari'. Mubari was the name of a ford on the River Kagera between Karagwe and Rwanda. Thus it is hardly

surprising that Nyiginya leadership should have assumed permanent form and been accepted by the Hutu and Batwa. The latter had nothing to compare or compete with the political and military institutions of the Tutsi. It is also important to remember the importance and value attached to cattle, both among pastoralists and agriculturalists. The great herds of long-horned cattle that the Tutsi brought with them added further to their status and power. This applied as much in Rundi as in Rwanda, though the particular form of Rundi's rise and growth is less certain. Traditions of Chwezi rulers and their successors do not include direct references to Rundi which may indicate a later and more indirect origin. Other traditions suggest that Rundi may have been founded by a Hinda dynasty, possibly from Karagwe. However, once established the rulers of Rundi assumed the title of Mwami, like their counterparts in Rwanda, and established a similar form of political and social society.

Both states developed centralised monarchies based upon their ruling Tutsi dynasties. Full use was made of their links with the god-like Chwezi kings in building up the power and prestige of the Tutsi monarchs. Many of the sacred symbols of royalty, the drums, spears, shields and beaded crowns, surmounted by tall copper cones and underhung with masks made from the skins of colobus monkeys, were either inherited from Chwezi forbears or copied from them. The Mwami was surrounded with all the ceremonial and ritual considered necessary for such a figure, the focus of all national loyalty, devotion and duty. From the Chwezi they had also inherited the system of 'orirembo' or royal enclosures with their elaborate reed palaces and large numbers of palace women and slaves. The centre or capital of Rwanda came to be at Nyanza while for Rundi it was at Kitega. From these centres they governed their kingdoms through a hierarchy of officials, reaching out into the provinces and districts. Alongside the civil administration there developed the military organisation that enabled the Mwami to call upon the services of those of military age. This in turn was linked with a system of land holding which ensured that certain areas were set aside for cultivation in order to support the army. The ownership of cattle was strictly controlled in the interests of the Tutsi overlords. Thus the whole pattern of political, social and economic society within the kingdoms produced a rigid class division, with the land and cattle-owning Tutsi aristocracy, a minority, on the one hand, and the Hutu and Batwa peasants and serfs, the majority, on the other. In a sense it was a racial as well as a social division, sharply distinguishing between the all-powerful Tutsi and the subordinate Hutu and Batwa in a way more lasting and permanent than in any of the other kingdoms of the interlacustrine region. As we shall see this was to have serious consequences in the twentieth century.

It would be wrong, however, to be left with the impression that the development of Rwanda and Rundi was solely due to the Tutsi rulers and their families. Factors such as climate, soil and vegetation may have attracted them to the area in the first place, and undoubtedly played an important part in the growth of population and the level of prosperity. But this very fact of a rapidly expanding population must have called for new and more intensive controls and techniques. The complementary roles of pastoralist and cultivator must have involved a certain degree of give and take between Tutsi and Hutu, just as problems of rinderpest and soil erosion must have been matters of mutual concern.

During the sixteenth to eighteenth centuries both kingdoms grew slowly but steadily, helped no doubt by their isolated and mountainous position. As they expanded so their influence in the neighbouring parts of East Africa increased, perhaps most notably in the development of the Bantu of Northern Tanzania. During the nineteenth century Rwanda emerged as the more dynamic and aggressive, both culturally and militarily. It outstripped even Buganda in its social structure and ceremonial and poetic heritage, but lacked the latter's administrative efficiency and ability to react to the new external challenges that were beginning to be felt. Writing about the situation in the interior of East Africa during the latter part of the nineteenth century Professor Oliver writes: 'Buganda and Rwanda remained the giants among the interlacustrine kingdoms.' (*History of E. Africa.* Vol. I: O.U.P.; p. 350.)

Indeed Rwanda's growth and consolidation continued well into the nineteenth century. Under Mwami Mutara II the neighbouring kingdom of Gissaka was conquered and absorbed in the 1840s, and although his successor, Kigeri IV, did not acquire much additional territory (apart from the strategically important large island on Lake Kivu) he raised his kingdom to a new peak of military and political prestige through a series of campaigns against his neighbours. To the south he failed to penetrate far into Rundi but to the north he got as far as Ankole and the shores of Lake Edward. Much of this military success was due to the aquisition of guns from Arab traders, but also to the Mwami's military reorganisation within his kingdom. He

arranged that men eligible for military service should not all serve at the same time, but at different periods, thus ensuring a regular and even supply of soldiers and making possible continuous military campaigns. Kigeri IV was apparently more concerned with the acquisition of cattle than land and in this he was undoubtedly successful. Relations between Rwanda and Rundi, however, did not improve. The Mwami of Rundi was handicapped by the trend towards separatism among leading members of the royal family, a recurrent threat to the unity and strength of his kingdom. Both Rwanda and Rundi were sufficiently strong, however, to prevent unauthorised entry by Arabs in search of ivory and slaves. Yet neither ruler appears to have realised the opportunity these Arabs offered to increase their wealth and power through trade. Instead they were by-passed by the principal trade route from Tabora, which crossed through Karagwe and Bukoba to Buganda. Although this may in part be due to geographical isolation it is true to say that neither Rwanda nor Rundi proved capable of responding, as Buganda did, to the new challenges and opportunities brought about by Arab and European intervention in the nineteenth century.

The Abaluyia and the Kingdom of Wanga

We now turn to the easternmost kingdom of this region, Wanga (see Map 22). Although situated in a very different part of the country and surrounded by people with entirely different cultures it nevertheless bears a strong resemblance to the kingdoms that we have been describing in this chapter. But first a little needs to be said about the Luyia, the largest single group in this area. They were an amalgam of people with various origins, being descendants of Kalenjin, Bantu and Maasai groups, and would appear to have converged during the seventeenth century. The Bantu culture predominated, though many features of Kalenjin influence can still be traced in certain areas. Luo influence was also felt at various times in the sixteenth and nineteenth centuries. The Luyia, like the Bantu, derived from an eastward movement from Uganda, as did the founders of what was to become the Wanga Kingdom, a group of Bahima people who moved from Western Uganda to Imanga hill, 6 kilometres (four miles) from the present township of Mumias. Some time between 1544 and 1652 their king, the 'Nabongo' brought together five different clans in this area. This Hima dynasty was replaced by the Abashitsetse dynasty

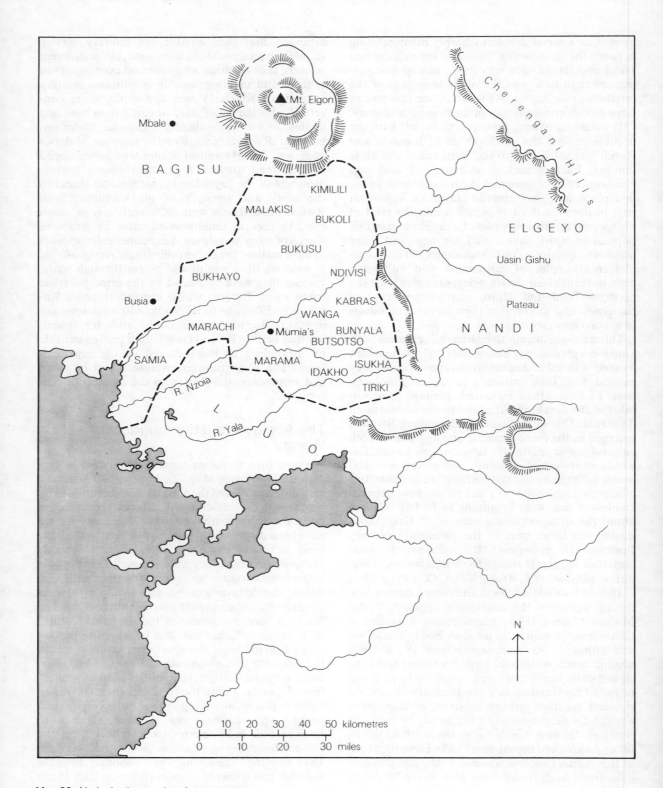

Map 22 Abaluyia clans and settlement areas

early in the seventeenth century. Their first ruler was called Wanga, after whom the kingdom was named. It is said that the Wanga people settled peacefully among the Bahima, and later staged a coup-d'etat against them. The new rulers introduced a period of warfare and conquest on a scale hitherto unknown in this area. They built up the institution of monarchy into a permanent system of government, adding prestige to it through the introduction of rituals and insignia, including the bushbuck totem of the ruling clan. By a successful series of wars and diplomatic negotiations they were able to consolidate their position.

In the mid eighteenth century the Nabongo Wamukoya Netya continued the process of centralisation and made use of Maasai troops to safeguard his kingdom from attacks by the Teso and others. The Maasai were rewarded with cattle, but eventually relations between the two deteriorated and led to a struggle in which the Nabongo was killed. His successor, Osundwa, who ruled from about 1787 to 1814 was obliged to placate the Maasai, but by skilful diplomacy he made use of both the Maasai and Abatsotso and was able to repel the advance of the Luo JoUgenya. He is also remembered for eliminating witchcraft from his kingdom. Further expansion took place under Nabongo Shiundu (1841–1882), when Kisa and Buholo were conquered and the people of Marama befriended. However the Luo Jo Ugenya and Jo Gem clans made serious inroads into Wanga, forcing Shiundu to sue for peace and hand over one of his daughters in marriage. The Luo would probably have weakened Wanga still further had it not been for the aid Wanga obtained from the Swahili and Arab traders with their guns. The latter had started to penetrate this area during Shiundu's reign. They were followed by the British who also propped up the Nabongo, and recognised Shiundu's successor,

Mumia, as paramount chief of the whole area including the Luyia and the Teso. The extension of this paramountcy into Luo areas such as Alego, Buholo and Gem caused much dissension.

Questions

1. What were the reasons for the decline of Bunyoro in the eighteenth and nineteenth centuries?
2. Why did Toro secede from Bunyoro?
3. Explain the reasons why the Kabakaship became such a powerful institution in Buganda.
4. What were the relations between the Bahima and the Bairu in Nkore?
5. What were the origins of the Wanga Kingdom in West Kenya?
6. How far do the Tutsi share the same traditions and origins as the people of Karagwe, Bukoba and Ankole?
7. Account for the greater success and strength of Rwanda as opposed to Rundi in the nineteenth century.

Activities

1. Discuss the reasons that made it easier for a centralised monarchy, such as Buganda, to become powerful and wealthy than for a state without a monarchy.
2. Make a diagram in the form of a pyramid and fill in the various positions and ranks among Baganda society—from the Kabaka at the top of the pyramid to the peasantry at the bottom.
3. Under the following headings make a list of the reasons why you think Buganda expanded while Bunyoro declined:
   a) Geographical (position)
   b) Economic (trade)
   c) Military
   d) Administrative

Chapter 8
The Eastern Bantu peoples, 1500–1850

Introduction

In this chapter we describe the people occupying the region to the east of the Rift Valley in Kenya and North-East Tanzania (see Map 24). Although defined as Eastern Bantu it should be remembered that there was as much merging and mixing of groups from different backgrounds here as in the rest of East Africa at this time. The Bantu-speakers are said to derive from a movement centred on the Katanga area in Central Africa. Part of this resulted in a spread eastwards to the Coast and then from south to north along the East African seaboard. This would have been early in the first millenium

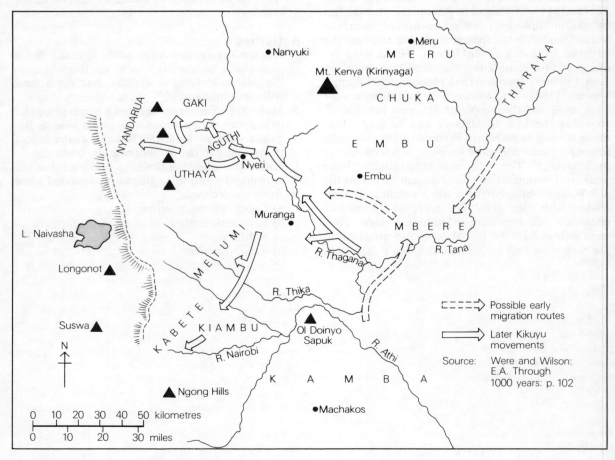

Map 23 Kikuyu, Embu, and Meru settlement

A.D. The area of East Africa into which they moved would have been one of strong Southern Cushitic influence and there followed a long period of interaction between these two cultures. There are still pockets of Cushitic speaking peoples, notably the Mbuguans in Usambara, though the general trend was for them to be absorbed into the Bantu communities. However the latter adopted a number of Cushitic customs, such as circumcision, linear age-sets, irrigation and possibly even the milking and bleeding of cattle. Particular traces of Bantu-Cushite contact have been found in the Taita Hills, in the Mt Kenya region, (dating as far back as the first millenium A.D.), and among the Pare traditions.

Much importance was attached, when tracing the pattern of migration among the Eastern Bantu, to the Shungwaya settlement and dispersal area, north of Lamu. No material evidence remains to help locate the site, but most coastal groups, such as the Nyika, Pokomo and Bajun, do have traditions of migration from such a place in the face of hostile pressure from the Galla and Somali. But among the inland Bantu there is no such tradition except in the case of the Meru. It seems more likely, therefore, that there was no single area of dispersal for the Bantu, just as there was no single movement inland for each of the present highland tribes. We must think of it rather as a gradual intermingling of people in the course of a process of continuous movement. Nor should we forget the part played by climate and geography in moulding the lives of these early migrants. For those moving inland there was the dry waterless 'nyika' to be tackled. For these and similar reasons the Eastern Bantu tended to form small, self-sufficient communities, going their own way and developing their own methods of government and society. The only things common to all of them were their language, their historical origin and their geographical proximity to one another. It is also noticeable that we do not find, among the Eastern Bantu, the strongly centralised political systems that were a feature of the Western Bantu.

There is still much research to be done on the histories of the Eastern Bantu peoples. Oral tradition and linguistics have so far been the chief sources, but it is likely that archaeology will in the future provide much of the material evidence that we still lack. For the early period of coastal migration and settlement we find some of the written accounts of early Arab travellers useful. The only members of the group that have so far been systematically studied by historians are the Pare, Shambaa, Kamba and Kikuyu.

Eastern Bantu groups
The Shambaa

The history of the Shambaa illustrates the point made above, that individual societies were often formed from successive waves of migration and settlement. The oldest clans in the Usambara area claim to have moved there during the initial movement of Bantu-speakers along the Coast. Later they were joined by migrants from Pare, Zigua and Taita; then finally the Mbughu and Nango clans moved in. But it was not until threatened by attack from outside, in this case Maasai raids in the early eighteenth century, that these clans formed any closer political union. The focus for this unity was provided by the Kilindi clan, whose recent arrival in Usambara under their leader Mbegha, was to have far-reaching effects for the Shambaa. There is still much uncertainty as to the origin of the Kilindi, but the direction from which they came suggests a link with the 'Ntemi' area of western and central Tanzania where systems of chieftainship had developed. But although they may have brought dynamic new ideas of political organisation to the Shambaa it is interesting to note that the Kilindi tended to adopt the customs of these people.

Mbegha established his capital at Vugha and assumed the title of Simba Mwene, the lion king. By starting the process of taking at least one wife from each clan and sending the sons of these marriages out as chiefs of the various provinces he began the process of centralisation. He also imposed large fines, and encouraged the Shambaa practice of granting asylum to any criminal or fugitive who took refuge at Vugha. He made sure of the support of the people by appointing Shambaa councillors to advise his Kilindi chiefs. The work of building up a centralised bureaucracy was continued by his son Bughe, while his grandson Kinyashi built up a strong military force and started the process of expansion towards the coast. This was carried to a climax by the famous Kimweri ye Nyumbai in the nineteenth century. During his reign the influence of the Coastal trade brought new challenges and opportunities. The first European missionaries and travellers were also encountered. Kimweri ruled until the 1860s when his brother Semboja, making use of foreign guns and mercenaries, broke away and established himself at Mazinde. The Bondei also declared themselves independent after marauding east Usambara. Weakened by an epidemic of jiggers in 1898 the Shambaa were further demoralised by the German intervention and their action in hanging Semboja's son, Mputa.

The Pare

According to certain archaeological evidence, the earliest Bantu speaking settlers in the Pare region, known traditionally as the 'Wagalla', were here some time before the sixteenth century. They appear to have been subsequently driven out or absorbed. Then from the sixteenth century a steady movement of Bantu people into north Pare took place, from the directions of Taita and Kilimanjaro. As the population expanded they moved into south and central Pare. Further Bantu groups came in from the Nguu Mountains, Usambara and the plains to the west. There is evidence that by the sixteenth century the Bantu societies in Pare were already organised in lineage systems, those in the north under the rule of an iron-smelting clan known as the Washana. Among the clans they ruled were the Wasuya, from whom the Washana ruler traditionally appointed his chief minister. With the growing problems of holding together an expanding population, the Washana lost control and, by means of a violent coup d'etat, the Wasuya seized power.

Under their rule the state of Gweno emerged as a stable and well organised unit that was to survive well into the nineteenth century. The founder's son, Mranga, established a centralised form of government: stemming from the paramount chief at the head, 'Mangi Mrwe', through councils, 'chila' and ministers, 'wanjama' to the district chiefs, 'wamangi'. He sent his own sons to rule outlying districts. But the key to control lay in the way he was able to command all the institutions connected with initiation, since these lay at the heart of Pare society. It should be noted that this whole process of political change came from within Pare, not from without as in the case of the Shambaa.

The areas of south and central Pare were not marked by the growth of any large states. The Wabwambo clan, who had moved there from the north, were one of the largest, but there were many other small independent groups around them. The tendency towards smaller units increased in the nineteenth century, in the face of external pressures. The extension of the coastal trade inland brought new strains and stresses in Pare society. Many chiefs, tempted by the new opportunities to acquire wealth and power, broke away or became rivals. There were, moreover, further kinds of intervention. The Chagga and Maasai came in search of iron, and the Shambaa in pursuit of their ritual antelope, the 'mpaa'. One of the most important items of regional trade was iron, and since the sources of iron ore were concentrated in Pare this gave the people of the area added importance, both as producers and as smelters. In return they obtained livestock. The salt obtained from plains between Kilimanjaro and Pare and to the west of the Usambara Mountains was yet another important item of trade. But, as Professor Kimambo has pointed out, one of the major effects of the long-distance trade from the coast was to weaken the authority of the states such as Pare and Shambaa, situated in the mountainous country away from the trade routes. The centre of political power in the nineteenth century was to be found on the plains alongside the caravan routes, as we shall see in a later chapter.

The Chagga

The southern slopes of Mt Kilimanjaro have attracted many different groups over the centuries. Fertile and well-watered, the area is ideal for cultivation of a variety of crops including bananas. This region has also proved a focal point for trade, both local and long-distance. The process of settlement here has extended over a long period and involved people from many different directions and origins. By the early nineteenth century there were over one hundred political groups in the area, with ruling families claiming descent from Taita, Kamba, Maasai and Shambaa ancestors. Recently archaeological evidence has been discovered of an Iron Age Bantu culture, known as the Kwale culture,

Fig. 8.1 Mount Kilimanjaro.

Fig. 8.2 Sina of Kibosho.

Fig. 8.3 Sina being attacked by the Germans.

extending from the hinterland of Mombasa as far as Pare and Kilimanjaro, and dating from between the third and ninth centuries A.D. It is quite possible that the River Pangani would have attracted early Bantu speakers inland to Kilimanjaro from the coast. The snow capped summits of this great mountain must have acted as a magnet for men throughout the ages, so that we would expect to find evidence of many cultures and ethnic groups around its slopes.

The Chagga are part of the Eastern Bantu linguistic group, but with strains of a number of other important elements, including Cushitic and Plains Nilote influence. From the fertile valleys on the slopes of the mountain they obtained all the food that they required with a sufficient surplus to trade for cattle, iron-ware and salt. Trade featured prominently among their activities from the earliest times. Among the most conspicuous of the chiefdoms was that of Rombo, centred on Keni. Under Orombo it expanded considerably as a result of raids to the north, extracting as tribute cattle, slaves, pots and eleusine. Another prominent chief

was Sina of Kibosho, an area that had benefited from a series of strong rulers in the nineteenth century. He equipped his standing army with guns and stabbing spears and built an impregnable fortress at his capital. He raided to the east into Taita country, carrying off women, children and cattle. But he was also anxious to encourage trade with the coastal Arabs, exchanging slaves and ivory for guns and cloth. His power remained unchallenged until 1891, when the Germans, encouraged by Rindi of Moshi, attacked and defeated him.

Chief Rindi of Moshi was perhaps the best known of the Chagga rulers in the nineteenth century. He became chief about 1860, and although no military leader, he made up for this by his shrewd diplomacy. Through a series of alliances, notably with the Arusha Maasai, he obtained military support and was able to use it against his rivals with considerable effect. He was skilful in the art of playing off one group against another, and if any Swahili caravan should attempt to cheat him he was

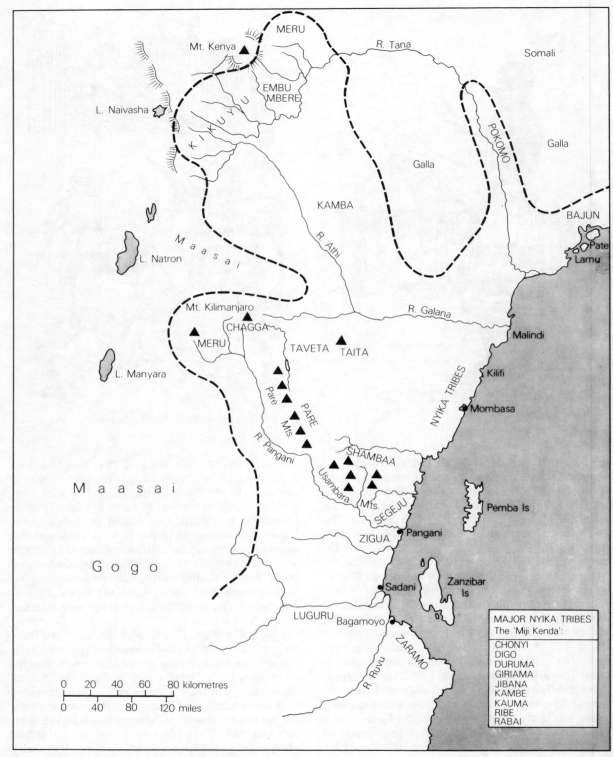

Map 24 The Eastern Bantu showing main groups and area of settlement

68

Fig. 8.4 Kikuyu country near Nyeri.

quick to turn his Maasai mercenaries against them. He succeeded in attracting the coastal caravan trade to Moshi, which became an important centre for the whole region. Close to his palace he had a little court erected for the Swahili residents and traders. Like Sina he exchanged slaves and ivory for cloth and guns, the most profitable items of trade during this period. Rindi impressed European visitors with his power, telling them that he was chief of all Kilimanjaro, a piece of bluff which many of them believed, and which successfully deterred them from visiting other chiefs in the area. Rindi ingratiated himself with the British Consul at Zanzibar, John Kirk, and even wrote letters to Queen Victoria and Kaiser Wilhelm. In 1885 he signed a treaty with the Society for German Colonisation, little realising where this would eventually lead him and his people. Another Chagga chief to win the support of the Germans was Marealle, in

Marangu. He was able to persuade German forces to march against the chiefs of Kilema, Kirua and Moshi by claiming that they had been disloyal. The impression we get of Chagga society, therefore, is one of rival factions competing for foreign support in order to further their own individual ends.

The Kikuyu

As we have seen, traditions of dispersal from Shungwaya do not feature at all among the histories of the inland peoples. The same is true of the Kikuyu, whose legends and myths refer to 'Mukurwe wa Gathanga', the place where God or 'Ngai' appeared and created their ancestors Gikuyu and his wife Mumbi. Another legend has it that a certain Mbere man had four sons who became the ancestors of the Kikuyu, Kamba, Athi and Maasai people. The latter contains an element of truth, since it does seem that by the sixteenth century the early Kikuyu had settled in Mbere and Chuka from the north. After some time the natural impetus of population growth, coupled with pressure from Galla forces, led them to move further to the Mwea Plains where they settled at Ithanga and were joined by the Kamba group, the Thagicu. These settlements, at Mbere and Ithanga, during the sixteenth and seventeenth centuries were important in the formative periods of the ancestral Kikuyu.

In the first half of the eighteenth century, urged on again by an increase in population, they moved north to Othaya and Aguthi in Nyeri, north east to Tetu and Mathira, southwards to Kiambu and west to Nyandarua (see Map 23). Expansion and consolidation in these areas continued through the nineteenth century. The only serious opposition came from the Maasai. But there were other groups encountered as well; the Gumba and the Athi. The former were hunters, bee-keepers, iron-workers and makers of pottery; extremely short in stature, they lived in caves and tunnels. The Athi were important in that it was from them that the Kikuyu acquired the skill of iron-working as well as cultural practices such as circumcision, clitoridectomy and certain features of the age-set system. The Athi in Kiambu sold their land to the Kikuyu in return for cattle, and elsewhere made themselves useful as middlemen in trade between the Kikuyu, Maasai and coastal traders.

In the political and social structure of Kikuyu society two units were of particular importance: the family and the age set. As the Kikuyu say: 'Nyumba na riika itiumaguo' or 'One cannot contract out of one's family or age set'. Everyone belonged to a family and each family had a family head. Above the family was the local territorial unit or 'Mbari'. As the Kikuyu came to occupy a land of steep valleys and ridges, each ridge constituted an Mbari.

Each Mbari was led by a Council of Elders, the head of which was called the 'Muramati'. He was not a chief, nor was his position hereditary; he was simply the most distinguished man.

Equally important was the age-set system, the 'Mariika'. Each riika consisted of those who had been circumcised at the same time as boys. For four or five consecutive years boys would be circumcised, then there would be a break for five to nine years before the next group. In this way each riika had time to grow up and learn the duties of a warrior, becoming a recognised age-set. Girls, however, were circumcised every year. The riika was important in

creating a sense of unity in Kikuyu society, since all those of a given age-set regarded each other as brothers and worked and fought together. The clan system also helped to bind the people together; there were ten clans and each had its traditions and legends. Periodically clan reunions would be held.

Clans also played a part in the system of land tenure. Land had always played an important part in the life of the Kikuyu. All the land in a single Mbari was considered as belonging to the descendants of one man, and it was the Muramati's duty to allocate plots of this land to each person. No such land could be sold unless everyone gave consent. Any non-descendant was regarded as a tenant, allowed on the land only by consent of the Mbari. New land was of course being opened up all the time and so the same system was extended. It was only the intervention of the British, with their alien treatment of land tenure, that put an end to the growth of the Mbari system.

The Giriama

The Giriama were one of the Mijikenda groups that share a common tradition of migration from

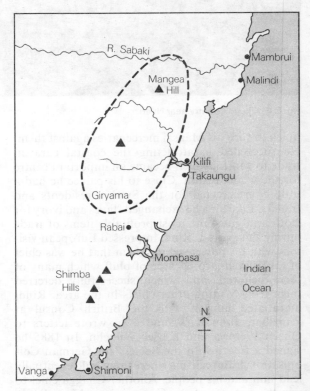

Map 25 Giriama settlement area

Shungwaya as a result of Galla pressure early in the seventeenth century. They moved south and eventually built a fortress on top of a hill, Kaya Giriama or more commonly Kaya Fungo, near Kilifi (see Map 25). Here they buried their sacred pots, symbols of religious and political authority. They lived in the neighbourhood, cultivating grain and keeping sheep and goats.

The political and social institutions of the Giriama were strongly interwoven with religious and magical features. Each clan had its own council of elders, known as a 'Kambi'. Senior elders of each Kambi formed the highest ruling Kambi which acted as a final court of appeal for all social, political and civil matters. Below the elders were the prophets and prophetesses, known as 'Wafisi', who had authority over all matters of religion and ritual. Only they had the power to administer oaths and to officiate at the many magical ceremonies that were called for, both at national and individual level. These might cover anything from protecting a home or averting an illness to ensuring a victory in battle or a favourable harvest. Another important group of officials were the 'Ways' who acted as the first level of authority in the hierarchy. Then there were the warriors, or 'Nyeri', who still lacked the age and experience to qualify for any of the more senior posts. During the second half of the nineteenth century population growth led to an extension of

Giriama territory northwards along both banks of the River Sabaki.

Questions
1. What cultural features did the Eastern Bantu have in common?
2. Trace the history of the Pare before 1900.
3. Describe the structure of Kikuyu society.
4. Compare the part played by trade in the growth of the Chagga and Shambaa states.
5. Give an account of the way in which the Giriama clans were organised.

Activities
1. Imagine that you were among the early Eastern Bantu peoples: describe the type of country that you would have moved through as you migrated from south to north along the coast, and the reasons that might have tempted you to settle around either Mt Kilimanjaro or Mt Kenya.
2. Make a list of the non-Bantu people with whom the Shambaa, Chagga and Giriama came into contact, and say whether this contact was friendly or hostile.
3. Draw a sketch map of the east coast of Africa from Kismayu to Bagamoyo and mark the main rivers and physical features. Compare this with the probable movements and settlements of the Eastern Bantu.

Chapter 9
The Bantu of Western and Central Tanzania

Introduction

In this chapter we examine the settlement and characteristics of the Bantu speakers who settled in this area. In contrast to the regions already covered in this book we find that it was entirely confined to Bantu people. There is little evidence of contact with groups of different origin. Moving in from the south and west there were already numbers of Bantu living here by 1500. The country into which they came was a vast upland plateau, a region of dry grasslands and open woodland with few rivers and rainfall that was either low or unpredictable. These geographical features were to have an important bearing on the way in which the Bantu people developed.

Since the land proved unable to sustain large and permanent concentrations of people, and because it offered such wide horizons for movement and expansion, the immigrants tended to remain in small, independent groups. The basic unit was the village, a self-sufficient community able to provide and fend for itself. However, in times of great danger or difficulty these villages found it necessary to combine to form a large and stronger group. This was known as the 'Ntemi'. At its head was a chief, originally chosen for his experience, to whom the people looked for leadership and guidance. In the course of time this system became a permanent feature of their life, and the Ntemi chief acquired certain political, judicial and religious powers and duties. He was usually assisted by a number of officials. A typical Ntemi unit might consist of no more than one thousand people. When the population grew too large, or was joined by a new group, there would be a division and a new Ntemi would be formed elsewhere, so that they remained small and compact. This was well suited to the needs of the people themselves and also to their surroundings, the kind of agriculture and pastoralism they

practised, and the constant process of migration and settlement that continued well into the nineteenth century (see Map 26). The Ntemi system was already in use by the fourteenth century among the Nyamwezi and Sukuma. Later immigrants adopted it and carried it with them. By the nineteenth century there were probably between two hundred and three hundred such groups in Tanzania. It has been said that the idea behind the Ntemi system came from the interlacustrine kingdoms, but this seems doubtful. It was not a highly centralised or bureaucratic structure as were the kingdoms to the north. Rather we should see it as being evolved in Tanzania as a direct response to the challenges and difficulties of their environment. It is therefore one of the features common amongst the Bantu groups in this area.

The Bantu groups
The Nyamwezi

The Nyamwezi would appear to have been among the early Bantu migrants into Tanzania. They occupied the central plateau around the present town of Tabora. By the eighteenth century they consisted of more than one hundred clans but without any form of central authority. Originally agriculturalists, supplemented by the raising of cattle, they were to become famous as pioneers of long distance trade in East and Central Africa. Organised in small self-governing units—the Ntemi—they shared associations based upon ties of kinship or else belief in common origins. Some of these associations were Unyangilwa, Usumbwa, Usagali, Ussongo and Usiha, each of which had its senior chief.

Among the Nyamwezi the Ntemi system achieved a highly organised and well regulated pattern, as will be seen from the diagram on page 74.

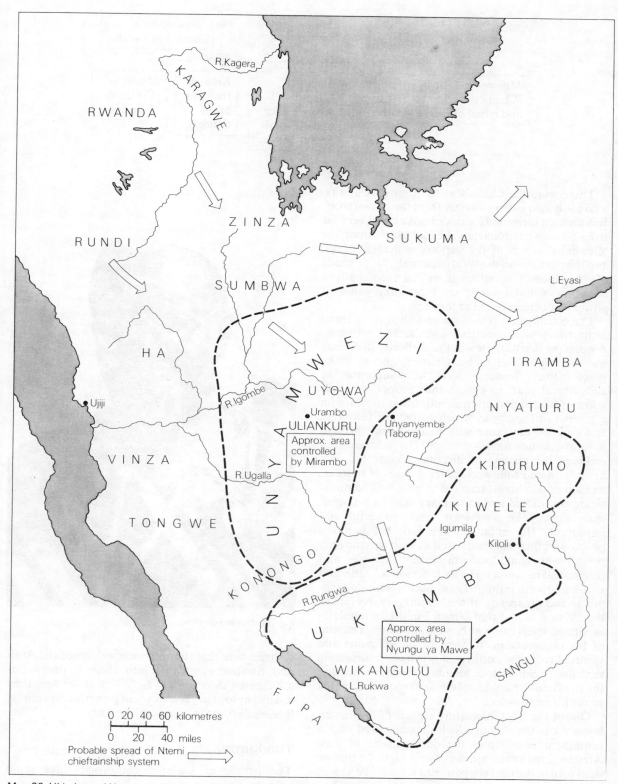

RWANDA

KARAGWE

R.Kagera

ZINZA

SUKUMA

RUNDI

SUMBWA

L.Eyasi

HA

U N Y A M W E Z I

IRAMBA

M U Y O W A

NYATURU

R.Igombe

Urambo

ULIANKURU

Unyanyembe
(Tabora)

Ujiji

Approx. area
controlled
by Mirambo

KIRURUMO

R.Ugalla

KIWELE

VINZA

U N Y A N G O

Igumila

Kiloli

TONGWE

U K I M B U

KONONGO

R.Rungwa

Approx. area
controlled by
Nyungu ya Mawe

WIKANGULU

SANGU

L.Rukwa

FIPA

0 20 40 60 kilometres

0   20   40 miles

Probable spread of Ntemi
chieftainship system

Map 26 Ukimbu and Unyamwezi showing the probable spread of the Ntemi chieftainship system

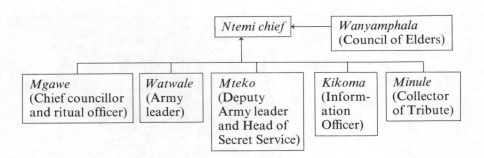

```
                              ┌─────────────┐      ┌──────────────────┐
                              │ Ntemi chief │◄─────│ Wanyamphala      │
                              └─────────────┘      │ (Council of Elders)│
                                     ▲             └──────────────────┘
         ┌──────────────┬───────────┼──────────────┬──────────────┐
```

| Mgawe (Chief councillor and ritual officer) | Watwale (Army leader) | Mteko (Deputy Army leader and Head of Secret Service) | Kikoma (Information Officer) | Minule (Collector of Tribute) |

These were the officials at the centre of affairs, who took their orders directly from the Ntemi chief. But his own direct influence did not extend very far from his own headquarters; he had to rely upon the 'Gungulis', heads of the various settlement areas, and they in turn on the 'Wazenga makaya' or heads of households. Thus although we can trace a pattern of authority, it did not by any means imply that all power was concentrated at the top.

The Ntemi chief possessed certain specific functions which were political, judicial and religious. Among the first of these was the authority to declare war, on the advice of his Council, and to make peace. Other functions were to inaugurate the agricultural year, to ensure that proper care was taken of land and of grain supplies, and to maintain a reserve of food with which to reward followers and compensate those who had suffered through natural disasters such as drought. His judicial duties included the settling of disputes among his own household and followers, hearing cases of murder, treason or witchcraft referred to him, and administering traditional and customary law. In his spiritual capacity he was even more powerful and important. He embodied the link between the people and their ancestors, and as such was the only person who could perform certain sacrifices and ceremonial functions. His own personal health and well-being were intimately connected with the happiness and prosperity of the community. As late as the 1920s it is said that Ntemi Fundikira regularly sacrificed seven cattle at Nsyepa, the former capital of his predecessors. In view of the religious and spiritual role they performed it is hardly surprising that the Ntemi system became hereditary, so that the chieftainship could only pass to someone related to the former holder.

One of the most interesting aspects of Nyamwezi history was the way in which they acquired such a prominent position in the development of East African trade in the nineteenth century. To this we shall turn in the next chapter. But it would be as well

Fig. 9.1 Ntemi Fundikira.

to stress here that they not only welcomed the Arab and Swahili merchants into their territory but anticipated their objectives. We shall see how they did this by looking at the lives of powerful Nyamwezi leaders during the nineteenth century.

The Kimbu

The people of Ukimbu comprised three main

groups; the Nyisamba, the Nyitumba, and the Nyangilwa. The first of these came from the north and were the earliest of the three to arrive, encountering a nomadic group called the Pantams, early in the seventeenth century. The Nyisimba were hunters and food gatherers as well as cultivators. They built their homes on hills for defensive reasons. The chief's ritual symbol was a wooden horn. The Nyitumba moved into the area during the eighteenth century; the majority of them from Usagara. They founded eight chiefdoms. They were iron smelters and made iron hoes, an important factor in the extension of agriculture in this area. Their Ntemi emblem was a conus-shell.

The Nyangilwa also migrated from Usagara, via Ugogo, late in the eighteenth century. Their ostensible reason for coming into this area was to hunt for elephant. They introduced cattle into Ukimbu, although their herds were wiped out by tsetse fly in the following century.

The nineteenth century brought a number of important changes to Ukimbu. During the first half of the century the Kimbu were harrassed by the Sangu and the Ngoni. In the 1830s a serious famine decimated the population, and shortly afterwards the Arab traders were coming into conflict with the Nyamwezi to the north. This new threat brought forth a leader who was to revive the fortunes of the Kimbu. His name was Nyungu-ya-Mawe, which literally means Pot of Stones. A soldier with only one eye, he was related to Mnwa Sele of Unyanyembe. In 1875 he staged a coup in Kiwale, the central chiefdom of Ukimbu. In a series of wars that followed he built up a large personal empire, with the aid of his standing army, the Rugaruga. Under his rule the whole of Ukimbu was united, and this he left to his daughter, Mgalula, on his death.

The Hehe

The people of this area were not originally known as Hehe; this was apparently a name used first by European visitors in the nineteenth century to describe the way they went into battle shouting 'Hee, Hee, Hee!' The area was occupied by various groups from Usagara, Ubena and Ukimbu. In the eighteenth century there were at least fifteen chiefdoms in the area and although they remained separate and independent until the nineteenth century they did share certain common features. For instance the chiefly clans buried their dead chiefs, while the commoners threw their dead out to be eaten by wild animals. A living man was buried with the dead chief, in a sitting position, supporting the

Fig. 9.2 The Hehe and the Ngoni meet for a peace conference.

head of the dead body. The Ntemi chiefs of this area were much respected and feared, since they were believed to be connected with the spirits of former chiefs and to possess potent war medicine.

Two important Hehe leaders emerged during the nineteenth century, Munyigumba and his son Mkwawa. The former came to power between 1855 and 1860 in the Lungemba chiefdom. Through force of personality and military ability he became a powerful ruler in this area, extending his rule into most of northern Hehe territory. By the time of his death in 1878 the whole of the Hehe plateau and highlands were for the first time under the rule of a single chief. Munyigumba's son, Mkwawa, expanded his territory still further, fighting against the Gogo in the north and the Usagara in the north east. Mkwawa's motive in these northern campaigns was to obtain access to the caravan trade in this region. By the 1880s the Hehe were threatening the traffic on the caravan route and by 1890 Mkwawa was a powerful monarch with headquarters at his fortress in Kalanga. His most famous exploits came with the fierce resistance he put up against the

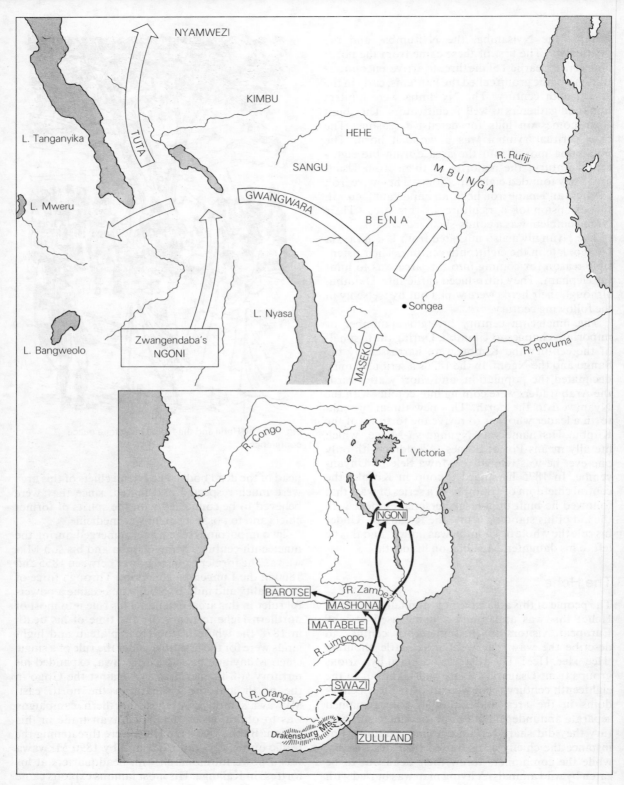

Map 27 The Ngoni invasion

Germans, and to this we shall return in a later chapter. The Germans certainly respected the determination and courage shown by Mkwawa and his Hehe people in their struggle to retain their independence.

The coming of the Ngoni

The people we have described so far in this chapter trace their origins, for the most part, to the Bantu migrations from Central Africa during the first and second millenium A.D. We come now to the last and latest of these great movements, the Ngoni invasions of the nineteenth century. In some ways their arrival in Tanzania was to send shock waves throughout the country.

In order to trace their origin we must turn to the Zulu of South Africa. Here, early in the nineteenth century, arose a powerful ruler named Shaka who became so feared and dreaded that his era came to be remembered by the people as the 'Mfecane', the time of troubles. Rather than submit to his tyranny many people sought refuge by escaping to the north. Some fled to Mozambique, others westwards, others to the north. Of the latter a group that came to be known as the Ngoni came eventually to East Africa (see Map 27).

The Ngoni were led by Zwangendaba. Starting from south of the River Limpopo they travelled north, destroying the old kingdom of Monomotapa as they moved. They crossed the River Zambezi in 1835 and defeated the Cewa people of present day Malawi. Learning of the renowned red cattle that were reared on the Fipa Plateau, Zwangendaba decided to make for this area. He finally settled and erected his capital in Ufipa, where he died some time between 1845 and 1848.

There followed a period of dynastic rivalry as a result of which the Ngoni split up into five groups. Two of these remained in East Africa, the Tuta and Gwangara; the former moving north into the valley of Lake Rukwa, then to the eastern shores of Lake

![Shaka treating with the British in 1824]

Fig. 9.3 Shaka treating with the British in 1824.

Fig. 9.4 Ngoni warriors.

Tanganyika. After defeating the Holoholo and twice attacking Ujiji they settled finally in the Runzewe district north-west of Tabora. Here they raided and plundered, disrupting Nyamwezi life. Those whom they took captive they put into their army, teaching them the famous Ngoni military tactics. Among these recruits was Mirambo from Nyamwezi of whom we shall hear more later.

The Gwangara Ngoni moved eastwards from the Fipa Highlands across southern Tanzania to the Songea area. Here they met the Maseko, a Ngoni group that had entered East Africa by a more easterly route. Being the larger and more established group the Gwangara accepted the leadership of the Maseko at first. But before long they revolted and drove the Maseko south across the River Ruvuma into Mozambique. Some Maseko people fled to the Kilombero Valley where they became known as the Mbunga, while others scattered to Tunduru, Masasi and Newala.

One may well ask how it was that such a relatively small group of migrants could enforce their authority in such a short time and make their presence felt so strongly. The answer would seem to lie in their emphasis on strong leadership, their outstanding military efficiency, and their capacity to absorb conquered people into their own clans and society.

Let us examine first their military achievements, much of which must have been due to their Zulu contacts. First, people of the same age were trained to fight together in territorial regiments. These formed compact and united units. The weapons they used included the short stabbing spear or assegai, rather than the long throwing spear. This meant that the warriors or 'impis' as they were called, could attack more effectively at close quarters, warding off arrows with their shields. This is how the traveller Burton described a Tuta Ngoni war formation:

'The arms are two short spears, one in the right hand, the other in the left, concealed by a large shield, disdaining bows and arrows, and they never use the assegai as a spear. Their thousands march in four or five extended lines and attack by attempting to envelop the enemy.' This was the famous 'cow's horns' formation by which they were able to surround their enemy. It needed a great deal of discipline and training to develop these tactics, but once perfected they were usually invincible.

The effects of the Ngoni upon the people of Tanzania

Together with the changes brought about by the coastal trade in the nineteenth century, the Ngoni invasion was to cause a fundamental shift in Tanzanian society. Many of the effects were destructive and damaging, but others led to more positive results. The immediate outcome was, of course, the destruction and devastation of many settlements and communities in southern Tanzania. Even in areas not directly affected the repercussions could be felt, as food supplies and trade routes were cut off or threatened. In the wake of such havoc followed chaos and anarchy, as organised society broke down and each survivor had to fend for himself. Bands of foot-loose mercenaries, 'Rugarugas', roamed at will plundering and killing. In such an atmosphere of lawlessness and uncertainty, disease and famine increased as crops failed to be planted or harvested and homes were destroyed.

But the people of Tanzania were not slow to learn the Ngoni military tactics and weapons. In Ufipa the local people in the 1850s were in a position to challenge the Ngoni, while the Sangu, under their leader Mwahawangu, fought hard for their independence. In the 1860s and 1870s Chief Merere of Sangu became famous in the use of Ngoni tactics. Similarly with the Hehe and Bena. In this way the new military power was used, not merely for robbing and pillaging by robbers, but as a means of establishing larger and stronger states.

The second positive result of Ngoni invasion was the move away from the small scale Ntemi system to the formation of bigger political systems under the control of strong rulers. Some rulers were themselves from chiefly families, others were self-made men. Whatever their personal motives or ambitions may have been, they succeeded in uniting many communities that had previously lived in isolation. This process was also due to the pressures from other directions, notably the Arab and Swahili coastal traders. But it did also enable African leaders, such as Merere, Mkwawa, and Mirambo, to negotiate with the traders as equals rather than as subordinates. No caravan could survive long without the security and supply centres that these rulers provided. Equally, rulers such as Mirambo knew that, in order to acquire wealth and power, they must not only assume all the traditional qualities and capabilities of an African ruler but must learn to match the coastal traders' skill in trade and commercial bargaining.

Mirambo

As a footnote to this chapter and as a link with the

Fig. 9.5 Mkwawa.

Fig. 9.6 Mirambo, Chief of Nyamwezi.

next we shall briefly consider the career and achievement of Mirambo. Although Nyamwezi by birth, he spent his early formative years among the Ngoni, acquiring much valuable knowledge of their military skills. He also gained experience of the caravan trade in which his people had already acquired such a reputation. By the 1860s he had become leader of his father's small Ntemi, Ugowe, which he later combined with the neighbouring Ntemi of Uliankuru from his mother's family. To his capital, Urambo, he attracted trade and traders. Although he had direct control over this area he extended his influence throughout most of Unyamwezi. Using Ngoni warriors and military tactics he secured control over the two principal trade routes from Tabora which ran to Ujiji in the west, and to Karagwe, Buganda and Bunyoro in the north. In the south his forces attacked Pimbwe, Tungwe and

Konongo during the 1870s in an attempt to extend the area over which he might demand tribute from trading caravans. To the north his presence was not felt directly as he raided this area mainly in search for cattle, and in 1883 to prevent the Ngoni from threatening the trade route to the north.

But his main troubles were with the Arab traders based at Tabora. They resented his demands for tribute and resisted forcibly between 1876 and 1880. Eventually they sued for peace and agreed to his terms. From then until his death in 1884 he remained the most powerful figure in north-west Tanzania. Although his empire was less compact and his methods of controlling it were less traditional his influence was none the less considerable. He modelled his army on the Ngoni but also made use of guns. While his position in Urambo stemmed from his authority as Ntemi, elsewhere in Unyamwezi he was famed and feared as a trader and controller of trade routes.

In his foreign relations Mirambo was no less successful. He knew that he could not do without the Arab trade from the coast however much he might dislike the influence of the traders. Thus, while contesting the claims of the traders at Tabora he also made friends with Tippu Tib (see page 93), one of the most powerful of the east coast traders, who was himself related to the Nyamwezi. Sultan Barghash of Zanzibar was also favourably inclined towards Mirambo, but owing to the opposition of the British Consul, Kirk, no formal agreement was actually signed. Mirambo also failed in his attempt to gain the Kabaka of Buganda's friendship, due in part to Arab interests at the court. Not a great deal is known of his relations with his fellow Nyamwezi ruler, Msiri of Katanga, but it appears that Mirambo allowed Msiri's caravans to pass through his territory unimpeded. European travellers were welcomed and missionaries invited to settle in Unyamwezi.

Following his death in 1884 Mirambo's Empire did not survive him. Nor was Nyamwezi unity and commercial supremacy to last much longer, faced as it was with the advancing interests of European imperialism. What then were Mirambo's lasting achievements? He symbolised the reaction of African people to the new external forces that were beginning to press upon them. By gathering his people under his control he tried to come to terms with these challenges. He showed that African societies could adapt and respond to change, both politically and economically. Had he lived longer he would have had to face the ultimate threat, the loss of political sovereignty to the Germans.

Questions
1. How did the Ntemi system of government operate?
2. Account for the rise to power of the Hehe.
3. Give an account of the Ngoni migration to East Africa.
4. How were the people of southern Tanzania affected by the Ngoni invasion in the nineteenth century?
5. Describe how Mirambo became the most powerful personality in north-western Tanzania.

Activities
1. Imagine that you were a Nyamwezi porter: describe a typical safari to the coast and back carrying ivory.
2. You have just been an eye-witness of an Ngoni military attack and have managed to escape. Describe what you saw.
3. Have a class discussion about the similarities and differences between the Ntemi chieftainship system and the monarchies of the interlacustrine area.

Chapter 10
The Portuguese and Arab rivalry on the Coast, 1500—1800

Introduction

Although the struggle between Portugal and Oman for control of the East African Coast and its trade takes us outside the main theme of mainland history, it was to have an important bearing on the development of trade in the interior during the nineteenth century. It also represents, in a limited form, the start of the process of intervention by foreign powers that culminated in the Scramble for

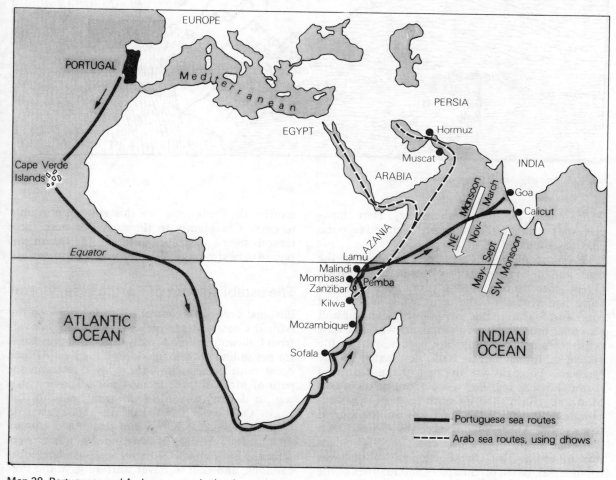

Map 28 Portuguese and Arab sea routes in the sixteenth century

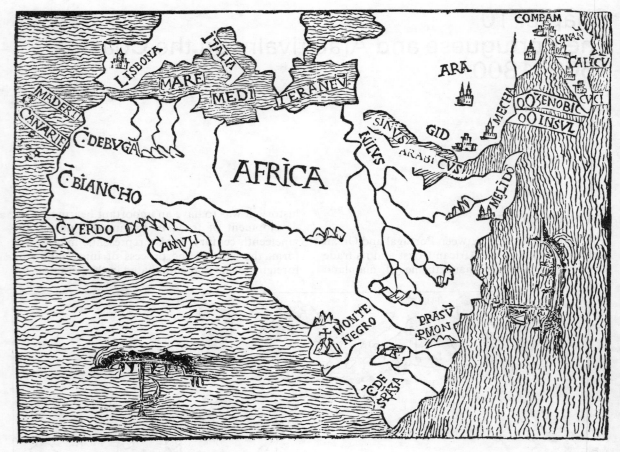

Fig. 10.1 An early map of Africa drawn in 1508.

Africa late in the nineteenth century. Here, however, the two contestants confined themselves to the coastal settlements.

Of course the Arabs had been involved in the trade and life of the east coast over many centuries. Omani merchants played a prominent part and some had settled on the coast while others had come as refugees. In this way political, dynastic and economic links had been maintained, while the East African Coast as a whole had become part of the system of Indian Ocean trade dominated by the Moslems. Portugal was the first of the European nations to seek and find a sea route to India (see Map 28). During the fifteenth century their sea-captains had struggled to find a way round the great continent of Africa, finally succeeding when Vasco da Gama sailed up the east coast in 1497 on his way to India. Thus the Portuguese motive was commercial, based on the spices and luxuries of the east rather than Africa. There was also a religious

motive: the Portuguese saw this as an opportunity to carry Christianity to the east. For both these reasons their appearance in the Indian Ocean was bound to be strongly resisted by the Moslem powers.

The establishment of Portuguese control

Portugal needed to control strategic points on the African Coast partly to prevent any European rivals from following her, and partly to act as supply bases for her sailing vessels. In addition the East African coast must be secured since it lay directly in the path of Moslem trade from Arabia. The first step was to destroy any Moslem strongholds on the coast. On his second voyage in 1502 Vasco da Gama bombarded Kilwa and demanded tribute, and in 1505 Sofala, Kilwa and Mombasa were attacked by Almeida. Superior weapons, including cannons, and skill in naval warfare gave the Portuguese the advantage. An eye-witness account of

82

one of these bombardments describes how the town of Kilwa was taken with little opposition, and then 'the Vicar General and some of the Franciscan Fathers came ashore carrying two crosses in procession and singing. They went to the palace and there the cross was put down and the Grand Captain prayed. Then everyone started to plunder the town of all its merchandise and provisions.'

This comment was typical of many such occasions and illustrates two aspects of Portuguese rule. First, the excessive zeal with which they attempted to force their religion upon all non-believers. This alone would guarantee them the bitter hatred of all Moslems. Secondly, the drastic and brutal way in which they put down the slightest sign of hostility, plundering and destroying as they went. This too earned them the undying hatred of all coastal people, who gave the Portuguese the nickname 'Afriti', or Devil.

In 1507 Mozambique became the headquarters of Portuguese authority on the coast, under the charge of a Captain who took his orders from the Viceroy at Goa. Later another Captain was appointed to take command at Mombasa, but it was not until 1588 that resistance from that town was finally overcome. The main functions of these Captains were the collecting of tribute from local rulers, the imposing of customs duties on all imports and exports, and the suppression of any resistance or rebellion. Due to a constant shortage of manpower the Portuguese were never able to provide sufficient troops to garrison their strongholds, so that it was difficult enough for them to secure their handful of settlements, let alone the coast or its hinterland. Disease, corruption and treachery made matters worse.

It may well be wondered whether the Portuguese had any allies on the coast; surprisingly enough they had. Malindi had always been favourably disposed towards them, ever since Vasco da Gama's visit in 1497 when he was permitted to erect one of his stone crosses on the seafront.

But this was perhaps due more to the traditional hostility that existed between Mombasa and Malindi. Vasco da Gama had not been warmly received at the former. Portuguese officials were quick to exploit the rivalries and feuds between local rulers and their followers. By pursuing a policy of divide and rule they maintained their foothold on the coast. In 1592, in order to strengthen this foothold they started the construction of Fort Jesus at Mombasa. This was to become their most powerful centre on the coast, and stands to this day. Built by Mateus Mendes de Vasconcelos, first Captain of Mombasa, to the designs of an Italian architect, Joao Batista Cairato, it was so well constructed and strategically situated that it could withstand siege and attack from any direction. Only twice was it captured by direct attack and once by bombardment from the sea. Today it is a national museum.

Fig. 10.2 Cross erected by Vasco da Gama at Malindi.

Fig. 10.3 Fort Jesus.

Fig. 10.4 Portuguese wall paintings in Fort Jesus.

You may well ask what profit Portugal made out of its possessions with such an oppressive regime. Having broken and disrupted the Moslem trade patterns the Portuguese discouraged the incentive of local traders to revive their traditional exports and imports. Nor did the heavy duties imposed encourage them. Some resorted to smuggling, but this was a risky business. The profitable gold trade from Sofala dwindled, despite Portuguese efforts to ensure that supplies were maintained. At one stage a Portuguese agent in Sofala even advised his king that what had been obtained was not worth the effort. What did reach Sofala was now shipped direct to Goa, and this in turn affected the towns further north whose decline continued.

Challenges to Portuguese control

At no time during the sixteenth and seventeenth centuries could the Portuguese claim that they had absolute control over the East African Coast. There were constant risings and revolts among the many small seaport and island states. There were also two notable attacks from different sources, the Zimba from the mainland and the Turks from the sea.

The Zimba were a warrior band that first appeared in the Zambezi Valley. Not much is known of their origin or the reasons for their sudden movement northwards and along the coast, which does not appear to have been connected with the movements of other Bantu groups in this region. At any rate they were reputed to be man-eaters, and attacked all who lay in their path. In 1587 they attacked Kilwa and apparently killed 3000 inhabitants before sacking the city. The following year they appeared outside Mombasa, just as the Portuguese were preparing to attack the town again. Faced with this combined assault Mombasa surrendered and was plundered yet again. In this case the Zimba would appear to have been allies of the Portuguese but they would doubtless have done the same had the town been in Portuguese hands. The Zimba headed north, still bent on destruction. But near Malindi they met their match in the Segeju, an equally warlike people, part of the Bantu dispersal southwards from Shungwaya. The Segeju destroyed the Zimba completely in 1589. Allied to the Sheikh of Malindi, the Segeju joined forces with him in the subsequent war against his old rival Mombasa. They surprised and defeated the Mombasan army and went on to occupy Mombasa, before surrendering it to the Sheikh and his Portuguese allies. It was after this that the Portuguese decided to construct Fort Jesus and to make Mombasa the strong point of their East African Empire, which it continued to be for the next one hundred years.

Fig. 10.5 Ali Bey.

The other external threat to Portuguese dominion came from a Turkish naval force that appeared in 1585 and 1587. Its captain, Ali Bey, called at Mogadishu, Brava, Kismayu, Faza, Pate, Lamu and Kilifi and was welcomed as a deliverer from Portuguese oppression. He told the people of these towns that he had been sent by the Sultan of Turkey, at that time ruler of the one remaining great Moslem power, the Ottoman Empire, to come to the aid of his fellow Moslems against their Christian masters. It was not difficult to persuade them to rise in revolt and he promised to return with a larger force. Meanwhile the Portuguese Viceroy in Goa had been informed and sent a force to suppress the rebellion. So ruthlessly was this done that Faza was said to have lost every living thing that did not escape, even dogs and parrots. Yet in spite of this, when Ali Bey appeared again in 1588, the towns rose again so that the Portuguese had to send a further reinforcement of 20 ships and 900 men from Goa. On this occasion the Portuguese were once again victorious: Ali Bey barely escaped with his life and the coastal towns were again savagely punished. In Manda, for instance, the Portuguese cut down two thousand cocoa-nut trees when they found that the inhabitants had fled, thus destroying a principal source of food and livelihood.

Having finally secured control of Mombasa and crushed their enemies the Portuguese rewarded their ally, Sheikh Ahmad of Malindi by making him ruler of Mombasa under their protection, in 1593. Before long however relations between the new ruler and the Portuguese Captain deteriorated, the former claiming that he was not receiving his share of the taxes and tribute collected. In 1614 he travelled to Goa to petition the Viceroy, without success. Instead local officials conspired with the mainland Nyika people to murder him. In an attempt to restore good relations with their old ally the Portuguese took the young heir, Yusuf Ibn Hasan, to Goa and brought him up as a Christian, hoping that he would then rule Mombasa in their own interests. In due course he returned to Mombasa and took up his duties as puppet king. But the strains of divided loyalty proved too great; he resumed his Moslem faith and in 1631 led an attack against Fort Jesus. He appealed for help but only Tanga and a few small townships responded. The revolt failed and severe punishment was meted out by the Portuguese. Yusuf escaped and took to a life of piracy, dying in Jeddah in 1637.

It is noticeable how often these challenges to Portuguese authority lacked coordination and thorough organisation. They also lacked the resources

Fig. 10.6 Francisco d'Almeida, Portuguese Governor General.

and military skills necessary, and above all the leadership that such an enterprise required. This was to come eventually from Oman. Meanwhile Portugal's monopoly of Eastern trade was beginning to be threatened from Europe. In 1595 Dutch ships appeared in the Indian Ocean, followed five years later by the English. With their commercial efficiency they brought also superior skills in naval warfare, both of which they used to compete against and eventually undermine the Portuguese power in the East. The Dutch and English showed no particular interest in the East Coast of Africa, since advances in navigation and ship construction made it no longer necessary to call there on the way to or from India and the Spice Islands. Thus Portugal's decline in this area was closely connected with the changing balance of power in Europe.

The rise of Oman

Since 1513, when Albuquerque had captured Ormuz, Oman had been subject to Portuguese domination. But early in the seventeenth century the Arabs were able to regain control in the Persian Gulf, taking Ormuz in 1622. One by one the Portuguese strongholds in the Indian Ocean fell. But it was some time before the authorities in Oman could carry the fight to the East African Coast. In the first place they themselves were divided by invasion from Persia and by dynastic rivalries. The Yarubi dynasty which had played a leading part in commercial and political relations with the East Coast lost power. Their successors, the BuSaidi, were more preoccupied with internal affairs although they did not abandon their claim to authority along the Coast. This was reinforced by the sending of occasional expeditions to support the coastal towns in their efforts against the Portuguese during the seventeenth century. But the Omani claim to overlordship was received with mixed feelings on the Coast; not everyone wanted to exchange a Portuguese master simply for an Omani one.

In 1652 Mombasa asked for Omani aid against Portugal. The Imam of Oman replied by sending an expedition to sack the Portuguese settlements in Zanzibar and Pate. Resistance came to centre on Pate, ruled by the Nabahani dynasty, who led five revolts between 1637 and 1687. On each occasion the Imam sent troops and supplies. Finally in 1698 after a siege lasting three years Fort Jesus was surrendered to a combined force from Oman and Pate. Of the original garrison only eight Portuguese soldiers, three Indians and two African women remained alive. A few years later Portugal's last ally, Zanzibar, was occupied by troops from Oman. Apart from a brief interlude in 1728–9 when they reoccupied Mombasa the Portuguese never returned north of Cape Delgado.

Expulsion of the Portuguese from the coast of East Africa did not mean the automatic establishment of Omani rule in their place. It was to take another century before this was finally achieved. At first the Omanis were content to station garrisons at strategic points along the coast, with their chief centre at Mombasa. It was not long, however, before resentment built up into open resistance; the people of Pate actually invited the Portuguese back in 1727, and it was this joint alliance that led to the re-taking of Fort Jesus and occupation of Mombasa. Between 1724 and 1765 the ruler of Kilwa made repeated requests to the Portuguese in Mozambique for assistance against the Omani governor of the town. The truth of the matter was that the coastal towns valued their own individual independence above everything else, and while they might welcome the Imam of Oman's presence in the struggle to throw out the Portuguese they were not prepared to submit to his permanent authority. The situation during the eighteenth century remained uneasy and uncertain. While the trade and Moslem culture along the coast revived, tension and rivalry between the local states remained. Nominally the Imams of Oman were still acknowledged, but in practice their authority was limited. In particular it was the rise of their Omani followers in Mombasa, the Mazrui, that was to prove the final obstacle to complete control over the East Coast.

The Mazrui of Mombasa

The Mazrui had come to Mombasa in the service of the Yarubi Imams at the end of the seventeenth century. They had taken part in the final assault on Fort Jesus and then settled in Mombasa, inter-marrying with the local Swahili. They became wealthy and influential as traders and 'Walis', or governors, of local settlements. In 1727 a member of the Mazrui family was appointed Deputy Governor of Mombasa, and in 1741 the Yarubi made Muhammad ibn Uthman al Mazrui Governor of Mombasa. Shortly after this the Yarubi were overthrown in Oman and replaced by the BuSaidi. This gave the ambitious Mazrui the opportunity they had been looking for. They declared themselves independent of Oman, the Governor declaring: 'The new Imam is an ordinary citizen like myself. He has taken power in Oman. I have taken it in Mombasa.'

Other towns, including Malindi, Pemba, Zanzibar, Pate and Mafia followed Mombasa's example.

Free of foreign domination and with no serious rivals to threaten their position the Mazrui set about strengthening their control both locally and further afield. They had already made peace between the two rival Swahili groups of Mombasa, the Thalatha Taifa and the Tisa Taifa, who now agreed to acknowledge the Mazrui as rulers of Mombasa. Many of these Swahili people had come as refugees from settlements further north. Through the Swahili of Mombasa the Mazrui were able to gain access to the manpower and trade of the Nyika groups in the hinterland. This was something that no other coastal state was able to do, and was made possible because the Nyika, with the exception of the southern Digo, used the Swahili leaders as their spokesmen with the outside world. Further afield the Mazrui seized Pemba from Oman and nearly took Zanzibar. Pemba was to become important as a principal source of food for Mombasa. An alliance was made with the Nabahani of Pate which enabled Mombasa to maintain a garrison in Pate, and which acknowledged the Mazrui as the senior of the two allies. This agreement survived, despite a rising in Pate in 1776. Mombasa's supremacy was also acknowledged by the Madiwani of Vumba, to the south, which gave the Mazrui a certain authority over the coast between Tanga and Mombasa.

The new Busaidi Imam did not turn a blind eye to

Fig. 10.7 The graves of the Mazrui.

these activities. In 1746 an Omani force succeeded in assassinating the Mazrui Governor, or Liwali, Muhammad, and imprisoned his brother Ali Mazrui in Fort Jesus. However, he escaped and gathered sufficient support to throw out the Omani. Under both Ali and his successor, Masoud bin Nasir, Mombasa was governed ably and energetically. The only check to this period of Mazrui supremacy came in 1785 when an Omani expedition, sent to deal with a rival BuSaidi claimant, Seif ibn Ahmed, who had come to seek support from the coastal towns, succeeded in getting the Mazrui to acknowedge the overlordship of the BuSaidi dynasty. In practice it made little difference, and for another twenty years or so Mazrui power remained unchallenged.

By this time the Mazrui had become thoroughly assimilated, through intermarriage and the adoption of local customs and language; still proud of their Arab ancestry, however, and of their Moslem heritage. Although the coastal settlements were never to regain their former wealth and prominence, there was a revival of building, crafts and other cultural activities along the coast. Some of the fine old buildings, such as the Kizimkazi mosque on

Fig. 10.8 Kizimkazi Mosque, Zanzibar.

Zanzibar Island, were restored. The Swahili language flourished in a variety of forms such as 'nyimbo' or songs; 'hadithi' or tales and histories; and 'utendi' or heroic poems recounting the deeds of famous men from the past. They revived the glories of the past, often with great imagination and talent. Though written in Swahili the script used was still Arabic.

By the beginning of the nineteenth century Mazrui rule was beginning to weaken. There were a number of reasons for this. Their own proud and contemptuous behaviour lost them the support of allies. Their own family feuds were another cause; the three principal Mazrui families became increasingly involved in conflicts over the succession to the position of Liwali. Their reputation suffered a serious setback at the battle of Shela in 1812, when they were defeated by a combined Lamu-Pate force. By 1822 they had lost control of Pate and Pemba to the new Imam of Oman, Seyyid Said, and in 1828 an Omani force landed at Mombasa, occupied the town but allowed the Mazrui to retain Fort Jesus provided they acknowledged Seyyid Said. Finally, in 1837 the Mazrui were expelled from Mombasa, their leaders arrested and deported. They had tried to avoid Omani conquest by appealing for protection to Britain, by now the major power in the Indian Ocean. In 1807 they sent an embassy to Bombay, the centre of British rule in western India. Two years later they offered Britain the overlordship of Pemba. Neither suggestion was taken up. In 1823 a further appeal was made, and early in the following year a British warship, engaged in surveying the coast, sailed into Mombasa just as an Omani fleet was about to bombard the town. Acting without official authority the naval officer in command, Owen, agreed to declare a British protectorate over Mombasa. It lasted for barely two years and in 1826 the British withdrew, leaving the Mazrui to their fate.

Seyyid Said, Sultan of Oman and Zanzibar

After a somewhat violent succession dispute involving the murder of his brother, Seyyid Said became absolute ruler of Oman in 1806. He was a shrewd and far-sighted man, combining great ambition with patience and caution. Until 1817 he was principally concerned with strengthening his position in Oman, although in 1813 Lamu had submitted to his authority. He realised that an alliance with Britain would be invaluable, both diplomatically and for reasons of sea power. Once this had been confirmed he set about the reconquest of the coastal towns, making skilful use of local quarrels and rivalries.

A dynastic struggle at Pate in 1823 gave him the chance to intervene and terminate Mazrui influence there. His forces were then able to exploit Shirazi dislike of Mazrui control in Pemba, further isolating Mombasa. A struggle for power between various Mazrui families then followed which, in spite of the able leadership of Liwali Salim bin Ahmad, added to Mombasa's troubles and helped Seyyid Said. As we have seen, the end came in 1837.

Seyyid Said's ambition, now that his authority on the East African Coast was established, was to create a great commercial empire. To this end he made the momentous decision to move his capital from Oman to Zanzibar. This was to have important political and economic consequences for East Africa as a whole. While keeping his links with Oman he turned his time and attention increasingly towards African affairs. Although he had no intention of building a large territorial empire on the mainland he strove hard to secure control or influence over the chief centres and routes of trade. 'I am nothing but a merchant', he is supposed to have said on one occasion. Zanzibar was to become the centre of this great network, and here again we note his shrewd judgment. Although it had never rivalled coastal towns such as Kilwa or Mombasa in the past, this island had certain special advantages. First, its position as an island gave it the security from mainland rivals and attack. Secondly, it possessed a good harbour with deep water, adequate not only for the dhows of the Indian Ocean but also the great ships of Europe and America which Seyyid Said hoped to attract. It was only 56 kilometres (35 miles) by sea from Bagamoyo on the mainland, the terminus for the overland route. Thirdly, the island offered an attractive climate, abundant rainfall and fertile soil.

Questions

1. What common interests did the Portuguese and Arabs have on the East Coast of Africa?
2. What methods did the Portuguese use to gain and then retain control of the East African Coast?
3. Account for the gradual decline of Portuguese power and influence in East Africa during the seventeenth century; how much of this remained after 1700?
4. Who were the Mazrui, and why were they so important in the history of Mombasa?
5. Describe the steps taken by Seyyid Said to establish himself as the dominant ruler on the coast of East Africa.

Activities

1. Imagine that you were a newspaper reporter on the Coast in 1498; how would you have described the arrival of Vasco da Gama at Mombasa and Malindi?
2. Describe what you would have done as Captain of Fort Jesus in 1587, faced with attack from the sea by the Turks and from the land by the Zimba.

Chapter 11
Zanzibar and the Interior, 1800–1880

Introduction

As a result of Seyyid Said's decision to move his capital to the island of Zanzibar it became the great terminus and outlet for East African trade during the nineteenth century. Not only was he determined to revive the traditional pattern of trade between the coast and the interior, but he sought to make Zanzibar an entrepot for international trade as well. In both these aims he was successful, thanks largely to his tact and diplomacy. He preferred to negotiate rather than fight, as we have already seen, and had the foresight to ally himself with the dominant power in the Indian Ocean at this time; Britain. When he moved his capital from Muscat to Zanzibar in 1832, he became in many ways more of an African than an Arab ruler.

Zanzibar itself had never been an important centre of coastal trade to the same degree as Kilwa or Mombasa. But it was to become so under its new Sultan. Seyyid Said saw the need to put the caravan trade onto a more regular basis; hence the need for traders from the coast to go inland themselves, something they had not done before. Meanwhile the demand for slaves on the coast was beginning to increase as Arab landowners acquired large plantations of coconut trees and, from 1818, cloves.

Indian business men, known as Banyans, had been encouraged to come to Zanzibar by Seyyid Said. They provided the financial backing and supplied the goods required for the caravans. In fact the bulk of the organisation was in their hands. They charged heavy rates of interest on the loans they advanced, in order to cover themselves against any risk of loss. Not all the caravans returned successfully. High prices were also charged for the

Fig. 11.1 Zanzibar, from the sea in the mid nineteenth century.

Fig. 11.2 The British and American consulates, Zanzibar.

goods and porters needed. It was a complex business, and it is not surprising to find that by 1860 there were over six thousand Banyans in Zanzibar, while others operated from the mainland. The other major function performed by the Indians was the collection of customs duties. A flat rate of five per cent was charged on all items. Heading this organisation was another Indian, the Customs Master of Zanzibar. In return for an annual payment to the Sultan he had almost complete financial control on the island. To ensure a profitable revenue the Sultan ordered that all imports and exports were to pass through Zanzibar.

Seyyid Said also encouraged European and American business interests. During his reign a number of Consulates were established on the island, with a view to developing international trade. The Americans were first, in 1837, followed by the British, French and Germans. Although anxious to attract their merchandise and money the Sultan made it clear that the development should be under his authority and not independent. These consular agreements were also a way of obtaining foreign recognition and confirmation of his position as ruler of Zanzibar and the East African coastal settlements. In particular he attached much importance to British recognition of this claim. In addition to the consuls Seyyid Said welcomed European travellers and even missionaries to his capital, and provided them with letters of introduction to his representatives on the mainland.

And so Zanzibar became a flourishing centre of commerce and business, a meeting place for men of many different backgrounds. The following diagram illustrates the range of goods passing through the island. Not all came with the caravans from the interior. Cloves and copra, for instance, were produced locally.

Imports

cloth	gunpowder
beads	guns
brass wire	provisions (for caravans)

Exports

slaves	cowrie shells
ivory	gum-copal
cloves	sesamum seed
rubber	maize, millet

The approximate figures for the growth in revenue from customs duties are also revealing:

Before	1828:	£10 000 p.a. approx
	1834:	£20 000 p.a.
	1859:	£50 000 p.a.
After	1869:	£65 000 p.a.
	1876:	£100 000 p.a.

The trade routes

Not all the principal trade routes had their terminus in Zanzibar (see Map 29). In particular the route into northern Uganda from the Sudan was under the control of the 'Khartoumers', nominally the subjects of the Khedive of Egypt. The main routes further south in East Africa had all been pioneered by African traders before the Arabs began to penetrate the interior. They covered considerable distances, and with the slow pace of caravans it took many weeks, even months, to reach their destination. Hence the need for regular stopping places, with facilities for storage of goods and supplies. This involved negotiations with local chiefs and rulers over a wide area, from Katanga and Zaire to the East Coast. Caravans varied in size from one hundred to one thousand or more men, including the Arab or Swahili leaders, their armed bodyguard and the porters. Apart from the articles of trade carried by the porters the chief items of equipment would be guns, ammunition, chains and gifts. It quite frequently took a caravan months or even years to complete its mission.

The main routes can be conveniently divided into north, central and south:

The southern route

This ran from ports on the southern coast of

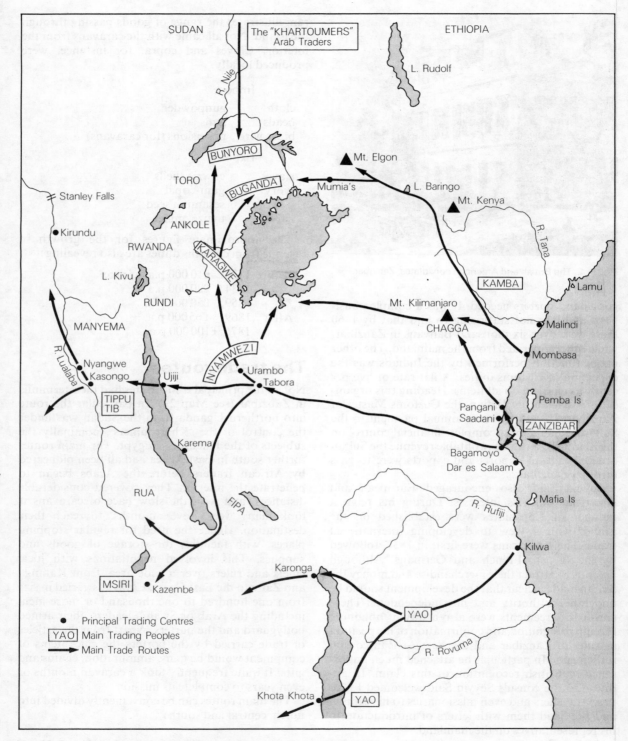

Map 29 East Africa showing principle trade routes of the nineteenth century

The "KHARTOUMERS"
Arab Traders

SUDAN

ETHIOPIA

R. Nile

L. Rudolf

Stanley Falls

Kirundu

BUNYORO

TORO

BUGANDA

Mumia's

Mt. Elgon

L. Baringo

Mt. Kenya

ANKOLE

R. Tana

RWANDA

KARAGWE

L. Kivu

RUNDI

MANYEMA

KAMBA

Lamu

Mt. Kilimanjaro

CHAGGA

Malindi

R. Lualaba

Nyangwe

Kasongo

Ujiji

NYAMWEZI

Urambo

Tabora

Mombasa

TIPPU
TIB

Karema

Pangani

Saadani

Pemba Is

ZANZIBAR

RUA

FIPA

Bagamoyo

Dar es Salaam

Mafia Is

R. Rufiji

MSIRI

Kazembe

Karonga

Kilwa

YAO

R. Rovuma

Khota Khota

YAO

● Principal Trading Centres

YAO Main Trading Peoples

→ Main Trade Routes

92

Tanzania, such as Kilwa and Lindi, inland through the country of the Yao, Makua and Makonde to Lake Malawi. This was the principal route for the export of slaves and was dominated by the Yao.

The central route

This led from the 'Mrima' coast, opposite Zanzibar, from ports like Bagamoyo and Saadani through Zaramo and Gogo country to the Arab stronghold of Tabora, in Unyanyembe. From here it divided:
a) north-west to Karagwe, Buganda and Bunyoro.
b) west to Ujiji (another Arab outpost) on Lake Tanganyika and thence to eastern Zaire.
c) south-west, round the southern shore of Lake Tanganyika towards Katanga.

The northern route

This led from Pangani, Tanga and Mombasa inland to the Kilimanjaro and Taita area, then divided:
a) west from Kilimanjaro to the eastern shores of Lake Victoria.
b) north-west to Mt Kenya, Lakes Baringo and Rudolf, and across the Rift Valley as far as the slopes of Mt Elgon.

The traders

As we have seen this trade on the mainland was by no means the monopoly of the coastal Arab and Swahili merchants. There were, in particular, three African groups who played a prominent part in developing and organising long distance trade: the Yao, the Nyamwezi and the Kamba. Let us consider each of these in turn.

The Arabs and Swahili

They first led their own caravans into the interior during the 1830s. Their activity varied from one route to another but was strongest on the central route. As the Sultan's subjects they carried his flag with them to impress those they met. But this does not mean that they always acted in his name. The most powerful of them made their own alliances. The chief Arab centres inland were Tabora and Ujiji, which became not only depots for storage and supplies but bases from which they could organise attacks. Among the more famous Arab/Swahili traders were:

Abdulla bin Nasibu, in Nyamwezi

Muhammad bin Khalfan, also known as Rumaliza
Said bin Abibu, of Nyangwe
Tippu Tib (Hamed bin Mohammed) of Manyema, in east Zaire
Mohara, of Nyangwe

A brief examination of Tippu Tib's life and career will show how these coastal traders operated.

Tippu Tib, or Hamed bin Mohammed to give him his proper name, was an Afro-Arab, born about 1830 in Zanzibar. His father had been a trader owning plantations around Tabora. He began his career by working for his father and then for a friend in the caravan trade.

In appearance he was more of an African than an Arab, though in dress and behaviour he adopted Arab ways. His great strength of character and self-assurance made him a natural leader, one who could inspire both respect and fear among his followers. But to his military qualities he added great skill as a diplomat and negotiator. Like Seyyid Said he was a realist and saw the need to come to terms with the Europeans. Although capable of great cruelty and ruthlessness he was noted for his

Fig. 11.3 Tippu Tib, Afro-Arab slave trader.

sociable and friendly disposition towards those he wished to please or impress.

After acquiring the necessary experience he started business on his own and in 1865 reached Ruemba on the eastern shore of Lake Tanganyika where he seized a local chief's supply of ivory and installed his brother as ruler. Moving into Zaire in search of ivory he then defeated and supplanted the chief of the Rua people, claiming to be related to him. He thus became a ruler as well as a trader, an ideal combination. He was now able to collect ivory as tribute due to him without having to pay for it. By 1883 he was established at Stanley Falls, having set up fifteen of his relatives as rulers and personal representatives in the Manyema area. He also secured safe passage for his caravans to the Coast by making agreements with Mirambo of Nyamwezi and Rumaliza of Ujiji. In the face of increasing European pressure and activity in the Congo basin Tippu Tib accepted the post of Governor of Stanley Falls from King Leopold of the Belgians, founder and head of the newly formed Congo Free State. He hoped to preserve his own position by doing so, but although he tried to keep out of the subsequent rivalries and quarrels between Arab and European traders, his influence inevitably declined. In 1890 he returned to Zanzibar for the last time and died there in 1905.

His career spanned a critical period of change in Africa, and it is interesting to note how he attempted to adapt and adjust to suit the times. In the early period he made much of his African blood and connections to establish influence or dominance over certain areas. Later, as Europeans began to upset the traditional balance of power in the interior, he attempted to join forces with them. But their aims and methods were too opposed to his own interests, nor could he hope to resist them. His death marks the end of the era of caravan traders.

The African traders

Before describing each of the three main groups engaged in the caravan trade we should point out that there had long been patterns of local trade between tribes in goods such as iron hoes, salt, livestock, food, tobacco and skins. But it was the long distance trade in basic commodities like ivory, slaves and copper that required the particular qualities and aptitudes that were shown by the Yao, Nyamwezi and Kamba.

The Yao

They were the first to develop this form of trade. As

agriculturalists they needed iron hoes, implements that only the iron-working Cisi group among them knew how to make. They started to travel about Yao country selling them. At about the same time, during the sixteenth and seventeenth centuries, Arab traders from the coast started trading in cloth with the Yao and their neighbours. As a result of the violent disruption that followed the Ngoni invasion early in the nineteenth century a new element entered the pattern of trade—slaves. Having themselves been raided for slaves by the Makua, the Yao began to do the same. As the demand for slaves at the coast increased, particularly at ports such as Kilwa, so the Yao became more and more heavily involved in supplying them. Under powerful chiefs such as Mpanda, Mataka, Machemba and Mtalika the trade along the southern route remained predominantly in Yao hands. Coastal traders who travelled inland came very much as clients of these rulers. They brought guns, cloths, beads and glass in exchange for slaves.

The Nyamwezi

They acquired a considerable reputation as porters as well as organisers of caravans. As J. B. Webster has noted: 'Skill in trading and porterage became symbols of status among the Nyamwezi, chieftaincy titles being conferred in recognition of unusual ability in either' (*Tarikh*, Vol. 1 (1) p. 64.). Helped by their own position in western central Tanzania, a region of intersecting trade routes, they were able to take advantage of the demand for salt from Uvinza in the north-west, for the iron ore from Usangi and Mtunze, and for the copper from Katanga. But in the nineteenth century the commodity most in demand was ivory. It found a ready market in India, Europe and North America. By 1800 the first Nyamwezi caravans had started to arrive at the coast with ivory. This trade became an essential part of Nyamwezi life and society, both economically and politically. Large Nyamwezi caravans moved annually to the coastal towns with their loads of merchandise; copper, ivory and later slaves.

They were to be found further inland as well, venturing as far as Katanga, Buganda and eastern Zaire. As Arab participation increased so the Nyamwezi were forced to share the traffic and business on the central route. But under powerful figures such as Mirambo and Nyungu ya Mawe they continued to play a prominent part. The central route became perhaps the busiest and largest of the three we have mentioned, and was certainly the one best known to European travellers and missionaries in the nineteenth century. It was also along this route that new crops were introduced: rice, maize and cassava, important additions to food supplies. The Nyamwezi themselves became increasingly cosmopolitan in outlook and began to lose their traditional ties of kinship. New loyalties to caravan groups, hunters' guilds or secret societies such as the Baswezi and Wayeye (snake experts) replaced the old. The proximity of Arab settlements such as Tabora also had a profound effect.

The Kamba

Living in an area of very uncertain rainfall the Kamba were frequently forced to go in search of food so that they developed from an early stage the practice of trading iron implements and poisoned arrows for food with their immediate neighbours the Kikuyu, Embu, Rabai and Giriama. They travelled even further afield and began to develop a tradition of trading. Early in the nineteenth century they made contact with Swahili and Arab traders on the coast and this led to a rapid extension of their activities. By the 1830s they were organising weekly caravans of from three hundred to four hundred people to the coast. They hunted for slaves, cattle and ivory as far as Lake Baringo and Samburu; exchanging these commodities at the coast for cotton cloth, blue calico, glass beads, copper, salt and zinc. But slaves were not as easy or profitable to obtain on this northern route. The chief outlets at the coast were Mombasa, Pangani and the important market centre of Kaya Rabai. By the 1860s Arab and Swahili traders were beginning to come inland in order to obtain direct access to this area. As a result the Kamba influence was weakened. But many of them continued to play an active role, among them Chief Kivoi of Kitui.

The slave and ivory trade

We have already referred to the greatly increased demand for ivory in the nineteenth century. There was a corresponding growth in the demand for

Fig. 11.4 The slave market in Zanzibar.

slaves from the mid eighteenth century. This came from four main sources: the French sugar plantations on Reunion and Mauritius islands in the Indian Ocean, Portuguese plantations in Brazil (as the supply of slaves from West Africa began to diminish), the new Arab clove and coconut plantations on the East African Coast and islands, and the Arab states. There had long been a steady trickle of slaves from east and north-east Africa, but it was nothing like the numbers enslaved during this period. Since few records were kept at the time it is not easy to calculate accurately how many slaves were taken to the coast. But by 1839 between forty and forty-five thousand slaves were being sold annually at the slave market in Zanzibar. Roughly half went overseas and half to local plantations. By the 1860s this total had increased to seventy thousand. The slaves came from a wide variety of places, the majority from the southern hinterland between Kilwa and Lake Malawi. The high prices

Fig. 11.5a Slaves in chains.

Fig. 11.5b Slavery in the Sudan.

paid for both slaves and ivory made them easily the most profitable items of trade in East Africa during the nineteenth century. It was a violent and destructive form of trade, as we shall see.

The slaughtering of elephants in order to obtain their ivory was carried out by bands of skilled African hunters or trappers as well as by Swahili or Arab traders armed with guns. Elephants were to be found in abundance throughout East Africa, particularly around the forested slopes of mountains, the lake shores and in the eastern part of Zaire. Guns also played an important part in the way that slaves were acquired. This might be either as a direct purchase from a local ruler, disposing of his captives, criminals or destitute subjects in exchange for guns and other articles; or by inciting one chief or ruler to attack a neighbouring group of people, and taking a share of those captured in return for the military assistance given; or through a direct attack on a settlement by the slave traders themselves. A number of eye witness accounts of such occasions have survived; they convey the true horror and brutality of the whole business. Thus David Livingstone writing in his journal:

'We passed a woman tied by the neck to a tree and dead. . . . We saw others tied up in a similar manner, and one lying in the path shot or stabbed for she was in a pool of blood. The explanation we got invariably was that the Arab who owned these victims was enraged at losing his money by the slaves becoming unable to march.' . . . and referring later to the preparation for a raid he wrote: 'The caravan leaders from Kilwa arrive at a Yao village, show the goods they have brought, are treated liberally by the elders and told to wait and enjoy themselves . . . then a foray is made against the Wanyasa who have few or no guns. The Yao who come against them are abundantly supplied with both by their coast guests. Several of the low coast Arabs, who differ in nothing from the Yao, usually accompany the foray and do business on their own account: this is the usual way in which a safari is furnished with slaves.' (D. Livingstone: Last Journals. London 1874, as quoted in *Missionary Factor in East Africa*, by R. Oliver: Longmans.)

The process of capturing and collecting together slaves and ivory often took many months. Hence the need for strongly fortified trading posts in the interior such as Tabora, Ujiji and Karonga. Having collected their caravan together the traders would then march slowly to the coast, often having to ward off attacks or fight their way out of ambushes. The missionary Frederick Moir gave this description of a caravan he met in 1885:

'First came armed men dancing, gesticulating and throwing about their guns as only Arabs can do, to the sound of drums, pipes and other less musical instruments. Then followed slowly . . . the great man himself . . . his richly decorated donkey walking along nearby; and surely no greater contrast could be conceived than that between the courteous and white-robed Arab, with his silver sword and daggers and silken turban, and the miserable swarm of naked squalid human beings that he had wantonly dragged from their now ruined homes. The men were driven, tied two by two in the terrible 'goree' or taming-stick, or in gangs of about a dozen each with an iron collar let into a long iron chain, many even soon after starting staggering under their loads. The women were fastened to chains or thick bark ropes. Many in addition to their heavy weight of grain or ivory carried babies. The double burden was almost too much, and still they struggled on.'

Those slaves that survived the journey and reached the coast were then disposed of by auction or sale. Zanzibar was the principal market for slaves; those destined for overseas would then be taken off by ship, facing yet another hazardous journey. Meanwhile the rest of the caravan would be disbanded, the porters paid off and preparations made for the next venture into the interior.

Although we have not made special mention of the Khartoum slave traders in northern Uganda, their methods and objects were very much the same. The 'Khartoumers' were moslems of the Sudan, at that time still part of the Khedive of Egypt's Empire. In 1841 an Egyptian expedition had reached Gondokoro, 50 kilometres (30 miles) north of the present border with Uganda. This and similar expeditions opened up the southern Sudan to possibilities of trade, which the merchants of the north were quick to seize, making Gondokoro their base. Originally ivory had been the main attraction, but it was not long before they turned to capturing slaves as well. Racial and religious attitudes gave an even sharper edge to these raids. The Khartoumers had no misgivings about raiding and enslaving the 'unbelievers' of this region. By the 1850s these raids had reached Acholi and in the following years they penetrated into Bunyoro and Lango, where they met with stiff resistance. The slaves were taken north to Khartoum to be sold.

The effects of the slave trade

The slave trade had far reaching effects that were to alter the lives of East Africans fundamentally. Quite apart from the immediate human suffering and misery it caused, there took place certain basic political, social and economic changes in society to which we must now refer. One must see these in conjunction with other movements and pressures to which we shall turn in the following chapters.

Political effects

The trade had the effect of strengthening the large and powerful states at the expense of the small and weak. In particular those with access to guns and ammunition through the coastal trade were able to dominate those without them. Guns were the key to both wealth and power. It is worth noting the comment of a minor chief in northern Uganda, with whom Sir Samuel Baker stayed: 'Most people are bad. If they are strong they take from the weak. The good people are all weak; they are good because they are not strong enough to be bad.'

Thus in the areas affected by the slave trade there was a move towards larger political units, often under the rule of men who owed their power and position to these new economic forces. At the same time traditional institutions of government were modified, with power moving more to the central authority and away from small, local bodies.

Economic effects

Famine, poverty and destitution were often the immediate outcome of slave raids. In the longer term there was much loss of agricultural production. Villages and fields laid waste were often not reclaimed for many years for fear of a similar fate. On the other hand, as we have seen, new food crops were introduced through this trade, and flourishing plantations established around trading centres. The size and scale of the trade brought new opportunities and livelihoods to many Africans. The Kamba are a good example of a group gaining rather than losing from the trade. At the same time it tended to discourage trade in certain traditional items since these proved less profitable than slaves and ivory. Similarly some of the old crafts and skills died out in the face of manufactured goods imported from overseas.

Social effects

Here again we find a mixture of negative and beneficial effects. There was the obvious suffering of those who lost relatives and had their homes destroyed. The security and protection afforded by their societies broke up, people lost confidence in their traditional leaders and customs. Fear and suspicion grew. But for those situated away from the trade routes life did not change noticeably, while those under the protection of powerful leaders often benefited considerably. Depopulation has been mentioned as a major factor, but it was more likely to have been serious in areas of persistent slave raiding, notably along the southern trade route.

Other consequences that might be attributed to the caravan trade were the introduction of the Swahili language to many parts of East and Central Africa, where it became the 'lingua franca' for many people engaged in business. The Arabs do not appear to have made any strong attempt to convert others to Islam. It spread more through inter-marriage and assimilation. Only in Buganda did Islam assume any prominence, when a group of courtiers formed a Moslem faction around the Kabaka. Belief in traditional African religion was, in many areas, demoralised by the effects of the trade.

Questions

1. Show how the establishment of Arab power on Zanzibar affected the East African mainland in the first half of the nineteenth century.
2. Compare the roles of the Nyamwezi and the Yao in the development of long distance trade during the nineteenth century.
3. Explain how Tippu Tib rose to power and describe the methods he used to do so.
4. Describe the principal trade routes established for long distance caravans in East Africa.
5. What were the main advantages and disadvantages brought about by the slave and ivory trade in East Africa?

Activities

1. Write an account of the life of a slave from the day he was captured to the time he was sold at the slave market in Zanzibar.
2. Draw a sketch map of East and Central Africa to show the principal trade routes and centres in the nineteenth century.
3. Find out more about the following:
   Mirambo of Nyamwezi
   Msiri (in Katanga)
   Kimweri of Vugha
   Sultan Seyyid Said
   You may find the historical journal *Tarikh* of use.

Chapter 12
European activity in East Africa, 1800–1880

Introduction

By the mid-nineteenth century the people of East Africa were coming into contact with visitors of a different kind—European traders, travellers and missionaries. In order to understand why they came to Africa we need to consider first what was happening in Europe at this time. Far reaching changes were taking place throughout western Europe and first and foremost in Britain. The Industrial Revolution was altering the whole way of life, from a predominantly agricultural and rural society Europe was becoming a continent of industrial cities, factory workers and machines. Coal and iron, the basic raw materials for this process, were easily obtainable and close at hand. But for many of these new industries raw materials were required from overseas such as cotton, wool, sugar and palm oil together with additional supplies of food to feed the rapidly growing population. There was also the need to find new markets for the manufactured goods produced by the factories. Hence the search during the nineteenth century for fresh outlets for these exports in America, Africa

Fig. 12.1 Early German traders in East Africa.

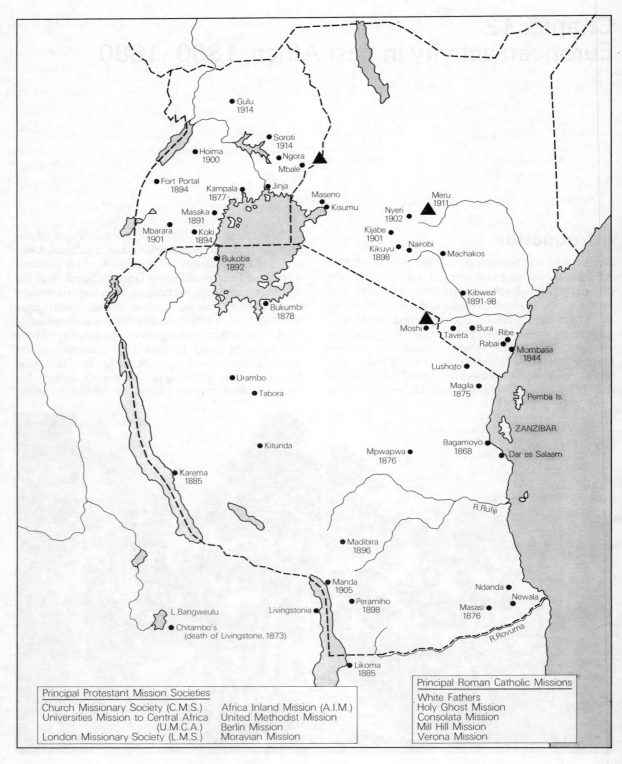

Map 30 Centres of early Christian missionary influence in East Africa

The labels on the map:

Gulu 1914
Soroti 1914
Hoima 1900
Ngora
Mbale
Fort Portal 1894
Kampala 1877
Jinja
Maseno
Kisumu
Masaka 1891
Mbarara 1901
Koki 1894
Bukoba 1892
Meru 1911
Nyeri 1902
Kijabe 1901
Kikuyu 1898
Nairobi
Machakos
Bukumbi 1878
Kibwezi 1891-98
Moshi
Taveta
Bura
Ribe
Rabai
Mombasa 1844
Lushoto
Magila 1875
Pemba Is.
Urambo
Tabora
ZANZIBAR
Bagamoyo 1868
Dar es Salaam
Kitunda
Mpwapwa 1876
Karema 1885
R. Rufiji
Madibira 1896
L. Bangweulu
Chitambo's (death of Livingstone, 1873)
Manda 1905
Peramiho 1898
Livingstonia
Ndanda
Newala
Masasi 1876
R. Rovuma
Likoma 1885

Principal Protestant Mission Societies
Church Missionary Society (C.M.S.)   Africa Inland Mission (A.I.M.)
Universities Mission to Central Africa   United Methodist Mission
(U.M.C.A.)   Berlin Mission
London Missionary Society (L.M.S.)   Moravian Mission

Principal Roman Catholic Missions
White Fathers
Holy Ghost Mission
Consolata Mission
Mill Hill Mission
Verona Mission

and Asia. In this enterprise Britain played the leading part, not simply because she had been the first to become industrialised but because she had the great advantage of sea-power to protect her ships and an established overseas empire.

But this does not explain the presence of missionaries in East Africa, although many of them were, consciously or unconsciously, furthering the interests of European commerce. They had come primarily to spread the Gospel and represented the powerful evangelical movement in the Church at this time. This was aimed not only at converting to Christianity those in foreign lands but also the many thousands of industrial and urban workers in Britain whom the Church had failed to reach. This revival of religious activity was particularly strong in Britain during the late eighteenth and early nineteenth centuries. It played a leading part in what came to be called the Humanitarian movement, campaigning for such things as the abolition of slavery and the slave trade, prison reform and the improved treatment of women and children in factories. Its leaders were men of influence and ability: Wilberforce, Buxton, Shaftesbury. Their sense of duty, of morality and of confidence in their own ideas was to become part of the character of the British people in the Victorian era.

While Britain was acquiring the benefits of industrial development the rest of Europe was in the grip of political uncertainty and unrest. From the outbreak of the French Revolution in 1789 until the mid nineteenth century European countries were involved in political struggles between the old reactionary monarchies on the one hand and the leaders of the new ideals of Liberalism and Nationalism on the other. Eventually the latter triumphed as, one by one, the nations of Europe acquired democratic institutions. It was this sense of national achievement and pride, coupled with the benefits and opportunities of industrialisation, that led nations like France, Germany and Italy to join in the search for overseas markets and colonies.

Let us see how these aims and ideas were applied in the case of those who came to East Africa in the period before 1880. By and large they came as individuals, or as representatives of some missionary or scientific society. Not until after 1880 did the governments of the states they came from intervene directly in East African affairs.

Missionaries

For the period covered in this chapter we may divide missionary activity into two phases. First the period from the early 1840s until about 1870. During this time the number of missionaries involved was small, their success limited and the sphere of their operations confined largely to the coast. Following the death of Livingstone in 1873 came a great wave of enthusiasm and support that led to the establishment of new mission stations in the interior, particularly in Buganda.

The pioneer missionary in East Africa was the German, Dr Ludwig Krapf. He had been sent by the Church Missionary Society in England to work among the Galla of southern Ethiopia in 1837. It was hoped that by doing so he might effectively spread the Gospel across much of north-eastern Africa, the area occupied by the Galla. It proved a disappointment, however, and so in 1844 Krapf came south to Zanzibar, hoping to obtain permission to cross to the mainland and approach the Galla from the south. A few months later he crossed to Mombasa and established a mission station at Rabai. Here he was joined by Johann Rebmann in 1846 and Jakob Erhardt in 1849. Krapf saw the Rabai station as the first of a series, 'the first link of

Fig. 12.2 Rabai church, built about 1886.

101

a mission-chain between East and Central Africa' he wrote in 1848. From this base these missionaries travelled inland; Rebmann to Teita in 1847 and Chagga the following year when he met chief Makinga. It was during these visits that he first saw Mt Kilimanjaro. In July 1848 Krapf visited Usambara where he was welcomed by the Shambaa king, Kimweri ye Nyumbai who asked for missionaries to come and teach his people. In 1849 Krapf travelled through Ukambani and met chief Kivoi and saw Mt Kenya. He made a second visit there in 1851 hoping to set up a mission station. But while travelling with Kivoi towards the Tana River he was attacked and Kivoi was killed.

The work of evangelism did not prove a success. When the British Consul, Colonel Playfair, visited Rabai in 1864 he found that only six people had been baptised and another six were being taught. Yet in another way their work had achieved something. From the experience of their travels inland and from information they gathered from Arab and Swahili traders, Erhardt compiled a map of the interior, including what he called the inland sea, 'Uniamuesi'. This, together with their reports of snow capped mountains on the equator, was to arouse much geographical curiosity and controversy. Could the inland sea be the source of the Nile? This led to the sending of several expeditions out to East Africa in search of the Nile's source. Finally, Krapf's work on a Swahili Grammar and Dictionary was to prove of great value to missionaries and travellers. Due to ill health he was forced to leave in 1853, Rebmann remaining for another twenty years.

One of the main concerns of the mission societies in East Africa during the 1860s and 1870s was the suppression of the slave trade and the subsequent problem of what to do with the freed slaves. In 1863 the Holy Ghost Fathers came from Reunion Island and started a mission in Zanzibar. In 1864 Bishop Tozer and the U.M.C.A. came to Zanzibar after an unsuccessful attempt to establish a station in the Shire area on the mainland. Much of their time and effort was taken up with the campaign for the abolition of the slave trade and plans for the resettlement of freed saves. One such centre was set up by the Holy Ghost Fathers at Bagamoyo in 1868 at which former slaves were taught basic skills such as agriculture and carpentry as well as how to read and write. In 1875 the C.M.S. started a similar centre at Freretown on the outskirts of Mombasa.

Livingstone's death in 1873 made him a national hero in Britain. Weakened by constant illness and lack of supplies he died at Chitambo's, near Lake

Fig. 12.3 David Livingstone.

Bangweolu. His faithful followers carried his body to the coast where it was taken by ship to Britain and buried in Westminster Abbey. The example of his life and death stirred the national conscience deeply. In a famous speech at Cambridge university in 1857 he had first made the appeal: 'I beg to direct your attention to Africa. I know that in a few years I shall be cut off in that country, which is now open; do not let it be shut again. I go back to Africa to make an open path for commerce and Christianity; do you carry out the work which I have begun. I leave it with you.' One of the immediate consequences of this speech had been the foundation of the Universities Mission to Central Africa. And now, in 1873, the response was overwhelming. Money and offers of assistance poured in. Livingstone's emphasis on 'Commerce and Christianity' united both religious and business interests and gave a new impetus to missionary activity in Africa, widening its aims and objectives. Typical of this new policy was the formation of the Livingstone Central African Trading Company by Mr James Stevenson of Glasgow, with the dual object of supplying the missionaries in the area and exporting ivory at a price that would undercut the Arab slave traders.

In East Africa the chief missionary objective was

Fig. 12.4 Henry Morton Stanley.

Fig. 12.5 A painting of a Mission Station in Zululand, 1880.

Fig. 12.6 Dispensary work on safari in 1924.

now the interior. The accounts given by travellers such as Henry Morton Stanley showed that the routes were accessible and conditions suitable for mission work. Following a report by Stanley from the Kabaka's court in Buganda the first C.M.S. party including Alexander Mackay arrived in Buganda in 1877 (see Map 30). The following year the first two White Fathers arrived there, while others of their party went to Ujiji. This important mission derived from the efforts of Cardinal Lavigerie in Algeria, and had been founded in 1868 as The Society of Our Lady in Africa. Meanwhile the U.M.C.A. had started operating at Magila and Masasi in Tanzania.

The impact of these early missionaries was at first limited to the immediate vicinity of their stations. Churches were built, schools and hospitals started. Work on translating the scriptures into the local languages began. Being the first Europeans to settle in the interior their houses and household goods attracted much interest and curiosity, as did their methods of cultivation and building. But their efforts to preach the Gospel and instil the Christian virtues often met with resistance, especially where they conflicted with tribal customs and traditions. In some areas the missions became involved in political issues. This was particularly true of Buganda from the 1880s, as we shall see in a later chapter. To many these first mission stations must have appeared to be the fore-runners of European domination.

Fig. 12.7 Speke and Grant at Mutesa's court.

The travellers

Those Europeans who came to Africa from motives of geographical or scientic interest have often been referred to as explorers. But since this description does not apply in our African context it has been thought more appropriate to use the word 'traveller'. Interest in the principal waterways of Africa had been a matter of major concern to Europeans since the late eighteenth century. In 1830 the mystery of the Niger's outlet had been finally settled by the Lander brothers, while Livingstone on his trans-Africa expedition of 1853–56 had followed the Zambezi down to the Indian Ocean. Somewhere within East Africa, it was felt, lay the solution to the question that had puzzled geographers from the time of Herodotus, namely the source of the Nile. News that Krapf and Rebmann had seen snow-capped mountains, and stories of great inland seas, revived this quest.

In 1856 The Royal Geographical Society picked two army officers, Richard Burton and John Hanning Speke, to lead an expedition from Zanzibar to trace the source of the Nile. With the aid of two experienced Yao guides, Sidi Bombay and Mwinyi Mabruki they travelled inland along the trade route to Tabora. Early in 1858 they reached Lake Tanganyika but were so weak with illness that they could not go much further. Returning to Tabora Speke decided to go north to examine stories of a great lake in that direction. Burton had a violent argument with him over this and remained behind. Speke alone found the lake and named it after his Queen, Victoria. He was convinced, though without sufficient proof, that it was the source of the Nile. The two men returned to the coast from Tabora still bitterly disagreeing. In 1860 a second Royal Geographical expedition came out, with Speke in command accompanied by Grant. Travelling north west round the shores of Lake Victoria they eventually reached Buganda and were welcomed by Kabaka Mutesa. Leaving Grant behind, Speke then travelled east and came across the place where the Nile leaves the Lake, where the modern town of Jinja now stands. Grant rejoined him and together they travelled north following the river to Gondokoro, where they met Samuel Baker coming south. To Speke the matter was settled, and he sent a telegram to this effect to London from Khartoum. Others remained sceptical, however, among them such respected figures as Livingstone. From 1866 to 1872 he travelled ceaselessly around Central and East Africa but without success. It was left to the journalist and adventurer, Stanley, to fill the missing gaps; between 1874 and 1877 he made a thorough survey of Lakes Victoria, Albert and Tanganyika, completing his journey by travelling down the River Congo to the Atlantic.

Another traveller of some note was the geologist, Joseph Thomson. His second journey took him, between 1883–84, through Maasailand, across the Rift Valley and into western Kenya where he saw Mt Elgon. This was essentially a scientific expedition whose purpose was to gather geological and biological information about this part of Africa. Among others to visit this area were Dr Fischer who reached Lake Naivasha in 1872 and Count Teleki whose hunting expedition took him as far as Lake Rudolf in 1888.

It is important to remember that these men came to East Africa for a very wide variety of reasons. Scientific and geographical interest was certainly a major factor, but this in itself was of more than mere academic concern. It provided European governments and business men with valuable information. In this way it was, in effect, part of the process of European intervention and conquest that was to culminate in the Partition of Africa in the last quarter of the nineteenth century. Thus a man like Livingstone must be viewed not simply as a missionary, but as a doctor, scientist, explorer and agent for the British Government during his long career in Africa. These missionaries and travellers saw themselves as carrying 'civilisation' into Africa, without doubting or questioning its advantages and disadvantages. This imposition of European civilisation upon African societies was not to prove as acceptable as they had imagined.

Traders

Missionaries and travellers had shown what the prospects were for trade. At first this was limited to Zanzibar and traditional exports such as ivory, gum copal, cloves, copra and skins. The Americans were the first on the scene, with traders from the ports of Boston and Salem bringing bales of cotton cloth or 'mericani' as it came to be called. In 1833 the Sultan had signed a commercial agreement with the United States, to be followed by one with Britain in 1839. French and German traders also became increasingly interested in trade with East Africa. The French had a particular concern in the export of slaves from the coast to their islands in the Indian Ocean. This was to bring them into conflict with both the Sultan, for encouraging the smuggling of slaves without paying the duties required, and with the British who were attempting to abolish the trade.

Following the establishment of a British Consulate in 1840 British influence increased steadily in Zanzibar. In the 1822 Moresby Treaty and the 1845 Hamerton Treaty Seyyid Said had reluctantly agreed to severe restrictions on the extent of the slave trade, in return for Britain's recognition of his position in East Africa and encouragement of what they referred to as 'legitimate' trade. We shall return to this below.

One of the major obstacles to the development of legitimate trade was the absence of any suitable means of communication or transport into the interior. The existing method of porters carrying head loads used by the caravans was slow and costly. Nor would it be adequate for the transport of the kinds of raw materials European traders hoped to find or produce in the interior. Nor were any of the rivers navigable for a sufficient distance to be of any use, though attempts were made to explore the possibilities on the River Tana. The only solution, as was

Fig. 12.8 Bargash Bin Said.

105

Fig. 12.9 Sir John Kirk after his retirement.

The abolition of the slave trade

The movement to abolish the slave trade started in Britain during the late eighteenth century and was aimed in the first place at the Atlantic slave trade, between West Africa and America. This was in the hands of European and American merchants. The abolition campaign was supported by various groups: religious bodies like the Quakers, humanitarians like Wilberforce and Clarkson, and writers such as the economist Adam Smith. Their object was to persuade Parliament to legislate against slavery both in Britain and her colonies, and to make use of her diplomacy and sea-power to persuade others to do likewise.

In 1772 slavery was declared illegal in Britain. There followed a series of parliamentary measures restricting the transport of slaves, culminating in the Act of 1807 which abolished the trade altogether, and finally in 1833 slavery itself was made illegal throughout the British Empire. But these measures applied only to British subjects and territories. An equally vigorous campaign was directed against other nations engaged in the trade, making use of British naval patrols, diplomatic agreements and consular officials in West Africa. It was therefore some time before Britain's efforts could be directed towards suppressing the East African slave trade which had been rapidly increasing as the West African trade declined.

The first step in the abolition of the slave trade in the Indian Ocean came in 1822. Captain Moresby concluded an agreement with Seyyid Said which forbade the sale of slaves outside the Sultan's dominions. Arabs were no longer permitted to sell slaves in India or to the French islands such as Reunion. This treaty also authorised British warships to stop and search Arab dhows suspected of carrying slaves, and to deal with smugglers. The Sultan was obliged to make these concessions in return for much needed naval and diplomatic support from Britain at a time when he was struggling to assert his authority on the East Coast. We have seen already how the Mazrui in Mombasa attempted to obtained British protection against Seyyid Said. The 1822 treaty did not abolish the slave trade but merely limited its sphere of activity. Moreover it was extremely difficult to enforce, as the small patrol of British naval ships proved quite inadequate.

The next step came in 1845 when Seyyid Said made a further agreement, this time with the British consul, Colonel Hamerton. The latter had become,

being proved in other parts of the world at this time, was to build a railway. But this was no light or cheap undertaking. Nor could it be undertaken without the Sultan's consent, so long as his authority along the East African coast was respected. Sultan Barghash turned down requests for concessions to develop trade and communications on the mainland from French and German interests, largely as the result of pressure from the British consul, Kirk. In 1877 William Mackinnon was granted a concession to develop some 1 536 000 sq. kilometres (590 000 sq. miles) of territory between Tungi and Warsheik and to construct a road from Dar-es-Salaam to Lake Malawi. This scheme had the support of both Kirk and the missionaries who saw it as a means to end the slave trade. But without adequate funds or the backing of the British Government it was not a success. Things were moving towards direct European intervention in East Africa, but before we turn to this mention must be made of the campaign to abolish the slave trade.

since his appointment in 1841, a close friend of the Sultan. It was this, together with a very real threat of French hostility, that persuaded Seyyid Said to impose yet further restrictions on the trade in slaves: they were no longer to be shipped or sold further north than Brava on the Mogadishu Coast. This was intended to cut off the supply of slaves to the Red Sea and Arabian ports. Elsewhere the trade might continue.

Seyyid Said died in 1856, and Hamerton the following year. In the struggle that followed over the succession to the Sultanate the issue of abolition was put aside, although British interests could not be entirely ignored. The rival claimants agreed to submit their dispute to British arbitration, and this was settled in the Canning Award of 1861, by the Governor General of India, Lord Canning. The new Sultan, Majid, was not however ready to make any further concessions over the slave trade, so that it was not until the accession of his brother Barghash, in 1870, that further progress could be made. Barghash realised how much he needed British support, both to make himself more secure within his own dominions and to resist pressures from rival European powers. He became the close friend and confidant of the new British consul, John Kirk; this relationship was to have a profound effect upon subsequent events in Zanzibar and East Africa.

Meanwhile the full force of the abolition campaign in Britain was being turned towards East Africa. In 1871 a Parliamentary Commission of Enquiry was set up to investigate and report on the slave trade in East Africa, and two years later Sir Bartle Frere was sent out to Zanzibar at the head of a special mission to persuade Barghash to make it illegal. This put the Sultan in a difficult position. He needed the support of Britain as much as ever. On the other hand supplies of slaves were vital for Zanzibar's economy, particularly at this time. In 1872 a hurricane had swept the island, devastating plantations, shipping and buildings; threatening ruin unless things could quickly be restored to normal. Moreover, any action on his part in abolishing the slave trade would provoke sharp hostility from his Arab and Swahili subjects. He therefore declined to sign any agreement with Bartle Frere and the latter departed empty handed. Kirk was not put off. By using various forms of persuasion, not least the threat of a blockade by British warships, he forced the reluctant but helpless Barghash to give way. On March 5, 1873 the decree was finally made, formally prohibiting the export of slaves from the mainland to any part of the Sultan's dominions and undertaking to close all the slave markets. Within twenty-four hours the main slave market on Zanzibar came to an end.

As with previous agreements it was one thing to make a decree and another thing to enforce it. Slaves were now marched northwards along the coast instead of being shipped across by sea. Some were smuggled into Zanzibar and Pemba. To check these evasions the Sultan decreed in 1876 that no slaves were to be transported overland, either from the interior or along the coast. To enforce this a small armed force was raised and stationed on the mainland, under the command of General Lloyd Matthews. Slavery itself remained legal until 1897, being considered indispensable to the society and economy of the Sultan's territory. This was even accepted by the British authorities after a protectorate had been declared over Zanzibar in 1890. The British Commissioner, Hardinge, argued that the final elimination of slavery must be done slowly if the stability and prosperity of Zanzibar were to be maintained. In the 1897 decree slaves were left to claim their freedom themselves. Many of them were unprepared to do so, while to others freedom offered more problems than it was worth. Thus emancipation came eventually but gradually.

Questions

1. What reasons led Europeans to take a greater interest in Africa during the first half of the nineteenth century?
2. Why is David Livingstone important in the history of East and Central Africa?
3. What part did the missionaries play in either the exploration of East Africa or the abolition of the slave trade and slavery?
4. What problems did the British authorities encounter in their efforts to end the slave trade in East Africa?
5. Compare the lives and achievements of Sultan Seyyid Said and Sultan Barghash.

Activities

1. Imagine that you are a page at the court of Kabaka Mutesa in 1862: write a letter home to your parents describing the visit of Speke and Grant to Mutesa.
2. Discuss the impressions that you think the first missionaries would have made on the African people they met.
3. Make a time chart of the major events mentioned in this chapter.

Chapter 13
The Partition of East Africa, 1884–1900

Introduction

During the first eighty years of the nineteenth century European interest and activity in Africa had taken many forms but had not yet resulted in any serious attempt to annex the interior of the continent. Colonial powers such as Britain, France and Portugal had acquired trading bases along the coastal perimeter over the centuries but, apart from Algeria and the Cape, there had been no interest in the occupation or settlement of the hinterland. This was to change abruptly in the last twenty years of the century, with a scramble for possessions and spheres of influence so intense that by 1900 only Ethiopia remained untouched. The remarkable feature of the partition was the artificial and arbitrary way in which boundaries were drawn and agreed between European leaders, with little or no reference to the people or the land of Africa.

The situation in Europe

In order to understand why the partition happened at this particular time and in this way we need to turn once again to the situation in Europe. We have seen in the previous chapter that new political and economic forces were at work, creating a need for fresh markets and raw materials. However, it had been possible to satisfy these needs, so far, without having to add to existing colonial possessions. Thus the scramble for Africa cannot be explained simply in economic terms, important though these were. The growth of nationalism became a significant feature of nineteenth century European society, encouraged by the development of democratic forms of government. Through public opinion and the press this could and did find an outlet in popular support for the policy of Imperialism. But perhaps the crucial factor was based on

strategic and diplomatic motives, and to understand these fully we need to look briefly at each of the main participants; Germany, France and Britain.

Germany had only recently achieved national unification, having been a collection of semi-independent states. The chief architect of German unification and strength was Bismarck, one of Europe's leading statesmen at this time. He had not only given Germany a thriving economy but also the most powerful army in Europe. In 1871 he upset the traditional balance of power in Europe by defeating France. As Chancellor of a confident and aggressive German Empire he now sought new outlets for German ambition and enterprise abroad. Germany wanted 'a place in the sun' i.e. tropical colonies. But Bismarck did not seek these simply for reasons of prestige and status but rather as bargaining counters to use in the diplomatic contest with his European rivals. Hence the skilful way he intervened in Togoland, Cameroon, South West Africa and East Africa.

France already had a foothold in parts of Africa. The conquest and settlement of Algeria had started in the 1830s. There were French posts in Senegal and along the West African coast. The Suez canal had been built by a Frenchman, Ferdinand de Lesseps, in 1869, and there were strong French financial interests in Egypt. But these alone would not be sufficient to explain why France carved out for herself vast areas of West and Central Africa after 1884. The reasons lay elsewhere. It was partly because of the humiliation suffered at the hands of Germany in 1871, resulting in a desire to recover her lost military reputation by engaging in a vigorous policy of imperialism abroad. Much of the territory annexed by France in Africa during the scramble turned out to be desert or semi-desert, but important for strategic reasons since it protected the hinterland of her West and North African colonies.

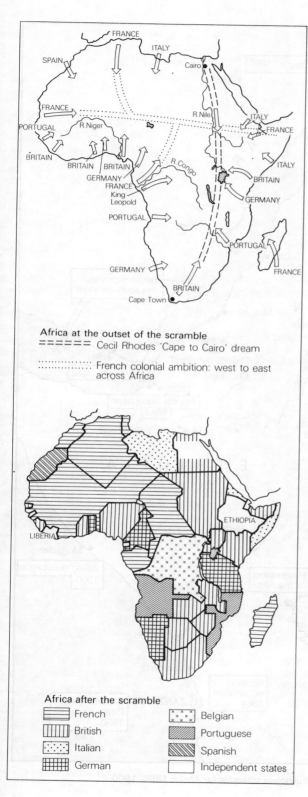

Africa at the outset of the scramble
====== Cecil Rhodes 'Cape to Cairo' dream

·············· French colonial ambition: west to east
across Africa

Africa after the scramble

▤ French	⊡ Belgian
▥ British	▨ Portuguese
⫶ Italian	▧ Spanish
▦ German	☐ Independent states

Britain also had a number of possessions along the coast of West Africa. Her confidence in the policy of free trade, however, made her reluctant to acquire colonies that were not essential. They were seen as a financial burden, and it was felt that Britain already had a sufficiently large and self-sufficient Empire. Hence the reluctance on the part of successive Prime Ministers to respond to requests for protection or intervention from abroad. Britain's chief concern lay in the protection and preservation of her Indian Empire, and of the sea routes leading to it. After 1869 the Suez Canal became the new gateway to India, so that during the 1870s Britain became increasingly concerned with this strategic area. In 1875 the Prime Minister, Disraeli, bought up a large number of shares in the Suez Canal Company giving Britain more control over this vital waterway. Inevitably this brought Britain into closer contact with Egypt, and ultimately with the Nile Valley, as we shall see.

Egypt and the scramble for Africa

Egypt was still nominally a province of the Ottoman (Turkish) Empire, but under successive Viceroys it had become virtually independent. Under Mohammed Ali, who ruled from 1806–1849, Egypt was strengthened and modernised so that she became a power in her own right. Mohammed Ali's armies were victorious in Arabia, Syria and the Sudan. In 1820 the Sudan was conquered and Egyptian authority established at Khartoum. It was felt that this would provide a steady supply of slaves as recruits for the army, together with sources of ivory. Very soon Khartoum became an important trading centre, attracting Arab merchants from a wide area. In 1841 an Egyptian expedition under the command of Selim reached Gondokoro, opening up yet further possibilities for trade in slaves and ivory. The 'Khartoumers' as the traders were called, raided and plundered at will throughout the southern region of Sudan and even into northern Uganda. Although they were subject to the authority of the Khedive of Egypt they did much as they pleased. Chaos and anarchy reigned in the area, and it was this impression that the European travellers like Speke and Baker conveyed in their letters and reports.

The Khedive was persuaded to intervene and restore order. He appointed Baker Governor

Map 31 The partition of Africa from 1885

109

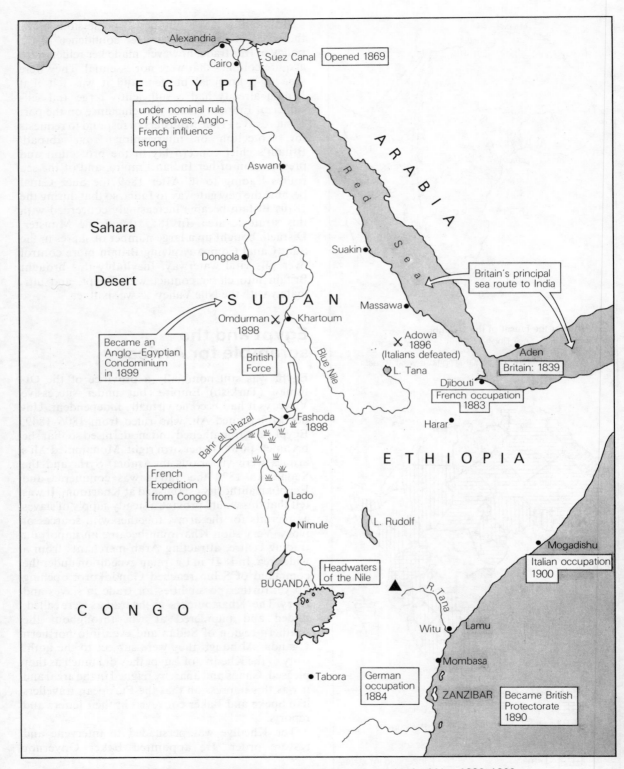

Alexandria

Cairo

Suez Canal · Opened 1869

E G Y P T · under nominal rule of Khedives; Anglo-French influence strong

A R A B I A

Red Sea

Aswan

Sahara

Desert

Dongola

Suakin

Massawa

Britain's principal sea route to India

S U D A N

Omdurman ✕ 1898 · Khartoum

Became an Anglo—Egyptian Condominium in 1899

British Force

Blue Nile

Adowa ✕ 1896 (Italians defeated)

L. Tana

Aden · Britain: 1839

Djibouti · French occupation 1883

Bahr el Ghazal

Fashoda 1898

Harar

French Expedition from Congo

E T H I O P I A

Lado

Nimule

L. Rudolf

Mogadishu · Italian occupation 1900

BUGANDA

Headwaters of the Nile

▲

R. Tana

C O N G O

Witu · Lamu

Mombasa

Tabora

German occupation 1884

ZANZIBAR

Became British Protectorate 1890

Map 32 The Nile Valley showing its strategic importance in the European scramble for Africa, 1886–1900

Fig. 13.1 General Charles Gordon.

Fig. 13.2 The Mahdi.

General of the Equatoria province in the Sudan in 1869, with the intention both of restoring order and extending his authority. Egypt too had imperial ambitions. Baker's dual task, to suppress the slave trade and enforce Egyptian authority, was not an easy one. He found that he could not do the latter without the aid of the traders. In 1872 he crossed into Bunyoro and attempted to annex it, but was met with such a defiant response that he was forced to retreat hastily. Kabalega was determined to be his own master. Baker was succeeded by General Charles Gordon, another Englishman in the Khedive's service, but one with an even greater determination to stamp out the slave trade. In order to do this he believed that Egyptian authority would have to be extended even further south, to the Great Lakes and across to the East Coast. He envisaged a string of Egyptian stations along the River Tana to Lake Victoria. Accordingly in 1875 Khedive Ismail sent a force to Kismayu while Gordon himself

marched south to Gondokoro. He sent emissaries to Buganda hoping to win the support of Kabaka Mutesa. Both ventures failed: the Kabaka was suspicious of Egyptian ambitions, and refused help, while the Sultan of Zanzibar's protests at the Egyptian occupation of Kismayu were supported by the British consul. In 1876 Gordon left Khartoum. Egypt's policy of African expansion was thus thwarted, and her authority in the Sudan further weakened in 1881 when the flag of revolt was raised by a religious fanatic, Muhammad Ahmed, 'The Mahdi'.

Meanwhile affairs in Egypt had gone from bad to worse. Owing to the Khedive's extravagance and financial mismanagement the Egyptian Government was bankrupt, and so French and British officials were appointed to oversee the country's finances. In 1882 rebellion broke out under the nationalist leader Arabi Pasha and Britain was obliged to intervene in order to protect the Khedive. Having

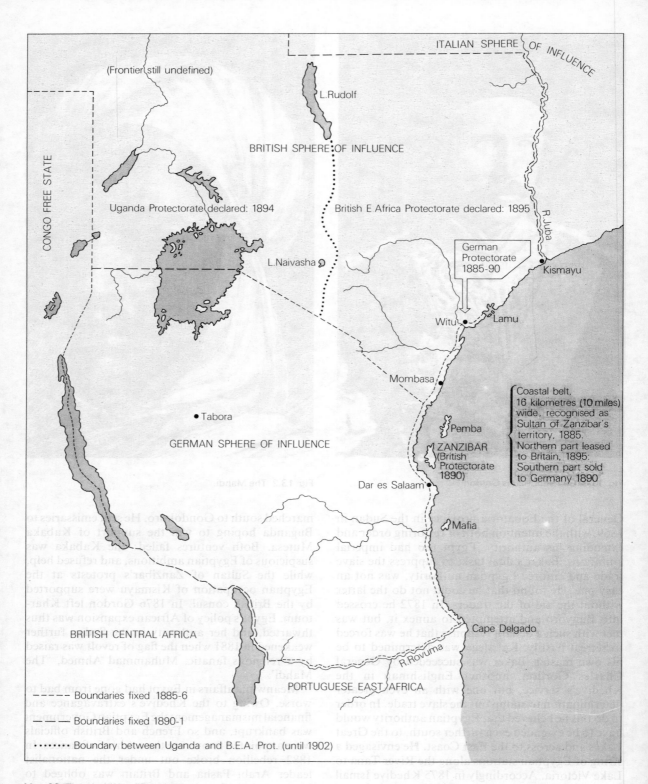

Map 33 The partition of East Africa

done so the British found that it was not as easy to withdraw. Inevitably they became more and more involved in Egyptian affairs and with their own strategic concern for the security of the Suez canal. Eventually, a combined Anglo-Egyptian army reconquered the Sudan and defeated the Mahdi in 1898. By this time the Sudan had become a matter of vital strategic importance to Britain, since the Scramble for Africa had brought new French and Belgian forces into this area. These are shown in Map 32. We have referred to the situation in Egypt and the Sudan in some detail since it played an essential part in the events that led to the British occupation of East Africa. It helps us to understand why, having been so reluctant to intervene directly in East Africa before 1884, they hesitated no longer.

The partition of East Africa

Germany and Britain were to be the main contenders in the scramble for East Africa (see Map 33). There had already been one attempt from a different source. In 1876 King Leopold II of the Belgians had formed the International African Association which would devote itself to the suppression of the slave trade and the establishment of Christianity and civilisation in the heart of Africa. In practice it was to be little more than a cloak for his own ambitions, to acquire wealth and status for himself. In 1878–79 he sent expeditions to establish a route into the interior from the East Coast of Africa. But when Stanley's reports reached him he decided to approach the Congo Basin from the Atlantic coast instead. This may have been a relief to the Sultan of Zanzibar but it led to a sharp reaction from those European powers with established interests along the African coast, such as France, Britain and Portugal. It can be said that King Leopold's intervention in the Congo (Zaire) was the spark that set off the rush for the interior.

Until 1884 the European powers with trading interests in East Africa had been content to direct their activities through Zanzibar and to respect the Sultan's territorial claims. But in September of that year Johnston had, with the Sultan's permission, obtained treaties with chiefs in the Kilimanjaro area on behalf of British commercial groups who planned to exploit the trade of that area by building a railway from the coast. Johnston was enthusiastic about the possibilities:

'Within a few years it must be either English, French or German. I am on the spot, the first in the field and able to make Kilimanjaro as completely English as Ceylon, should I receive the necessary authorisation.' ... The newly formed British East African Association was ready to take up this challenge, but the British Government refused to support it. The reason given was that it did not wish to antagonise German interests in this area, being more concerned to obtain Germany's agreement to British influence in Egypt and the Nile Valley. Therefore when Carl Peters arrived in Zanzibar in November, 1884 with two companions, all three disguised as mechanics, he was able to cross over to the mainland and obtain treaties from chiefs in the Usagara, Uzigua, Nguru and Ukami areas without any reference to or consent from the Sultan. The latter's protests went unheeded and his appeal for British support was useless. Following their return to Germany, Bismarck declared these areas a German protectorate to be administered by the German East Africa Company.

Thus the first round in the contest for East Africa had been won by the Germans (see Map 33). It should be noted that the contest was based upon the securing of treaties with individual chiefs rather than direct military confrontation. This was typical of the method used during the Scramble for Africa. The chiefs often had little idea of what they were doing; some saw it simply as a means of obtaining presents, while to others it was a way of playing off one power against another. To the Europeans the treaties were written proof of their claim to territory.

The effect on the Sultan of Zanzibar was humiliating. Forced by the guns of a German naval squadron to recognise all the German claims on the mainland, including Witu in the north, he was then obliged to give way to a German demand for a commission to enquire into the exact extent of the Sultan's dominions. The work of the commission resulted in the first Anglo-German Agreement, of 1886. This limited the Sultan's mainland possessions to a 16 kilometre (10 mile) strip of land from Tunghi Bay in the south to the mouth of the River Tana in the north, together with the towns of Kismayu, Brava and Merka further north. At the same time the hinterland was divided into British and German spheres of influence either side of a line from the mouth of the River Umba to the foothills of Mt Kilimanjaro and thence to the eastern shore of Lake Victoria. The islands of Pemba, Zanzibar and Mafia were to remain under the Sultan. Although the area left to the Sultan was probably not much less than he had effectively controlled before, the treaty marked a turning point for the Sultanate. The centres of power shifted to the mainland and were now in the hands of the Europeans.

The next phase in the partition was taken up by commercial companies entrusted by their respective governments with the task of occupying and administering their spheres of influence. These were The Imperial British East Africa Company and The German East Africa Company. The former grew out of the British East Africa Association formed by Mackinnon. In 1888 it was granted a royal charter under its new title, with the power to administer the areas it occupied on behalf of Britain. Mackinnon himself had rather mixed motives which were religious, philanthropic and commercial. He saw the company as an instrument to stamp out the slave trade, as a means of supporting the efforts of the missionaries, and as a body for developing whatever opportunities for trade they might find in the interior. But he was not an effective administrator, nor did the Company ever have sufficient capital to undertake all the tasks assigned to it. The German Company, on the other hand, had a much more positive and aggressive leader in Carl Peters. It had developed from the earlier German Colonisation Society and had received a charter from the German Emperor in 1885. Apart from exploring all the possibilities for commerce Carl Peters was determined to see that German rule was established permanently on the African continent. In particular he intended to prevent any encirclement of German settlement in East Africa by British forces from the south (under Cecil Rhodes) joining up with those to the north (I.B.E.A. Company). He was prepared to go to almost any length to achieve these aims and to

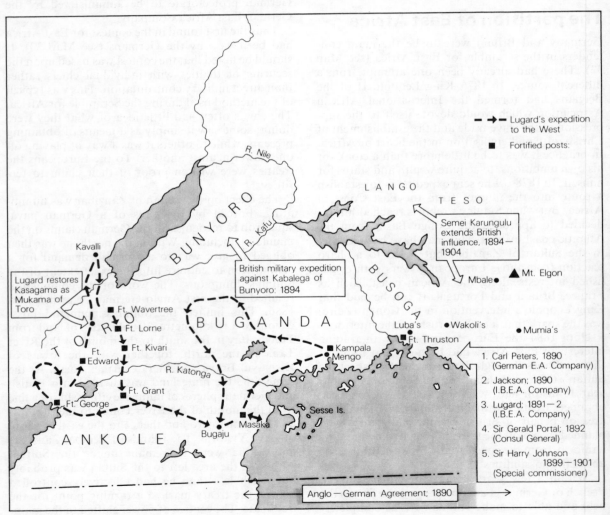

Map 34 Uganda, 1890–1900

use any means, however ruthless.

The chief prize in the period after 1886 was undoubtedly Buganda. Since the 1886 Agreement had not defined the western limit of their spheres of influence beyond the eastern shore of Lake Victoria, Uganda still lay open to whichever power got there first. Its position at the headwaters of the Nile made it an area of vital strategic importance for Britain. There was also increasing concern for the safety of British and French missionaries in Buganda. Rivalry between the three groups at the Kabaka's court, the Catholics, Protestants and Moslems, had become political as well as religious, as each competed for the Kabaka's favour. In 1884 Mutesa had died and been succeeded by his son Mwanga. Young and inexperienced, the new Kabaka was faced with serious new problems, both external and internal. He lacked the qualities of leadership and determination needed to unite his people at this critical time. He wavered and hesitated, favouring one group and then another. To make matters worse the factions at his court were identified with foreign interests: thus the Catholics became the 'Wafranza', the Protestants the 'Ingleza' and the Moslems were linked with the Islamic forces to the north. There were other tensions as well, such as the struggle for power between the young men at the Kabaka's court and the traditional 'bakungu'. Into

A LITTLE PARTY IN EAST AFRICA ONLY GOING TO COLLECT A FEW BUTTERFLIES AND FLOWERS FOR THE DEAR KAISER, THAT IS ALL!!

"We came very near to having Kilima-Njaro attached to the British Empire, only the German Emperor said he would very much like it, because he was so fond of the *flora* and *fauna* of the place . . . Would the English have expected to get any territory on account of their great interest in the *flora* and *fauna* here."—*Stanley speaking at Chamber of Commerce, May 21.*

Fig. 13.3 A satirical cartoon on imperialism in East Africa.

this explosive situation came the rival British and German imperialists. Carl Peters was the first to reach the Kabaka's court, early in 1890. He secured an agreement with Mwanga placing Buganda under German protection. The I.B.E.A. representative, Jackson, arrived shortly afterwards but was unable to make Mwanga change his mind. However, events in Europe were to determine the outcome.

Lord Salisbury was already engaged in diplomatic negotiations on behalf of Britain with the German authorities. This culminated in the second Anglo-German Agreement of 1890, sometimes referred to as the Heligoland Treaty. The terms of this agreement, and the way in which matters had been settled, showed how little attention was paid to affairs on the African continent that did not directly affect the European powers. The 1890 settlement extended the line of demarcation from east to west across Lake Victoria, thus confirming Uganda as within the British sphere and ignoring Peters' treaty with Mwanga. Germany also agreed to give up her claim to Witu and to accept a British protectorate over Zanzibar and the rest of the Sultan's territory. In return Britain surrendered the North Sea island of Heligoland to Germany, for whom it was of strategic importance. Germany was permitted to purchase her part of the coastal strip from the Sultan, thus leaving the latter with just the 16 kilometre (10 mile) wide strip on the coast of British East Africa and the islands of Pemba, Zanzibar and Mafia. Although the British Consul General continued to reside in Zanzibar, its days as the focal point of political and commercial power in East Africa had come to an end. Thus the period of the Scramble and partition was virtually over. All that remained for Britain was the adjustment of boundaries with other powers involved in East and North East Africa: Portugal (1890), France (1890) and Italy (1891). We must now examine the effects upon the people of the mainland.

The African response to partition

1. Uganda, 1890–1900

The full impact of partition was not generally felt until the actual establishment of colonial rule. There were areas such as Buganda, however, where it had an immediate effect. Following the signing of the 1890 Agreement the I.B.E.A. Company sent Capt. Lugard to establish British control in Uganda. He arrived at Mengo on December 18th, 1890 and the following week signed a treaty, in which Kabaka

Mwanga recognised the Company's authority. Lugard built his fort on Kampala hill, close to the Kabaka's palace (see Map 34). He found a tense situation in the kingdom, with four major political factions competing for power and influence around the weak-minded Kabaka. These were the Catholics, Protestants, Moslems and 'pagans'. Lugard was able to unite the Christian groups temporarily in a campaign against the Moslem forces in Bunyoro. Having successfully defeated them he moved on to Toro where he restored Kasagama to power and then succeeded in persuading Selim and 600 Sudanese troops to join him, thus adding to his small force of Company soldiers. The Sudanese, or Nubians as they were sometimes called, were the remnants of a force left behind by Emin, a former Governor of Equatoria Province. Lugard then returned to Kampala via Toro and Ankole, constructing a chain of forts along the route.

On his return Lugard found that Protestant and Catholic parties were on the verge of war. The Catholics were overrun and fled to the Lake, taking the Kabaka with them. Eventually peace was restored and the Kabaka returned. A fresh treaty was made in which Lugard took account of the claims of the various religious and political groups in the distribution of lands and chiefdoms. Meanwhile the Company had found that the cost of maintaining a military presence in Uganda was too great and announced that it would have to withdraw. This led to an immediate reaction from the missionary societies, notably the C.M.S. Public opinion in Britain was aroused and sufficient funds were raised to enable the Company to carry on for another year. Lugard himself left Uganda in 1892 and helped campaign in Britain for the retention of Uganda. The British Government was persuaded that it might have to intervene directly and despatched the Consul General at Zanzibar, Sir Gerald Portal, to report on the situation. Portal travelled to Buganda in 1893 and quickly came to the conclusion that a British Protectorate would have to be declared. A new agreement was signed with the Kabaka and in 1894 the British Parliament formally approved the declaration of a Protectorate over Buganda.

The situation remained extremely uneasy. To the north Bunyoro remained hostile, a refuge for all anti-British groups. The Sudanese left in charge of the forts had become a law unto themselves. In 1893 the British Commissioner's first task was to lead an expedition against Bunyoro. While militarily successful it did not prevent Kabalega from evading capture. He continued to wage guerilla warfare against the British and their allies for the next five years. In 1896 the Protectorate was formally extended to include Bunyoro and the country to the East of Buganda. But British control was far from secure; in 1897 two new threats emerged. Mwanga revolted with some of his chiefs and, after being driven out of Buddu, fled north to join Kabalega. In Eldama Ravine a contingent of Sudanese troops mutinied and marched to Uganda where they were joined by others. Faced with this double challenge reinforcements had to be brought in from India. Only then could the mutineers be rounded up and an expedition be sent north to capture Mwanga and Kabalega. Both rulers were deported to the Seychelles. It had been a difficult and costly operation, and it was this that made the Government decide that some permanent settlement must be found; hence the appointment of Sir Harry Johnston as Special Commissioner in 1899.

2. German East Africa

In 1887 the Germans had established a base at Dar es Salaam and proceeded to extend their influence along the coast. Two revolts were quickly sparked off by German interference with the coastal trade and 'hongo', or duty imposed on caravans in transit. Abushiri of Pangani rose against the Germans, and with him others as far south as Kilwa. It was considered sufficiently serious for a German officer, Major Von Wissmann to be sent from Germany to suppress the rising. The German force consisted of six hundred Nubians, fifty Somalis, three hundred and fifty Zulus and twenty Turkish police. In 1889 Abushiri ran short of manpower and supplies and so took refuge in Usagara. He was eventually captured and hanged at Bagamoyo. The other rising was led by Bwana Heri of Saadani. After six months of fighting he retreated into the interior in June 1889, but while attempting to rally support the following year he was defeated. One of the weaknesses of this resistance to the Germans was lack of unity and coordination.

In the interior the Germans came across sporadic resistance but none more persistent than Mkwawa, the Hehe chief. Realising that the Hehe were the most powerful group in southern Tanzania the Germans attempted a peaceful approach at first but this broke down when Mkwawa felt that his messengers were being treated contemptuously. He then closed the caravan route that ran through his country. The first armed clash came in 1891, then in 1894 the Germans attacked and captured the Hehe capital but Mkwawa escaped. For the next four years he

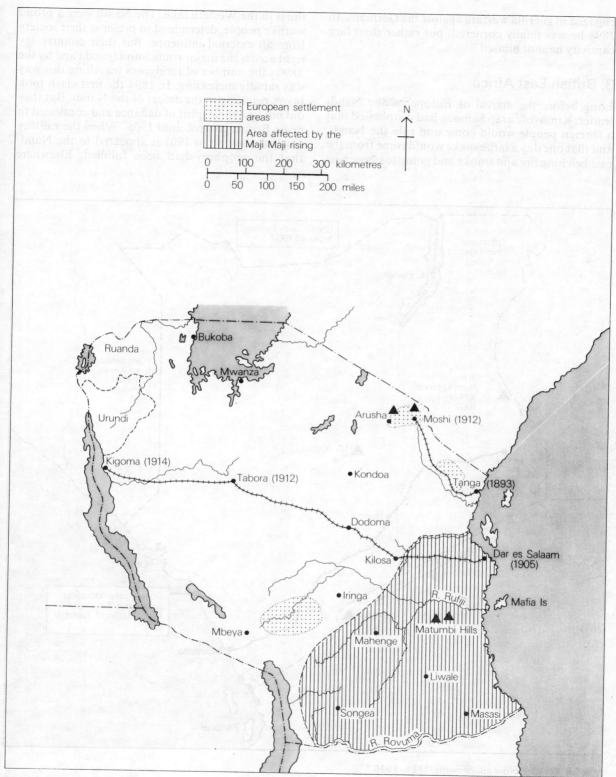

Map 35 German East Africa

engaged in guerilla warfare against the Germans. In 1898 he was finally cornered, but rather than face captivity he shot himself.

3. British East Africa

Long before the arrival of Europeans the Nandi leader, Kimnyole arap Samoei, had prophesied that a foreign people would come and rule the Nandi, and that one day a large snake would come from the east belching fire and smoke and going to quench its thirst in the Western lake. The Nandi were a proud warlike people, determined to preserve their society from all external influence. But their country lay right across the major route into Uganda and by the 1890s the number of foreigners travelling this way was rapidly increasing. In 1894 the first clash took place, resulting in the defeat of the Nandi. But they did not lose their spirit of defiance and continued to resist British control until 1906. When the railway reached Kisumu in 1901 it appeared to the Nandi that the prophecy had been fulfilled. Elsewhere

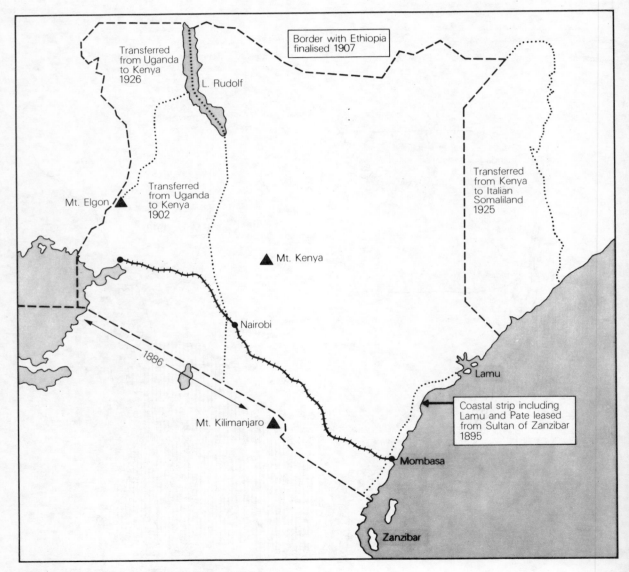

Map 36 Kenya: border adjustments, 1886–1926

resistance was limited because British influence was as yet hardly felt. It was the railway that brought with it the administrators, traders and settlers.

Questions
1. With the aid of a sketch map show where the various European interests in Africa existed before 1884. Explain how these had changed by 1900.
2. Show how and why Egypt and the Nile Valley played such a significant part in the Partition of Africa.
3. What were the reasons for the unrest in Buganda between 1884 and 1900.
4. Compare the terms of the two Anglo-German Agreements of 1886 and 1890, and show how they affected those two powers.
5. Give three examples of African resistance to European rule and explain the outcome of each.

Activities
1. If you had been a radio commentator on one of the following occasions how would you have described the scene?:
   a) The signing of the Treaty between Lugard and Kabaka Mwanga.
   b) The closing of the slave market on Zanzibar in March, 1873.
   c) The outbreak of the Uganda Mutiny in 1897.

Chapter 14
The establishment of colonial rule in Zanzibar and Uganda, 1900–1914

Introduction

The establishment of colonial rule followed the partition of Africa. In order to make their occupation effective and to be able to exploit the resources they required, the first necessity for the European powers was an effective means of communication and transport into the interior. This involved the construction of roads and railways, expenditure that the colonial governments were often reluctant to make. They were determined to see that their colonies became as profitable as possible, by providing the raw materials needed for their industries. The emphasis during these years was on economy and exploitation: to administer their possessions as cheaply and effectively as possible while extracting the maximum benefit from the mineral and natural resources available. This policy was seen at its most blatant and extreme form in King Leopold's Congo Free State. The methods used by the Europeans to impose their authority were a combination of force and persuasion, to which the inhabitants reacted either with armed resistance or submission and cooperation. In this chapter we shall examine the methods used by the British and German authorities in East Africa and the ways in which the African people responded.

Zanzibar

In 1890 Zanzibar had been declared a British Protectorate. The chief effect of this was that while the Sultan retained his position and control over his government, responsibility for all external matters passed to Britain. In practice Britain had already become the power behind the throne in Zanzibar, so that it did not make a great deal of difference at first. In 1900 Zanzibar was placed under the authority of the Commissioner and Consul General for East Africa whose headquarters were at Mombasa. He became increasingly preoccupied with affairs on the mainland, and in 1904 Zanzibar was once more made the responsibility of a Consul General on the island. He also held the post of First Minister to the Sultan. In 1902, on the accession of the seventeen year old Sultan Seyyid Ali, the Consul General, Mr Rogers, was appointed to act as Regent for the Sultan. This enabled him to introduce a number of internal reforms, including the appointment of a financial adviser. In 1905 an official from the Foreign Office, Edward Clarke, came out to Zanzibar and made proposals for the reorganisation of the administration. These included closer control and supervision of Zanzibar'a finances and judiciary, improvements in communications and provision for education. Departments of Education and Agriculture were set up, the latter with the particular aim of improving the yield and quality of Zanzibar's two main staple crops, cloves and coconuts. Additional revenue was to be raised by increasing the duty on imports from 5 % to $7\frac{1}{2}$ %.

These reforms and changes inevitably meant an increase in the number of British officials since it was felt that the Arab ruling class, or aristocracy, was incapable of handling such matters efficiently and honestly. They naturally resented many of the changes, as did the Sultan. But there was little they could do. The Sultan had become virtually a puppet; although government was still carried on in his name the real decisions were made and implemented by the British Consul General and his officials. In 1913 responsibility for the Sultanate of Zanzibar was transferred from the Foreign Office to the Colonial Office. The Consul General assumed the title and position of Resident, the powers of which were little different from those of a Governor. A Protectorate Council was formed, presided over by the Sultan, and including the Resident and a number of officials. Its function was purely advisory.

The construction of the Uganda Railway

For Britain to make her presence in Uganda effective it was essential that a railway be constructed from the coast (see Map 37). This had been made clear by the efforts and failures of the I.B.E.A. Company. A survey had been carried out in 1892 by Capt. J. R. L. Macdonald. But the Company lacked the capital and resources for such a project which was estimated to cost about £2 million. Following the declaration of a Protectorate over Uganda by Portal in 1893 the need became even more urgent, for both strategic and economic reasons. But the matter was bitterly contested in the British Parliament; some doubted whether it would ever repay the cost of construction, others dismissed it as 'the lunatic line'. However, eventually a start was made and the first line was laid at Mombasa on May 30, 1896. George Whitehouse was the chief engineer. Labour was provided largely by coolies brought over from India, while many of the skilled craftsmen and clerical staff were also Indians. It was found that Africans were not available for such work, or else openly hostile.

The survey had revealed the formidable physical obstacles that would have to be overcome. These included the dry waterless 'Nyika' country behind the coast, the ascent to the highlands, the steep escarpments of the Rift Valley and the numerous river beds to be bridged. To make matters worse much human misery and suffering was caused by malaria, sleeping-sickness, small-pox and jiggers, especially among the coolies. At Tsavo the construction parties were attacked in their camps by man-eating lions, so that at one stage, in 1898, all work was brought to a standstill for three weeks. Eventually the lions were hunted down and shot by Colonel Patterson. There were problems over water and food supplies, often difficult to obtain in country where the attitude of the local people was uncertain or unpredictable. In some areas there was fierce resistance, notably from the Nandi. Camps were raided, workers killed and stores carried off.

All these problems slowed down progress, but in June 1899 the railhead reached Nairobi. This was to

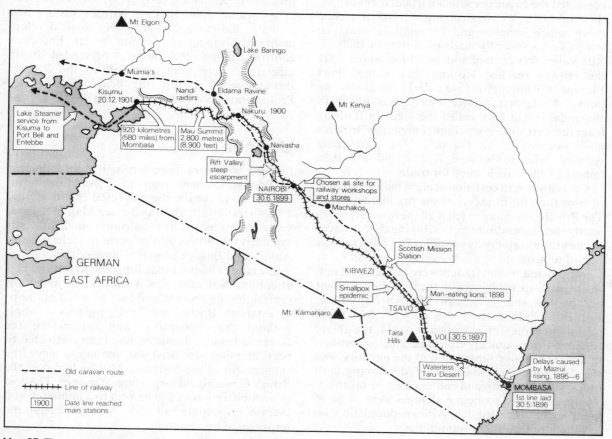

Map 37 The construction of the Uganda Railway, 1896–1901

121

Fig. 14.1 The railway reaches the edge of the Rift Valley.

be the site for a supply base before the ascent into the highlands. There was little thought at the time that it would become the capital. The Rift Valley presented the engineers with a particular challenge; they solved it by constructing a vertical incline down which supplies and locomotives could be lowered on a specially made platform. In 1900 the Rift Valley was crossed and on 20 December 1901 the railway reached Kisumu then named Port Florence 870 kilometres (543 miles) from its starting point. A steamer service linked Kisumu with Buganda. It had been called the Uganda Railway from the start since it was in that area that Britain's main interests lay at the time. The intervening country, later to become Kenya, did not then appear to offer much scope for trade.

The railway had cost almost eight million pounds to construct, far in excess of the original estimate. The British Government felt it all the more urgent to justify such expenditure by developing the resources of the area as rapidly as possible. The railway itself helped to generate new commercial possibilities, as European and Indian traders were attracted inland, towns grew up, bringing with them all the attendant occupations and services of Western civilisation. For the administration the railway gave rapid communication with the outside world, the ability to move troops quickly from one area to another, and more effective supervision of the territory. For the first time the possibility of developing cash crops, such as cotton and coffee, could be taken up. These social and economic changes were to be of great significance for the African population no less than for the other communities.

There were of course many areas still untouched and unaffected by the railway, which did not reach Kampala until 1931. It is important not to exaggerate its effect in these early years, but it can be seen as a turning point in East Africa's history and probably did more than any other single development in bringing the region under European control. Among other things it persuaded British officials to turn their attention to the country through which it ran, the British East Africa Protectorate (as it became known in 1895).

Uganda

In 1899 Sir Harry Johnston had been appointed as Special Commissioner to Uganda, with instructions to settle the confused political and administration situation there (see Map 38). Three years previously Lord Salisbury had officially extended the British Protectorate to include Toro, Ankole and Busoga as well as Buganda. But it was to the latter kingdom that Johnston first turned his attention. Not only was it the largest and most central, but he also realised that he could not hope to establish British rule in Uganda as a whole without the cooperation and support of the Baganda leaders. Johnston had been instructed to bear in mind the need for economy, since the suppression of the Sudanese Mutiny had cost the British Government large sums of money. The cost of administration had to be kept to a minimum and everything possible had to be done to develop the resources of the country.

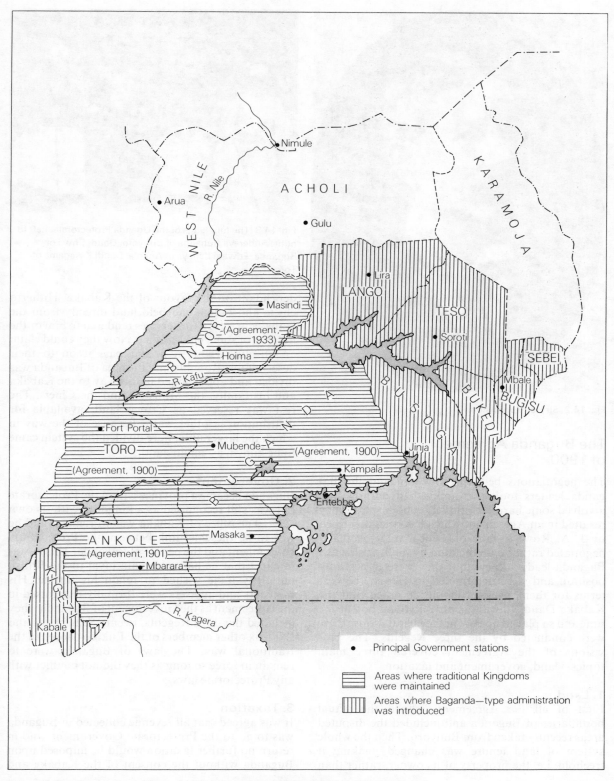

Map 38 The Uganda Protectorate showing the establishment of British administration

Key labels on map:

WEST NILE
ACHOLI
KARAMOJA
• Nimule
• Arua
• Gulu
• Lira
LANGO
TESO
BUNYORO
• Masindi
(Agreement, 1933)
• Hoima
R. Kafu
• Soroti
SEBEI
• Mbale
BUKEDI
BUGISU
BUSOGA
• Fort Portal
TORO
• Mubende
BUGANDA
(Agreement, 1900)
• Jinja
(Agreement, 1900)
• Kampala
• Entebbe
ANKOLE
• Masaka
(Agreement, 1901)
• Mbarara
KIGEZI
R. Kagera
• Kabale
R. Nile

Legend:

• Principal Government stations

Areas where traditional Kingdoms were maintained

Areas where Baganda—type administration was introduced

Fig. 14.2 Sir Harry Johnston.

Fig. 14.3 The four kings of the Uganda Protectorate. Left to right: Andereya Ruhanga of Bunyoro. Daudi Chwa of Buganda. Edwadi Kahaya of Ankole. Daudi Kasagama of Toro.

The Buganda Agreement of 1900

The negotiations between Johnston and the Baganda leaders took two and a half months and involved some hard bargaining on both sides. They resulted in an Agreement which has been described by J. A. Rowe as 'the only local treaty actually negotiated rather than dictated by the British'. The Baganda leaders knew that they were in a strong position and were determined to extract the best terms for themselves. It should be noted that the Kabaka Daudi Chwa was only a young boy at the time and so played no part in the negotiations; these were conducted by the three Regents. The provisions of the Agreement covered three main topics—land, government and taxation.

1. Land
First of all the Agreement defined the actual boundaries of Buganda and included the disputed areas recently taken from Bunyoro. Then the whole system of land tenure was changed, making it freehold, i.e. the property of its owner, rather than

dependant on the favour of the Kabaka. Hitherto chiefs and others had held land directly from the Kabaka in return for services rendered to him or the holding of some public office. Now they could claim an absolute right to it and pass it on to their descendants. Roughly half the area of Buganda was divided and apportioned in this way to the Kabaka and his family, the Ministers and the Chiefs. The rest was reserved as Crown land, available for distribution in other ways. Because of the way in which the larger units were divided the system came to be known as 'mailo' land.

2. Government
Buganda became a province within the Protectorate but was still recognised as a kingdom with its own ruler. The office of Kabaka was to remain, and he was to be the chief link between the Protectorate government and the people of Buganda. This meant in effect that he had to remain loyal to the British authority if he wished to retain his throne. His ministers and advisers were formally recognised in the Agreement as the Government of Buganda: they included the three Regents, twenty Saza chiefs and sixty-six other members of the Lukiko chosen in the traditional way. The laws of Buganda were to remain in force so long as they did not conflict with any Protectorate laws.

3. Taxation
It was agreed that all revenue collected in Buganda was to go to the Protectorate Government, and in return no further taxation would be imposed upon Buganda without the consent of the Kabaka and

Lukiko. The existing taxes were the hut and gun taxes.

The Buganda Agreement was to have a major effect on the development of Uganda right up to the time of Independence. In the first place it gave Buganda itself a prominence and status that none of the other kingdoms or provinces ever had. Within Buganda it gave new power and influence to the chiefs and leading ministers, and correspondingly reduced the role of both the Kabaka and the clan heads (the Bataka) in matters of government and land. In particular the land settlement was to lead to much bitterness and envy among the peasantry and those whose claims had been overlooked. This was to become even more acute when the introduction of cash crops such as cotton and coffee brought added signifance to the ownership of land. Finally, as the Lukiko became more and more the centre of power in Buganda it became the focus of all Baganda political activity, thus making it more difficult in later years to create a legislative body that would represent the interests of the Protectorate as a whole.

The Toro Agreement of 1900

This was signed in June 1900, following the main outline of the Buganda Agreement in giving recognition to the local ruler, or Mukama, in return for the collection of revenue and incorporation within the Protectorate. All land was declared Crown land but freehold grants were made to the Mukama and his leading chiefs. Again there was more emphasis on the interests of the ruler and his chiefs than on the needs of the peasantry. The Mukama, Kasagama, was not in as strong a position as the Baganda leaders and needed British support to remove the old threat from Bunyoro.

The Ankole Agreement of 1901

Johnston was at first reluctant to recognise the Mugabe as paramount ruler as he did not appear to exercise sufficient influence over the other chiefs. However, by 1901 the Ankole chiefs agreed to acknowledge the Mugabe as their ruler and a limited agreement, similar to that made with Toro, was signed by Wilson on behalf of the Commissioner.

The extension of British rule in Uganda

Since Bunyoro was at this time still regarded as conquered territory there was no question of an agreement with its ruler. Instead, use was made of Baganda agents to establish British authority in the area, as they did in the districts to the east of Buganda. This was much resented in Bunyoro where it was felt to add insult to injury, and in 1907 the Baganda agents were forced to take refuge in the district headquarters at Hoima. In the dispute that followed a number of Banyoro chiefs were deported, but no further Baganda agents were appointed. This use of Baganda agents to carry out British policy was considered to be a temporary stage in the process of training local chiefs, but inevitably it gave further prominence to the Baganda and allied them more strongly with British authority. It also led to considerable misunderstanding, as agents such as Kakungulu were to discover.

Semei Kakungulu

This man was perhaps the most outstanding of these Baganda agents. He was a Ganda general who had taken part in the religious wars and had assisted the British in their defeat and capture of Kabalega and Mwanga. With his band of armed followers he moved into the Teso and Lango districts and brought them within the authority of the Protectorate government between 1894 and 1904. He introduced the pattern of administration used in Buganda, dividing them into counties, 'sazas', and sub-counties, 'gombololas', with Baganda agents in each. He set up his headquarters at Budaka in Bukedi and erected forts in newly conquered country. He also recruited local labour to build roads. So securely had he established himself that Johnston nicknamed him 'Kabaka of Bukedi', a title he was only too anxious to acquire and one that had been the object of his ambitions. But this was not what the British authorities intended. In 1901 his headquarters at Bukedi was taken over by a British officer and Kakungulu moved to Mbale which became the headquarters of British administration in 1903. When the British took over the administration of these districts they retained the system that Kakungulu had introduced, making the Baganda agents advisers to the local chiefs they now sought to appoint.

Kakungulu himself was appointed President of the Busoga Lukiko. Here again he introduced the Buganda method of administration, but he became increasingly disappointed and bitter as the British failed to support his ambitions. Transferred back to Bukedi in 1913 he became involved in a religious sect, the 'Abamalaki', which rejected missionary preaching and Western medicine and demanded a return to the ways of the past. This lost him the prestige and respect he had once enjoyed among the British who removed him from office. He died in 1929.

On the whole the British officials and their agents did not meet with a great deal of armed resistance after 1900. It took some time, however, to establish regular administration in the north and north-east. A series of boundary agreements made clear the exact extent of the Protectorate for the first time. Between 1907 and 1912 the Uganda-Congo border was made clear and in 1914 the West Nile district was added to Uganda from the Sudan. In 1902 the whole of the Eastern province of Uganda was transferred to the East African Protectorate. These boundary changes are shown in Map 39.

In 1907 responsibility for Uganda was transferred from the Foreign Office to the Colonial Office, so that the Commissioner became Governor. The policy and methods of government did not alter. As revenue from taxation and customs duties increased so the functions of government were extended and the number of officials increased. But the main emphasis in the period up to 1914 lay in establishing a firm foundation of administration and making the Protectorate as financially self-supporting as possible. The fact that by 1914 Uganda no longer needed financial assistance from the British Government was due to the rapid growth of cash crops based on peasant agriculture. Of this we shall have more to say later in this chapter.

The pattern of administration in Uganda was based upon direct and indirect rule. It was headed by the Governor of the Protectorate, with his headquarters at Entebbe, with Provincial Commissioners and District Commissioners in their respective areas, supervising the activities of chiefs and the collection of revenue. In the Kingdoms of Buganda, Toro and Ankole much was left to the rulers and their traditional advisers, but even they were subject to the 'advice' of British officials. Perhaps the most outstanding figure of the time was Sir Apolo Kagwa.

Sir Apolo Kagwa

Kagwa's career serves as a good example of African cooperation in the early period of colonial rule. Born in 1869 he served in the courts of Kabaka Mutesa and Kabaka Mwanga and thus learnt the art of political survival in those dangerous times. He was converted to the Protestant faith and became the leader of the Protestant group that eventually

Fig. 14.4 Sir Apolo Kagwa.

played a part in Mwanga's downfall. He came out openly in support of the British in their campaign against Kabalega and Mwanga in 1899. This was followed by Mwanga's exile to the Seychelles and in his place his young son Daudi Chwa was proclaimed Kabaka. Of the three Regents appointed to rule for him during his youth Apolo Kagwa, as Katikiro, was the senior. He therefore played a leading part in the formulation of the Buganda Agreement, receiving the largest single grant of land outside the royal family. He was granted 78 sq. kilometres (30 sq. miles). He continued to work closely with the British authorities, encouraging the establishment of schools and the adoption of new agricultural methods and crops. His influence was particularly valuable when Sir Hesketh Bell decided on the evacuation of all people living on the shores of Lake Victoria, in order to eliminate sleeping-sickness. He was not afraid to stand up for the rights of traditional Buganda institutions, such as the Lukiko. This brought him increasingly into conflict with the Protectorate government whenever he felt that the independence of his group, the 'Bakungu' chiefs, was being threatened. He had other rivals and enemies within Buganda, including the Bataka and the new generation of chiefs. Moreover the

Fig. 14.5 Coffee drying at Mulanje in 1902.

Kabaka had grown up and was anxious to assert himself. Finally in 1926 Kagwa resigned, angry and disappointed, and died in the following year. He had outlived his usefulness both to the British officials and to his own people.

Trade and agriculture

The urgent need for the British to make Uganda pay for its own upkeep has already been mentioned. But before people can pay taxes they must have money and some way of earning it. Traditional methods had been based upon a subsistence economy, with payment in kind and trade through barter. The authorities had therefore to stimulate the need for and use of currency before anything else could be done. In 1903 the principal export was ivory, valued at £2600. There were no obvious mineral resources and so agriculture offered the best solution, with the introduction of cash crops.

The question was whether this should be based on large-scale plantations run by European settlers or whether development might be possible through small peasant holdings owned by Africans. In the neighbouring East Africa Protectorate, later

to become Kenya, Sir Charles Eliot was already successfully encouraging European settlement on a large scale. Sir William Morris Carter, Chief Justice, and other officials felt that the same policy should be followed in Uganda, and steps towards implementing it were taken. However the Governor, Sir Hesketh Bell, did not share this view and was supported in his belief by Mr S. Simpson, Director of Agriculture from 1912 to 1928. In the end Sir Hesketh Bell's opinions triumphed; Uganda was not to be another 'white man's country'. It was shown that small scale production of cotton and coffee could be profitable and beneficial both to the Protectorate and its inhabitants.

Cotton had been found growing wild in Uganda but it was not until 1904 that the first serious trials with imported cotton seed were made by the Uganda Government and Mr K. Borup of the Uganda Company. In order to protect the Uganda crop from disease and criticisms of poor quality strict measures were taken by the Government. Only approved seed was made available. New ginneries were set up in different parts of the country to process the raw cotton, and a good system of roads was started to facilitate transport. Thus by 1914 cotton had become the major export,

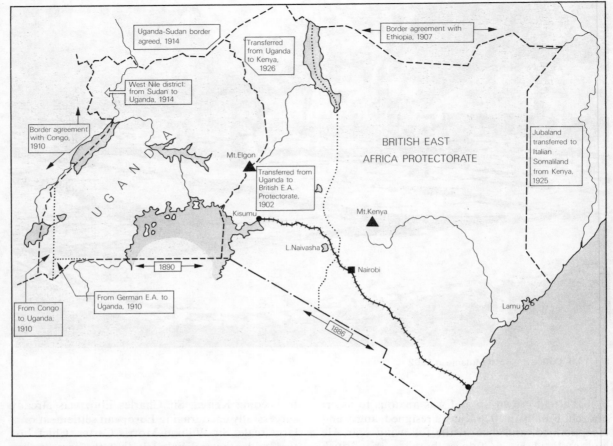

The map contains the following labels:

Uganda-Sudan border agreed, 1914

Transferred from Uganda to Kenya, 1926

Border agreement with Ethiopia, 1907

West Nile district: from Sudan to Uganda, 1914

Border agreement with Congo, 1910

BRITISH EAST AFRICA PROTECTORATE

Jubaland transferred to Italian Somaliland from Kenya, 1925

U G A N D A

Mt.Elgon

Transferred from Uganda to British E.A. Protectorate, 1902

Kisumu

Mt.Kenya

L.Naivasha

Nairobi

1890

From German E.A. to Uganda, 1910

From Congo to Uganda, 1910

Lamu

1886

Map 39 The borders of Uganda and British East Africa (Kenya) finalised between 1900 and 1926

a new source of wealth for the people and an additional source of revenue for the Government. The principal cotton growing areas were in Buganda and Busoga.

Other cash crops tried out at this time included coffee, rubber, sugar, groundnuts and simsim. Of these coffee was the most successful, grown at first by European planters. By 1914 there were one hundred and thirty coffee plantations, most of them in Buganda, although the Bagisu had already started experimenting with the Arabica variety on Mt Elgon. All such crops were dependent on the world market; a sudden fall in the price paid could ruin a country whose economy depended on a single crop. But Uganda was fortunate in that the demand for both cotton and coffee was rising steadily at this time.

A major problem that faced the producers and Government was the lack of adequate transport facilities. Sir Hesketh Bell started a programme to extend and improve communications within the

Protectorate. He also encouraged the import of motor vehicles and bicycles. A rail link was built between Kampala and its nearest point on the lake, Port Bell, and further east a start was made on the Jinja-Namasagali line so as to serve the cotton growers of Busoga. All exports and imports still had to cross by lake steamer from Kisumu.

Towns and trading centres grew rapidly around the administrative centres and along the lines of communication. Here the Asians set up their shops and business concerns, having come in to Uganda with the establishment of British rule. They were quick to gain control of the commercial opportunities being offered in the retail trade, as importers and exporters, or as mechanics, clerical officials and craftsmen. Perhaps the most prominent of them all was Allidina Visram who had first arrived in Zanzibar as a boy in the 1870s. There he had acquired and built up his own business, extending this to the mainland with a string of trading posts along the main route from Bagamoyo. In 1898 he

128

Fig. 14.6 The landing stage at Jinja showing Kenyan and Ugandan steamers.

had set up his first business in Kampala and before long had a number of successful enterprises there, including a soda factory, cotton ginnery and workshops and mills.

Questions

1. Describe the methods used to establish British control in Zanzibar between 1890 and 1912.
2. What were the main reasons for the construction of the Uganda railway and why did it take so long to build?
3. Outline the main features of the Buganda Agreement of 1900, and explain why it was significant for Uganda as a whole.
4. What part did either Semei Kakungulu or Apolo Kagwa play in the establishment of British rule in Uganda?
5. What were the main steps taken to develop the resources of Uganda between 1900 and 1914?

Activities

1. Arrange to show the film 'Permanent Way', which can be hired from the East African Railways and Harbours Corporation.
2. Draw a map of the route taken by the Uganda Railway, marking the chief physical obstacles.
3. Compare the characters and achievements of Apolo Kagwa and Semei Kakungulu.

Chapter 15
The establishment of colonial rule in the British and German East Africa Protectorates, 1900–1914

Introduction

In July 1895 the area between Mombasa and the Rift Valley had been declared a British Protectorate, but for the first seven years of its existence it was regarded as little more than the main supply route to Uganda. Administered first by the Consul General in Zanzibar and then from Mombasa, there was no attempt to do more than maintain and protect the railway line. However, the construction of the line added to the strategic importance of the area, and the realisation that it must be made to pay for itself led to a greater interest in the Protectorate.

One of the first to show interest was Sir Charles Eliot, appointed Commissioner in 1900. He already had decided views about the civilising mission that Europeans could perform in Africa. He felt that most Africans were not yet capable of developing their own resources and needed the example and guidance of Europeans. The solution both to this and to the need to make the railway profitable was, he thought, to open the Protectorate to European settlement. So he started an official campaign to encourage settlers to come to East Africa. In 1902 the whole of Uganda's Eastern province was transferred to the East Africa Protectorate, thus adding to it much of the highland country that Eliot considered ideal for European farming. He instructed his Land Officer to reserve all land between Machakos Road station and Fort Ternan for this purpose. The Crown Lands Ordinance of 1902 made it possible for land to be sold on easy terms to Europeans provided they occupied and developed it. Eliot's successor, Sir Donald Stewart, gave further assurances to prospective settlers and obtained from the Colonial Secretary, Lord Elgin, an assurance that the highlands would be reserved primarily for them.

Fig. 15.1 An early picture of Delamere Avenue (now Kenyatta Avenue) Nairobi.

British East Africa
The establishment of administration

With the growing number of European settlers and Asian traders coming into the Protectorate it became necessary to make the administration more effective. In 1907 the government headquarters was moved from Mombasa to Nairobi and in the same year a Legislative Council was established, consisting of five officials and three unofficials nominated by the Governor. Two years earlier the Foreign Office had transferred control of the Protectorate to the Colonial Office, since it was rapidly becoming more of a colonial and less of a consular responsibility. The Governor, Sir James Hayes Sadler, was faced with the task not only of extending

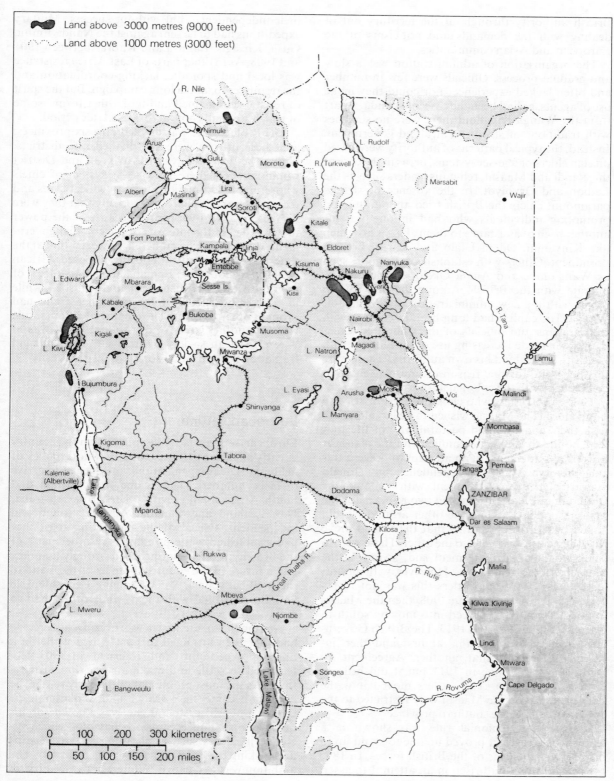

Legend:
- Land above 3000 metres (9000 feet)
- Land above 1000 metres (3000 feet)

R. Nile
Nimule
Arua
Gulu
Moroto
R. Turkwell
L. Rudolf
Marsabit
Wajir
L. Albert
Masindi
Lira
Soroti
Kitale
Fort Portal
Kampala
Jinja
Eldoret
Kisuma
Nakuru
Nanyuka
Entebbe
Nyeri
L. Edward
Mbarara
Sesse Is.
Kisii
Kabale
Bukoba
Nairobi
R. Tana
Kigali
Musoma
L. Kivu
Mwanza
L. Natron
Magadi
Lamu
Bujumbura
L. Eyasi
Arusha
Moshi
Voi
Malindi
Shinyanga
L. Manyara
Kigoma
Mombasa
Tabora
Tanga
Pemba
Kalemie
(Albertville)
Lake Tanganyika
Dodoma
ZANZIBAR
Mpanda
Kilosa
Dar es Salaam
L. Rukwa
Mafia
R. Rufiji
L. Mweru
Mbeya
Kilwa Kivinje
Njombe
Lindi
L. Bangweulu
Great Ruaha R.
Lake Malawi
Songea
Mtwara
Cape Delgado
R. Rovuma

0   100   200   300 kilometres
0   50   100   150   200 miles

Map 40 The main physical features of East Africa

131

British authority throughout the territory but of dealing with the demands and criticisms of the European and Asian communities.

The organisation of administration was a slow and gradual process. Officials were few in number and often lacked experience; nor could they make use of agents, as had been the case in Uganda. Apart from the Wanga Kingdom there were no societies with traditions of strong, centralised government. Instead, the typical patterns of authority were based on clan elders or age-set systems, or, as in the case of the Nandi and Maasai, religious leaders such as the Laibon and Orkoiyot. In the absence of strong, paramount chiefs the British tried appointing and promoting individuals who had in one way or another been of assistance to them. This is how men like Kinyanjui, Odera Ulalo and Karuri became prominent. Others with established positions, such as Wang'ombe and Anam Okelo, decided to co-operate with the British. Among the first to join forces with the new administration was Mumia of Wanga. His capital had long been in contact with the caravans and officials of the Chartered Companies. He made increasing use of his alliance with the British to extend his own authority. These were the men who, for one reason or another, chose to collaborate with the colonial authority.

There were others who chose to resist or tried to stand aloof. The Maasai wished to be left alone but with their nomadic and pastoral way of life they were bound to come into conflict with the plans for European settlement. In an attempt to prevent this and preserve Maasai independence Sir Donald Stewart signed an Agreement with Lenana, the Oloiboni, in 1904. This created two reserves for the Maasai, one in Laikipia the other around Narok, linked by a strip of land so that they could move with their cattle from one to the other. These were to belong to them, the Agreement said, 'so long as the Maasai as a race shall exist'. However, with mounting pressure from the settlers this was not to be. First the strip was closed in 1908, then the Maasai from Laikipia were coerced into moving south to Narok between 1909 and 1913. The British Government was unaware of this at first and then intervened, insisting that another Agreement be made. This was done in 1911 but it did little to protect the Maasai. The settlers moved into the Laikipia area and the Maasai were restricted to the dry grasslands of the southern province.

Resistance to colonial rule was shown in a number of areas, but proved unable to stand up to the superior firearms of the British forces. In 1895 the coastal tribes had risen in an attempt to assert their independence, but without success. Military expeditions had to be sent against the Nandi, Embu, Gusii, Kipsigis, Bukusu and Kabras between 1901 and 1908. As in other parts of East Africa resistance was local and sporadic, lacking coordination and the resources to fight a long campaign. But the spirit of resistance remained and took other forms, some of which we shall come across in a later period.

The Protectorate was divided into six provinces, and these in turn were sub-divided into districts. Under the watchful eye of Provincial and District Commissioners there grew up a system of chiefs whose principal functions were to collect taxes and recruit labour. It is hardly surprising that they were disliked by their own people because of the power they wielded in the interests of the colonial government. It should be remembered, however, that at the time British authority was being imposed African society was not static. In many areas the process of migration and settlement had barely finished, while in others the effects of long distance trade had brought other changes. The coming of colonial rule was yet another cause of disruption, but it was to 'freeze' African society by imposing its own rigid framework of tribal divisions and restrictions.

European settlement

European settlers had first appeared in the country as early as 1896 but it was not until Eliot's policy of deliberate encouragement that they began to arrive in large numbers. They came from Britain and South Africa mainly, with others from Australia, New Zealand and Canada. All were tough and independent, typical of the pioneering spirit that had established white dominions in other parts of the British Empire. They believed strongly that they had a future in the country, both as farmers and in the political sphere. Some brought a considerable amount of capital with them, while others had to make a start with very little.

Among the first to arrive was Lord Delamere. He had first been attracted to East Africa while on a hunting expedition, and returned in 1903 determined to settle and make a success of farming there. As the most prominent of the early settlers he quickly became their leader and spokesman. A typical English aristocrat, he was known for his quick temper and eccentric behaviour, which included incidents such as shooting at street lamps and locking the hotel manager in his meat safe. His ambition was to create a 'White Man's Country' in

Fig. 15.2 President Kenyatta and the second Lord Delamere at a meeting in Nakuru.

Fig. 15.3a A European farmer stands beside his wheat.

Fig. 15.3b A typical settler's homestead in the Highlands of Kenya.

East Africa and to achieve this he was prepared to spend his own considerable fortune in developing new forms of agriculture. He was also prepared to exert all his influence with the Governor and with the British Government to see that the settlers' views were listened to.

Delamere acquired land at Njoro and around Lake Elmenteita, and here he started to experiment with various strains of wheat and with different breeds of livestock. Much time and money was spent in overcoming the problems of disease, climate and rainfall. At first the wheat was attacked by 'rust' and it took much patient research to find a resistant strain. Cattle, sheep and pigs were imported, but many of these were attacked by East Coast fever and other diseases. It was found that by crossbreeding with local stock animals could be reared that would withstand local diseases. A Government experimental farm at Naivasha also played an important part in this stage. In 1912 Delamere produced his first successful wheat crop, proving that it could be grown profitably. Four years previously he had formed a small company, Unga Ltd, to start a mill for the wheat growers. He continued to play an active part in the development of European agriculture but became increasingly preoccupied with political affairs, representing the interests of settlers on the Legislative Council and elsewhere. As official British policy became less favourable towards the Europeans in later years he grew more critical and outspoken, but remained the acknowledged leader of the settler community until his death in 1931.

In 1906 Major Leggett had been sent to investigate and report on the economic possibilities in the Protectorate. He recommended that both European plantation agriculture and African peasant farming should be encouraged. Official support was given to cotton growing in Nyanza and copra at the coast, but inevitably this was overshadowed by developments in the 'White' Highlands. Nevertheless it should be remembered that it was some time before European agriculture made a significant contribution to the economy. In the years before the First World War the African population continued to produce at least half the total value of the country's exports. By 1912 the Protectorate had become self-supporting, and no longer required annual grants-in-aid from Britain. Another major reason for this growing prosperity was the success with coffee production. First grown at mission stations in the 1890s, notably St Austin's Mission near Nairobi, it quickly became popular with European farmers, encouraged by the rising price on the world market. In 1908 the Coffee Planters Association was formed. By 1913 coffee exports were worth £18 000.

The problems of land and labour were to become major issues in the 1920s and 1930s, but already they were the cause of friction between the immigrant communities and the officials. The latter had insisted that all land allocated for settlement must be properly registered and marked out before it could be occupied. This inevitably led to delays and frustration as the government failed to keep pace with the flood of new settlers. There was uncertainty and misunderstanding also between officials and Africans over the question of land tenure, leading to considerable resentment and bitterness, particularly among the Kikuyu, who saw much of their land taken from them for European settlement. The Asian community was also anxious to secure the right to acquire land, and petitioned the British and Indian Governments in 1906, but without success.

Trade, transport and the Asian community

The growth of trade and the development of towns in the East African Protectorate were closely linked with the Asian community. These were not the coolies who had built the railway, most of whom had returned to India. They were mainly Gujarati Indians whose associations with East Africa and its trade went back many years. Following the construction of the railway and the British occupation they set up trading posts at Kibwezi and Machakos in the 1890s, then in Nairobi and further west. They were the first to carry European and other manufactured goods into the remoter areas, often far from the nearest road or railway. With their commercial skills they were quick to seize and dominate much of the business and trade of the country. They tended to congregate in the townships where they preserved their own culture and way of life. Being a largely urban community, and having been discouraged in their attempts to acquire land, they concentrated on the skilled and semi-skilled occupations as well as business and commercial enterprises of all kinds. One of the most successful was A. M. Jeevanjee, who became head of a firm of building contractors and shipowners. He had first come to Nairobi in 1899 to construct a house for the government official John Ainsworth. Among his other ventures he started a newspaper which he sold in 1903; it still flourishes today as *The Standard*.

The railway proved to be the life-line for the

Protectorate. Not only did it provide transport for the immigrant settlers and traders, enabling them to establish themselves, but it provided the Government with a steady source of revenue. All the new towns and centres of trade were situated on or close to the main line, and it was not long before branch lines were added to serve other areas. An extension to Magadi enabled the valuable soda deposits to be extracted; another line to Thika and eventually Nanyuki served the sisal and coffee plantations in that direction. From the administration's point of view the railway made communication and control quicker and much more effective, though there were still many districts that could only be reached on foot. For the African population the railway was one further change in the adjustment they were making to a cash economy and the new demands of colonial rule.

German East Africa including the Kingdoms of Rwanda and Rundi

When the German Government asserted responsibility for its East African territory in 1890 it was inexperienced in colonial rule; the Germans had only recently begun to acquire colonies. Their overriding concern was to extract the maximum benefit from whatever resources they could find, within the shortest possible time. In this respect they were more dedicated, thorough and ruthless than their British neighbours. While the British authorities were anxious to make their new colonies pay their way, the Germans had an even more positive aim—to make their colonies produce a profit. This was considered more important than anything else.

The establishment of German administration

We have seen how the attempt of the German East Africa Company to control the coast provoked revolts in 1888. The German Government had been obliged to send out reinforcements to suppress these risings, and in 1891 they took over responsibility for the government of their East African territory. It took them fourteen years to extend their control throughout the country, using force on many occasions but making use of support whenever they could. Among those who allied with the Germans were Merere of the Sangu, Marealle of Marangu

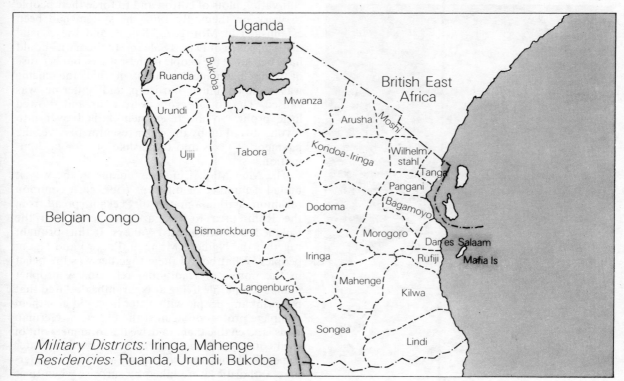

Map 41 German East Africa showing administrative divisions

135

and Kahigi of Kianja. They did so in order to increase their own territory and power in much the same way as those who collaborated in Uganda and Kenya. Of those who resisted, mention has already been made of men like Abushiri, Bwana Heri and the Hehe chief Mkwawa.

The pattern of German authority that was established during the 1890s was similar in some ways to the British system, though different in the methods used. At the head was the Governor with his headquarters in Dar es Salaam. In 1904 a Governor's Council was set up to advise him, consisting of officials and unofficials. Prominent among the latter were German settlers who came to exercise a strong influence over official policy. The territory was divided into districts, of which there were twenty-two by 1914; two of these, Iringa and Mahenge, were under military control. In the north-west the traditional rulers of Ruanda and Urundi were left to themselves, subject to the advice of German Residents. Distances were so great and communications so poor that much power and responsibility rested with the District Officers or 'Berzirksamtmann'. They had the duties of collecting taxes, appointing and controlling local chiefs or agents (Akida), presiding over the courts and administering punishment. They were assisted by small forces of police or troops. Wherever possible the Germans made use of African chiefs to assist in governing the districts, but in the areas where these did not exist they appointed coastal Arab or Swahili men as Akidas. Often the latter were hated and resented as much as the Germans for their cruel and harsh behaviour. This tendency towards brutal methods of administration was due partly to the fact that the Germans often over-reacted to the slightest sign of discontent. They felt isolated and heavily outnumbered. But this does not explain or excuse the conduct of officials such as Carl Peters who had responsibility for the Kilimanjaro area. So oppressive and cruel did he become that in 1896 he was brought to trial, found guilty and dismissed.

The Maji Maji Rising and its effects

The last and most serious revolt against German rule broke out in July 1905, in the area of the Matumbi Hills. The immediate cause of discontent was the government's cotton scheme. In 1902 the Governor decided that cotton must be grown in the southern districts. Headmen were ordered to start cultivating plots of cotton and to force their people to work on them. By 1905 the system had been established in Morogoro, Kilosa and the coastal districts south of Dar es Salaam. In theory it should have benefited the people of these areas, but because of the harsh and inefficient way in which the scheme was handled much hardship and suffering was caused. The cotton crops were poor and showed little profit. So the resentment boiled over into revolt, stirred up by the other resentments over the payment of taxes and the dislike of foreign domination.

The Maji Maji rising was unique in the way it united a number of different tribes in a common rebellion. Within a matter of weeks it spread from the Rufiji area to Uluguru, Mahenge and the Lukuledi and Kilombero Valleys. It thus brought together the Ngindo, Mbungu, Pogoro and Ngoni peoples. What bound them together was the belief in the power of traditional religion. A prophet named Kinjikitile living at Ngarambe declared that by sprinkling people with water he could give them complete protection against the bullets of German guns, and enable them to drive the foreigners out of their country. His messengers then carried the water to people throughout southern Tanzania. The German authorities were taken by surprise when their headquarters and officials were attacked at the end

Fig. 15.4 Dr Carl Peters.

of July 1905. But they soon had reinforcements on the way and set about crushing the rebellion. The courage and determination of the Maji Maji fighters, armed only with spears, was no match for the machine guns and rifles of the German forces. They died in hundreds, and without adequate leadership or organisation they were defeated. The last group to hold out were the Ngindo, under their leader Abdalla Mapanda, who survived until January 1907.

The immediate consequences of the rising were tragic. The German forces left behind them a trail of destruction and devastation that led to three years of the most terrible famine. This was the period known as the Fugafuga, when survivors took to eating insects and wild fruit. Villages had been destroyed, families broken up. It has been estimated that seventy-five thousand Africans died as a result of the fighting and the famine.

As for the Germans, they had been badly shaken by the intensity of the revolt, and the German Government was led to reconsider its attitude towards the local population. Dernberg, the Minister in charge, appointed a new Governor in 1906, named Rechenberg. His instructions were to see that no such rising ever occurred again. Accordingly he curbed the settlers' demand for forced labour and tried to find better way of encouraging the population to grow cash crops. He also attempted to put an end to some of the more brutal habits such as the use of corporal punishment.

These were the immediate effects of the rising, but there were other more profound results that affected the course of Tanzanian history. The Africans realised that armed resistance was no use; instead other methods must be found. And in particular they were to learn the importance of organisation and leadership in any campaign against oppressive foreign rule. As John Iliffe has pointed out: 'A mass movement needs strong organisation, and the religious organisation of Maji Maji was not strong enough.' Henceforth they were to seek other ways of resisting colonial rule, but they were never to forget the spirit that had been kindled by the Maji Maji rising.

German settlement and the development of agriculture

It was not until after 1900 that settlers began coming to German East Africa in large numbers. By 1905 there were 180 and by 1913 the number had grown to over 5000. Not all came from Germany; there were Greeks and Italians among others. They were attracted mainly to the Usambara and Kilimanjaro areas, though some chose the Rufiji Valley. They were as determined as the government to make the country economically successful and profitable. It was felt that plantation methods of cultivation were the best way to do this, supported by a steady supply of forced labour. One of the most outspoken advocates of this policy was Paul Rohrbach. Like their counterparts in British East Africa the settlers wanted to make the colony into a 'White Man's Country'. In 1907 the settlers of Usambara and Tanga formed the Northern League under the leadership of Carl Feilke, to press their demands upon the government.

The government, however, had its own views and these were clearly expressed by Dernberg in the same year. 'We have not gone to East Africa to find plantations for three thousand to four thousand people but to make a vast country bloom, to find raw materials and create markets for German trade and German industry. East Africa's economy cannot be based on the activities of plantations and settlers . . . but must be developed through its natural products and through the natural experience of its inhabitants.'

Fig. 15.5 A sisal plantation on the slopes of Kilimanjaro near Moshi.

Fig. 15.6 A Lutheran mission school built by the Germans at Marangu.

Nevertheless the government realised that it could not develop the resources of the territory to the full without the enterprise and capital of the settlers. In 1902 a Biological & Agricultural Institute was established at Amani for research into tropical agriculture. The results were made available to the settlers and also passed on to African cultivators. In 1905 a centre for showing Africans how to cultivate cotton was set up at Mpanganya in the Rufiji Valley. Encouragement was also given to African coconut plantations on the coast. But for new cash crops such as sisal and coffee reliance was placed primarily on the settlers.

Sisal was first imported from Florida in 1892 and soon proved ideal for the climate and soil over a wide area. Helped by the rise in world prices it became the territory's most valuable cash crop, earning 1 368 000 marks in 1906 and 7 359 000 marks in 1912. With the construction and extension of railways new areas for cultivation of sisal were opened up. Coffee was first grown in the Usambaras in the 1890s, but was hindered by poor soils and shortage of labour. With the extension of the railway to Moshi in 1912 and the rise in world prices, new opportunities in the Kilimanjaro area for coffee production were taken up by Greek and Italian

planters and also by certain Chagga chiefs. So successful did African coffee growers become that in 1907 the European planters complained of the threat to their labour supply. Whereas the Arabica variety was grown on Kilimanjaro it was the Robusta variety that the Africans in Bukoba produced, developed from the crop that chiefs in that district had formerly grown for ceremonial purposes. Cotton cultivation met with some resistance, as we have seen, but by 1914 it was being grown successfully by the Wasukuma in Mwanza and in parts of the Rufiji Valley. Rubber plantations were started in Tanga and Morogoro districts to supplement the collection of wild rubber, but after the drastic fall in the world price of 1913 it declined in importance.

Transport and trade

In a territory as vast as their East African colony it was obviously essential to develop a system of road and rail transport if they were to exploit its resources effectively. The first to be built was the Usambara line; work started at Tanga in 1893 and in 1905 it reached Mombo. It served the settlers in Usambara and, after its extension to Moshi in 1912 the planters and African growers on Kilimanjaro. Work on the central line from Dar es Salaam started in 1905, reaching Tabora in 1912 and Kigoma in 1914. It was hoped that by linking up with the western districts in this way it would now be possible to tax the people of Rwanda and Urundi as well as those living along the line. Rechenberg also hoped that a railway through Nyamwezi country would encourage them to grow groundnuts as a cash crop. The line was also strategically important should the need arise for troops to be moved into the interior. New areas for sisal production were opened up around Morogoro and Tabora.

As in other parts of East Africa the railway brought new opportunities for trade, and the first to take advantage were the Asians. Rechenberg gave encouragement to the Asians as he attached importance to the role they could play in the colony's commercial expansion. He resisted settler demands for restrictions on Asian immigration. The largest of the Indian trading concerns was that of Alladina Visram. The German East Africa Company remained the major European firm in the country. Modern techniques of trade and transport had all but put an end to the caravan and porterage system that had flourished in Tanzania during the

Fig. 15.7 Bukoba: a steamer entering the harbour on Victoria Nyanza.

nineteenth century. Consequently the role of such traditional traders as the Nyamwezi declined. But there were still areas untouched by rail or road so that for many years the remoter areas continued to depend on the old methods.

Rwanda-Urundi under German rule

As a result of the Anglo-German Agreements of 1886 and 1890 and a subsequent agreement between Germany and Belgium, the area covered by the kingdoms of Rwanda and Rundi fell within the German sphere of influence. But it was some time before the Germans could visit it, let alone start to make themselves felt. The first German to reach Rwanda-Urundi, as this part of German East Africa was now called, was Graf von Goetzen in 1894. Cut off from the rest of the territory by its isolated position and its history and traditions, Rwanda-Urundi remained a distinct and separate unit throughout the colonial period. German officials were quick to realise this and to accept the fact that, short as they were of administrators and manpower, they would have to retain the existing rulers of the two kingdoms. Accordingly Mwami Musinga of Rwanda and Mwami Mutuga of Rundi were given official recognition and allowed to retain their traditional forms of government. The only other area where the Germans followed a similar policy of indirect rule was in Bukoba. In return these rulers had to accept the advice of German Residents.

In fact there was little the Germans could do at first to interfere with the internal affairs of the kingdoms. Their time and attention was taken up with risings elsewhere in the territory, culminating in the great Maji Maji rebellion of 1905. Distances were so great and communications so poor that it was as much as they could do to retain even a nominal presence in Rwanda-Urundi. As late as 1914 there were still only six officials in Urundi and five in Rwanda, with small military units in support. Officials were frequently transferred elsewhere, thus making it difficult to pursue a consistent policy. The most outstanding of the German Residents was Dr Kandt who remained in Rwanda from 1907–1913, longer than any of his colleagues and long enough to be able to understand the particular needs and problems of the area. He saw the possibility of developing coffee as a major cash crop, along with other products such as cotton and hides. But little could be done without adequate communications. Plans for a railway to Rwanda-Urundi never materialised, the nearest being the Central line from Dar es Salaam to Kigoma on Lake Tanganyika, completed in 1914. Although a start was made to develop new products the Germans were disappointed with the progress made. Consequently attempts to collect taxes were largely ineffective, since few had yet moved from a subsistence to a cash economy. Not until 1914 was it possible to organise anything like an effective tax system.

German administration was noted, as we have seen, for its authoritarian and at times ruthless methods. But this was probably less evident in

139

Rwanda-Urundi owing to the retention of authority by the rulers and the shortage of German officials. In fact it may be that the rulers, notably Mwami Musinga of Rwanda, gained from the German presence. The sudden decline in intertribal warfare that followed the establishment of colonial rule usually benefited those chiefs and rulers who held power at the time, and could use European authority to their own advantage.

The policy followed by the Residents in Rwanda-Urundi was contained in the Gotzen Instructions of 1905, a document worked out by the German Government. This made it clear that they were not to interfere with the traditional pattern of government and customary law except where it conflicted with basic European laws and ideas. The Resident was expected to be an adviser rather than an administrator, using persuasion rather than force to get the ruler to accept gradual reforms, particularly in the field of economic development. At the same time they were not to disrupt the traditional system of land tenure. One may wonder whether these two policies were compatible; was it possible to preserve old institutions while introducing new techniques? Nor can we tell whether the Germans would have found a solution, since their presence in Rwanda-Urundi came to an abrupt end during the First World War. Certainly in matters relating to external affairs the Residents were given greater freedom to act on their own initiative, particularly with regard to the entry of foreigners into the kingdoms and in the recruitment of local labour for areas outside Rwanda-Urundi.

Although German authority was not challenged on quite the same scale as in other parts of East Africa it was found necessary to organise small punitive expeditions on a number of occasions. Very often this was to deal with a challenge to one of the Mwamis. In 1910 Muhumusa, the widow of a former Mwami of Rwanda, attempted to regain the throne for her son but failed and withdrew to Kigezi in Uganda. In 1912 a more serious uprising occurred when Ndungutze, a member of the Rundi royal family, stirred up ancient Hutu hatred of the Tutsi in an attempt to overthrow the Mwami. This threatened a widespread breakdown of law and order and was met by swift German counter-measures. The revolt was put down ruthlessly and its leaders severely dealt with. German administration was probably more effective and efficient in Rwanda than Urundi, a reflection of the relatively

stronger position of the Mwami of Rwanda. Urundi still suffered from disunity and rivalry within the royal family, a weakness that was not made any better by the tendency of German officials to play one faction off against another. From 1911 the Residents began to play a larger part in local affairs through the appointment of government chiefs, to act as intermediaries between the local police authorities and the Residents themselves. Rwanda was divided into seven districts for this purpose. Gradually German influence was beginning to make itself felt throughout Rwanda-Rundi and not simply around the main administrative head-quarters, Bujumbura, and its outposts. But this was cut short by the outbreak of the First World War and the occupation of German East Africa by British and Belgian forces. In 1914 the Germans in Rwanda-Urundi found themselves threatened from two directions; from the North by the British in Uganda and from the West by the Belgians in the Congo. In 1916 a Belgian force crossed over and drove out the remaining Germans, thus effectively bringing to an end the period of German rule.

Questions
1. Why did it become necessary for the German and British Governments to take over from the commercial companies in their East African territories?
2. Compare the methods used by the British and German authorities to establish control over their territories.
3. What problems faced European settlers in Kenya before 1914 and how did they attempt to solve them?
4. Why did the people of southern Tanzania revolt against German rule and what were the results of this revolt?
5. Describe the role played by the railways in the establishment and development of colonial rule in East Africa.

Activities
1. Compare the methods of agriculture practiced by Europeans and Africans in the early part of the twentieth century in East Africa.
2. Find out all you can about the earliest Mission school or hospital in your area.
3. Write an imaginative account of the last days of the Maji Maji rising and describe the effects of the 'Fugafuga'.

Chapter 16
The inter-war years: Tanganyika, Zanzibar and Rwanda-Urundi

Introduction

The First World War lasted from 1914 to 1918 and was primarily a struggle between the major powers of Europe. Britain, France and their allies were fighting against Germany, Austria and Turkey. Although it took place for the most part in Europe and involved purely European issues it was inevitable that the overseas empires of the two sides would be involved, directly or indirectly. In East Africa there was bound to be some conflict between adjacent German and British colonies. For the Germans it offered a useful way of pinning down British forces and resources that might otherwise have gone to the main area of operations. Although Britain had command of the sea routes she could never be sure that German supplies might not get through to East Africa.

The First World War and its effects

The military campaign that started in East Africa involved both European and African personnel and severely disrupted the economic development of all three mainland territories, particularly that of German East Africa. It was here that most of the fighting took place. The German forces under the able command of General von Lettow Vorbeck first sought to cut the main line of communication between the coast and the British hinterland. After some fighting in the Taveta and Voi area the Germans were forced back after the arrival of Smuts and the South African forces. Meanwhile Belgian troops were attacking German positions in Ruanda and marching on Tabora, while from the south General Northey was approaching with a contingent of Rhodesian and Nyasaland soldiers. By 1917 the British forces had control of the ports, main line and the whole of north-east German East

Fig. 16.1 General von Lettow Vorbeck.

Africa. However, so stubborn and skilful was the German resistance that von Lettow was able to evade both capture and defeat until after the German surrender in Europe in 1918.

There were important political, social and economic consequences for the peoples of East Africa. In the first place the war had completely devastated the economy of German East Africa. European farms

Fig. 16.2a A German field gun from the 1914–18 war. It now stands outside Fort Jesus.

and plantations had been abandoned and neglected. In many areas African cultivation had suffered equally badly, and there was famine and disease among those who survived. Large numbers of troops and carriers on both sides had been killed or wounded, and inevitably the majority were African. For the survivors there was the memory of a new type of European warfare; they had seen Europeans fighting against each other and they had learnt that Europeans were not invincible. In the British territories there had been a loss of agricultural production and shortages of various kinds but not the physical destruction seen in the German colony.

The immediate political outcome was that Germany had to surrender all her overseas colonies, which were handed over to the newly formed League of Nations. This body then entrusted them as mandated territories to various member nations, to be administered and developed in the interests of the inhabitants on behalf of the League. The nations responsible for these mandates were instructed to pay special attention to the economic, social and moral welfare of the inhabitants and to submit annual reports on the progress made. Britain thus took over responsibility for German East Africa in 1920 and renamed it Tanganyika. In fact there had been British administration in part of the country since 1916, under the command of Horace Byatt.

Fig. 16.2b A German column in British and Portuguese uniforms during their 4000 kilometres, four year long march.

Tanganyika

Post-war reconstruction in Tanganyika

Byatt became Governor in 1920 with an Executive Council of four officials to advise him. His total staff was small and resources barely adequate. The task facing him was formidable. Not only had he to establish a new British form of administration in place of what was left of the German system, but he had to restore to life an economy that had been shattered by the war, as well as regain the confidence and loyalty of the people. Wherever possible he sought to retain and use local authorities, even the Akidas. He was cautious and suspicious about letting the new settlers have things their own way, with the result that the abandoned German plantations were slow in coming back to life. New leases of land to Europeans were limited in time and area. This was in sharp contrast to the influx of soldier-settlers into Kenya at the same time. Byatt and his officials were aware of their primary responsibility under the mandate. A grant of £330 000 had been made by the British Government to assist with reconstruction. Many roads, railways and bridges had been destroyed during the War, so that there was a great need for funds to meet these costs. A start had already been made in encouraging African agriculture; as District Officer in the Kilimanjaro area since 1916 Charles Dundas had revived interest among the Chagga in coffee growing.

Sir Donald Cameron and indirect rule

By the time Byatt's term of office came to an end in 1924 the process of reconstruction and recovery was still under way. There had not been time to do much about establishing a stable system of administration. The new Governor, Sir Donald Cameron, had already had a long career in colonial service including ten years as secretary to the government of Nigeria. This had given him considerable experience of Lugard's methods of indirect rule in that country. He saw this as the solution to the problem of local administration in Tanganyika. Not only would it assist the British officials but it would help to fulfil one of Britain's obligations under the League of Nations' mandate.

Basically indirect rule meant governing African people through their own traditional institutions. In northern Nigeria Lugard had applied it to the powerful Moslem Emirates with their strong tradi-

tions of authority, law and custom. In Buganda it had been embodied in the 1900 Buganda Agreement, and to a lesser extent in the Toro and Ankole Agreements. In these areas there were strong centralised authorities, so that all the British had to do was to harness them to their own administration. In Tanganyika the position was different in that there were no powerful rulers, but Cameron was none the less determined to apply the same principles in developing what he called 'Indirect Administration'.

As so many of the units of local government in Tanganyika were too small or poor, Cameron tried to get them to come together in federations of larger groups. Between 1927 and 1931 this took place in several areas including Sukumaland, Nyamwezi and Bukoba. Chiefs agreed to combine to form councils where they would then discuss and make decisions. This system was formulated in the Native Authority Ordinance of 1926, which set up various forms of authority, varying from chiefs to federations of chiefs and tribal councils. These were to be entrusted with executive, financial and judicial functions. Executive duties covered a wide range, from the maintenance of law and order to the control of animal diseases. Financial matters covered the collection of hut and poll taxes and the setting up of local treasuries, which would keep records of revenue and expenditure. The revenue would be used to pay the salaries of chiefs and other local officials and for the provision of public services and works. Judicial powers were extended in 1929 to include criminal and civil offences. The courts were graded into various categories of responsibility, and were subject to the supervision of Government officials.

There were problems in putting this policy into practice. One was the lack of trained and experienced personnel. Since most of the chiefs were still illiterate they could hardly be expected to manage all the judicial and financial tasks given to them. This invariably meant that British officials had to play a more prominent part than was desirable. Indeed, Cameron insisted on close supervision as part of his policy of guardianship. And yet so long as British officials remained so close at hand the chiefs and councils had little chance of displaying any initiative. It also tended to make them appear as little more than the agents of colonial government in the eyes of their own people. Nor was the emphasis on chiefs alone a very effective method of training for modern local government. Another weakness of the system was that it tended to ignore progress and development in other fields, and held up the growth of greater national unity and understanding. For instance, the Tabora school for the sons of chiefs was planned and run entirely on tribal lines.

On the credit side we must acknowledge that the system of indirect rule in Tanganyika did survive the effects of the economic depression and the Second World War. Schools and dispensaries were kept going despite the fall in revenue. The treasuries worked well and there were over three hundred in operation by 1938. Moreover the 1926 Ordinance stressed the importance of allowing local authorities to develop and adjust in their own way to meet the changes brought about by modernisation. This was significant in that it recognised the fact that African society ought not to copy European methods slavishly.

Central government and economic development

Cameron believed that African participation in government should develop in stages, starting at the local and regional level. He was not enthusiastic about the appointment of a Legislative Council but in the face of pressure from settlers and immigrants for a share in the formulation of government policy this was established in 1926. It consisted of thirteen officials and seven unofficials at first, meeting under the Governor's chairmanship. Of the unofficials nominated to the Council by Cameron, five were European and two were Arab. As with other Legislative Councils its function was mainly to deliberate government policy; it had no executive powers.

One of the matters with which it was chiefly concerned was the economy. Unlike Byatt, Cameron gave encouragement to European farming in the territory as he saw it as a means of setting an example to African cultivators. In spite of the poor conditions on the world market the production of cash crops continued to recover: the output of sisal increased from 20 834 tons in 1913 to 45 828 tons in 1929 while coffee increased from 1 059 tons in 1913 to 10 000 tons in 1928. Undoubtedly much of this was due to the extension and improvement of roads and railways. A rail link between Tabora and Mwanza was completed in 1928, and another from Moshi to Arusha in the following year. A steamer service on Lake Tanganyika enabled the central line to tap much of the trade to and from that area.

A matter over which there was usually less agreement in Legislative Council was the question of labour. Aware of their responsibility under the mandate the officials refused to give in to settler demands for forced labour to work on their plantations. The 1923 Masters and Servants Ordinance laid down detailed instructions for the hire and employment of labour, requiring a written contract signed by both parties. In 1926 a Labour department was set up with the task of checking on housing and health facilities for labour and providing camps for migrant labourers on their way to and from work. Nevertheless there was still a certain amount of coercion used to obtain labour for public works.

Education and health

The Germans had shown keen interest in education, encouraging the missions and starting their own schools. By 1903 there were already eight Government schools, twelve run by local authorities and fifteen by various missions. While the latter tended to emphasise the training of readers and catechists for religious purposes they did provide a basic education in reading and writing which could prove useful in other occupations as well. The government schools concentrated on training clerks, interpreters and minor officials. The British continued this basic

Fig. 16.3 Tabora: a mission worker conducting the High School band.

pattern of education, appointing a Director of Education in 1920 to coordinate educational policy. Great stimulus was given to African education by the Phelps-Stokes commission and its report but there was still little provision for secondary level education. But the main need at first was to provide Africans with sufficient education to participate in Cameron's pattern of local administration. The school at Tabora for the sons of chiefs was the first to start secondary education.

Similarly in the field of health and medicine it was the Christian missions that paved the way. Many had their own hospitals and dispensaries long before the government took action. The training of orderlies and nurses was another aspect of mission work that was later copied by the government. In major projects such as combating sleeping sickness it was obviously government money and direction that was required, and as revenue increased so did the provision of government hospitals and dispensaries.

The beginning of African politics

In Tanganyika after the First World War there was not the same resentment and bitterness over matters such as land and labour as in Kenya. Consequently African opinion was not as easily roused or united. However there were signs of a new consciousness, limited and local at first, that was to have important results in the future. One of the main disadvantages in this period was that the leaders lacked, or were out of touch with, the mass support they needed in order to make themselves felt.

The Bukoba Buhaya Union was one of the first African movements to be started, in 1924. Its leader was Klemens Kiiza who had worked for both the government and missions, and saw this as an organisation for social and economic improvement by means of encouraging literary education and coffee growing. It opposed the privileged and protected position of the chiefs under the new system of indirect rule, and the 'nyarubanja' land tenure system, not unlike the 'mailo' system in Buganda. Then there was the Kilimanjaro Native Planters Association formed in the same year, a Chagga enterprise formed to organise the growing and marketing of coffee. The Usangi Sports and Welfare Club founded in 1935 was for social and recreational purposes but had a strong underlying motive of educational and economic self-improvement. All came into conflict with the chiefs in one way or another since they were often led by the new generation of young educated Africans.

Martin Kayamba might be taken as a typical example of this generation. Born in Zanzibar in 1891, the son of a schoolteacher, he was educated at Kiungani UMCA school and then became a clerk and trader, travelling in Kenya and Uganda. After being imprisoned by the Germans he was appointed by the new administration after the war as chief clerk of the Tanga District Office. He did well and was promoted. On two occasions he visited Europe. In 1922 he founded, with the support of the Government, the Tanganyika Territory African Civil Service Association. This was primarily a club for African clerks and teachers, with its own newspapers and football team. Although limited in its aims and objectives it did become a meeting point for educated Africans of different tribes and religions, and helped them to think of themselves and of their country as a nation rather than a collection of tribes. Kayamba believed in the need for self-improvement and unity. He was no politician or nationalist but created the organisation and conditions that enabled a nationalist movement to emerge in later years. Members of his organisation took part in the formation of the Tanganyika African Association between 1928 and 1929, in Dar es Salaam. It soon had branches in nine centres, including Zanzibar. It was from this body that T.A.N.U. developed in 1954.

Zanzibar

Zanzibar was little affected by the First World War, in spite of its proximity to the German territory. Its form of government had continued little changed and was by the 1920s typical of any British colony. In 1926 Executive and Legislative Councils were established, the latter including ten officials and six unofficials (three Arabs, two Indians, one European). No African member was nominated until 1945. This was because the British authorities saw Zanzibar as primarily an Arab settlement, and gave special encouragement and emphasis to Arab participation in government. This was to be the cause of much hostility and trouble in years to come. The Arabs formed the landowning aristocracy of the island, headed by the Sultan himself. Sultan Khalifa II ruled from 1911 to 1960 and was throughout this period content to leave the direction of affairs to the British Resident. But the Arabs were in a minority and lacked the energy and drive to dominate the economic and political progress of the Protectorate.

To protect their chief source of income the Arabs had formed the Clove Growers Association in 1927.

This body became increasingly powerful and influential, so that when the clove producers were badly hit by the world depression they were able to obtain from the British authorities special protection and support. This annoyed the Indian and European traders who handled much of the export business, as they suffered from the new export tax imposed to help the C.G.A. In 1937 the Indians refused to have anything further to do with the clove trade, thus threatening the clove growers with economic collapse. The new Resident, Sir John Hall, intervened and worked out a compromise that

Fig. 16.5 His Highness Khalifa II, Sultan of Zanzibar.

Fig. 16.4 The streets of Zanzibar around 1920.

Fig. 16.6 Clove trees in Zanzibar.

146

enabled business to be resumed. But the incident had served to show the powerful role of the Indian community in the commercial sector and the declining power of the Arabs. Cloves and copra continued to be the two main exports from Zanzibar, the former being considerably boosted during the Second World War when the Japanese occupied the only other area of clove production—the East Indies. The island's revenue increased considerably, enabling the Government to impose an income tax for the first time.

Arabs and Moslem Africans were understandably suspicious of the schools set up by the Christian missions on the island, so that for many years these schools relied on the mainland for their pupils. In 1907 the Government had set up an Education department and government schools were started. But here too the response was poor, until the 1920's. The policy was to develop schools for the different races so as to help overcome the suspicions, particularly of the Arabs. In 1923 a Teacher Training College was opened, and in the same year a commercial school for Asians. The following year an industrial school for Africans began. Educational progress was, however, very gradual.

Although placid and quiet on the surface Zanzibar in this period was becoming more divided and insecure as the African majority felt increasingly left out and ignored. In 1934 the African Association was formed on the island to protect the rights and interests of educated Africans. Though only a small and limited start it was to become increasingly significant in the years after 1945.

Rwanda-Urundi under Belgian rule

The Belgian Government hoped that by occupying Rwanda-Urundi it might be in a stronger position in the post-war negotiations to bargain for concessions around the mouth of the River Congo. However in this they failed and eventually had to accept Rwanda-Urundi as a mandate from the League of Nations. Thus in May 1919 this area passed into Belgian control while the rest of German East Africa was mandated to Britain as Tanganyika. The term mandate implied that these territories remained the ultimate responsibility of the League and were entrusted to various 'protecting powers' to administer and develop in the interests of their inhabitants. But unlike its successor, the United Nations, the League of Nations was more concerned with the social and material well-being of the people than their political advancement. This suited Belgian colonial policy which followed much the same pattern.

For administrative convenience it was felt suitable that Rwanda-Urundi should be linked with the Congo, under the control of the Governor General in Leopoldville, though with its own budget and a Resident in each of the kingdoms. The Belgians decided to keep the system of indirect rule adopted by the Germans and thus retained the kingdoms and gave official recognition to the rulers. But while retaining the structure of traditional authority they also developed their own administrative machinery which gradually assumed more and more power.

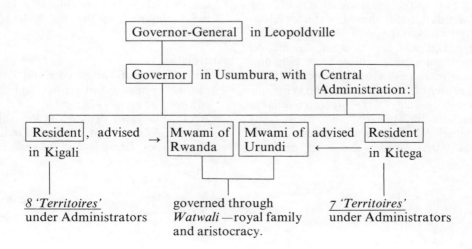

147

Apart from the authority exercised by the Tutsi rulers and their advisers there was little or no provision for African participation in government except at the lowest level. Nor did the Belgians consider it necessary to educate or train Africans for positions of responsibility in the administration, the professions or commercial life of the country. In the first place Belgian policy was marked by a considerable degree of paternalism. The attitude was that the colonial government knew what was best for its people, that it would provide for their material needs and that they need not concern themselves with anything else, least of all the government of the country. Secondly, it was highly centralised, with authority coming from above and controlling every major decision, leaving little opportunity for initiative or variation at the local level. Thirdly, the Belgian officials were noted for their bureaucratic and theoretical approach to problems. The result of these three characteristics made Belgian Colonial Government cautious, suspicious of change and inflexible. This might not have mattered so much at first, but after the Second World War the whole tempo of international events brought new forces to bear on Africa which were bound to be felt by those in authority.

Belgian social and economic achievements

The social and economic achievements of the Belgians in their African territories, notably the Congo, were considerable. They were much in advance of other colonial powers in their provision of medical and community care for workers in the towns and mining centres. The Church also played an important part in the provision of schools and hospitals. Rwanda-Urundi shared in this development, although it lacked the great mineral resources of the Congo and was for most of this period dependant upon an annual subsidy from Belgium. Coffee was the main cash crop, producing 15 000 tons in 1955, in addition cotton, hides and skins and pyrethrum were exported. Of the minerals available only wolfram and tin appeared to exist in commercial quantities. With all these products, as with the potential tourist trade, the chief problem

appeared to be the remote and land-locked position of the country. Although much had been done to improve roads and communications by lake to the rail-heads at Kigoma and Albertville, Rwanda-Urundi was still heavily dependant upon the transport systems of neighbouring countries.

Meanwhile the population was increasing rapidly. In 1918 it was estimated at 2 300 000; by 1940 it had risen to 3 200 000 and by 1956 to 4 400 000. When one compares these figures with those of the much larger territories of Tanganyika or Uganda at the same time it is clear that the population density was far greater than anywhere else in tropical Africa. And since it was not matched by a corresponding increase in employment opportunities or sources of income many inhabitants were forced to go outside the country to seek their livelihood, particularly in Uganda and Tanganyika. Population pressure also placed new demands upon the country's food supplies, increasing the risks of soil erosion and cattle disease. Attempts were made to find additional sources of food for the population, notably fish from Lake Tanganyika.

Questions

1. How did East Africa become involved in the First World War and what were the results of the war in East Africa?
2. Discuss the policies of Sir Donald Cameron and assess their effect on Tanganyika.
3. Trace the development of African opinion and political feeling in Tanganyika from 1920 to 1945.
4. What administrative and economic changes took place in Zanzibar between the Wars?
5. What part did the Christian missions play in medical and educational work before 1945?
6. Compare the systems of colonial rule imposed by the Germans and the Belgians in Rwanda-Urundi.

Activities

1. Draw a map of Tanganyika and Zanzibar and put in the main crops grown, and the railways constructed up to 1928.
2. Arrange a class debate on the subject: The advantages and disadvantages of indirect rule in Tanganyika, Zanzibar and Rwanda Urundi.

Chapter 17
The inter-war years: Uganda and Kenya

Introduction: The world depression and the economic slump

During the 1920s and 1930s the world was affected by a series of economic crises that hit the African colonies particularly severely. We have noted already how the price paid for cash crops could vary from year to year, with the producer unable to do anything about it. In times of scarcity or great demand prices would rise, while the reverse could also happen. This affected the cost of imports, and reduced the revenue earned by the government. As a result there would be less money available for schools and hospitals and public works. All this was the result of the move to a cash economy during the colonial period, and showed how dependant colonies were on the industrial and capitalist systems of Europe and America. But the alternative would have been to revert to subsistence economy, which by now was quite impossible. Thus the depression of 1920–21 and the even more severe slump of 1929–1930s affected all sections of the community in East Africa, but particularly the African and European producers.

To add to the troubles caused by the general fall in prices there was a currency crisis in East Africa shortly after the First World War. In 1905 the Indian rupee had been adopted as the basis of currency in British East Africa, with a rate of exchange fixed at fifteen rupees to one pound sterling. Due to various economic factors the value of the rupee increased against the pound during the war, making exports to Britain far less profitable than they had been. In 1920 the East African Currency Board was set up in order to stabilise and reorganise the system of currency. Eventually it was decided to drop the rupee and make the shilling the

standard of currency. But in the meantime many European farmers in Kenya had lost money or gone bankrupt, while large numbers of African troops and carriers who had been paid their wages in paper currency found that their money was worth little or nothing.

Gradually the position improved as prices paid for cash crops increased in the 1920s. But then came the great 'crash' in the financial centre of Wall Street in America that spread to the capitals of Europe and so throughout the world. The effects were drastic. Government plans for development and expansion were cut back or abandoned. Unemployment increased as firms and employers lost business and reduced their output. The prices obtained for raw materials dropped so sharply that it was hardly worth producing them. For example in 1930 the price of coffee dropped from about £120 to £70 a ton, while sisal fell from £40 a ton in 1929 to £20 a ton in 1930. There was little assistance of any kind available to help producers. While many African farmers could subsist on their own food crops, large numbers of Europeans had to sell up and leave, or seek alternative employment. It took many years for the world market to recover. As far as East Africa was concerned the crisis showed the danger of over-dependance on one cash crop alone, and the need for greater protection and security in the marketing of produce. The other solution was to speed up the growth of local industries so as to be less dependant on imported goods. The hardships brought about by the slump also had their political effects among the various racial groups in East Africa.

Uganda between the wars

In contrast with Kenya, Uganda continued to develop in the inter-war years as a primarily African

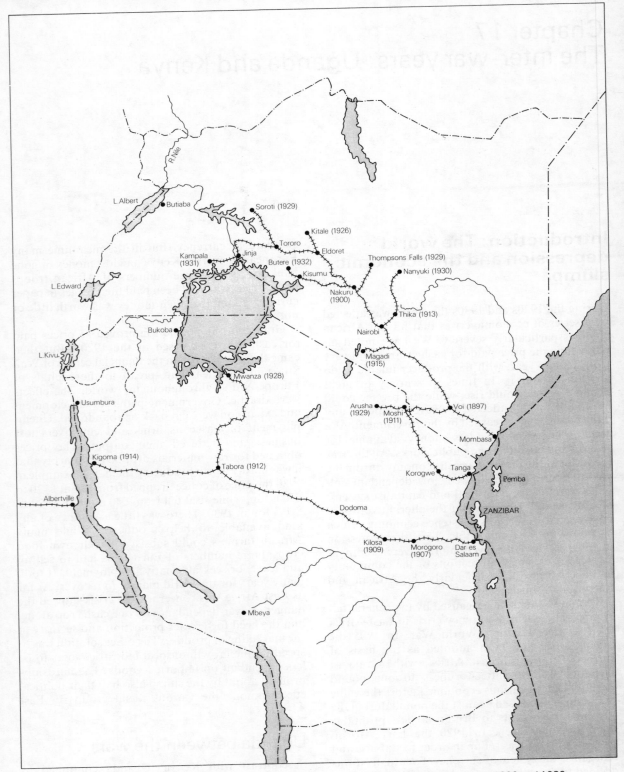

L.Albert
Butiaba
R.Nile
Soroti (1929)
Kitale (1926)
Tororo
Eldoret
Kampala (1931)
Jinja
Butere (1932)
Thompsons Falls (1929)
L.Edward
Kisumu
Nanyuki (1930)
Nakuru (1900)
Thika (1913)
Bukoba
Nairobi
L.Kivu
Magadi (1915)
Mwanza (1928)
Usumbura
Arusha (1929)
Moshi (1911)
Voi (1897)
Mombasa
Kigoma (1914)
Korogwe
Tanga
Tabora (1912)
Pemba
Albertville
ZANZIBAR
Dodoma
Kilosa (1909)
Morogoro (1907)
Dar es Salaam
Mbeya

Map 42 East Africa showing the development of communications and economic resources between 1900 and 1939

country, with an economy based on peasant agriculture. Buganda affairs tended to dominate the headlines and it was here that much of the political activity among Africans took place.

The administration

In 1921 the Governor, Sir Robert Coryndon, had established Executive and Legislative Councils for the Protectorate. The latter comprised five officials, including the Governor as chairman, and three unofficials, two Europeans and one Asian. The Governor was favourably inclined towards European settlement but resisted the Asian demand for equal representation with the Europeans. The Asians boycotted the Council until 1925, and eventually won their extra seat in 1933. No African was nominated until 1945. It is doubtful whether the Baganda, the most likely candidates, would have agreed to serve on the Council. They were determined to cling to their own institutions and not to acknowledge any others.

The Governor administered the Protectorate through his officials, Provincial and District Commissioners, though continuing to recognise the kingdoms and their rulers, but in theory more than

Fig. 17.1 Sir Robert Coryndon.

in practice. In Ankole, Toro and Bunyoro District Commissioners dealt directly with chiefs and agents in carrying out government business. An Agreement had been signed with Bunyoro in 1933 recognising the Omukama. At first the chiefs and agents were all government appointments, responsible directly to the British authorities. They had little local sympathy or following. As education increased and the training of chiefs improved the Baganda agents who had played such an important role were steadily replaced by local men. In the 1930s and '40s it was the deliberate policy of the Governors, notably Sir Philip Mitchell and Sir Charles Dundas, to select traditional leaders as chiefs rather than appoint outsiders. It was felt that only in this way could local government develop on a sound and popular basis. The same was done with District Councils which had been set up in order to recommend changes in customary laws and appropriate punishments for breaches of such laws.

The principal functions of the chiefs were:
1. To maintain law and order.
2. To regulate and control the consumption of alcohol.
3. To assist in the collection of taxes.
4. To recruit labour for public works.
5. To assist in the enforcement of government measures; this might cover anything from disease control to agricultural improvements.
6. To take part in the jurisdiction of the local Courts, within defined limits and subject to the District Commissioner's power of review and correction.

The District Comissioners played a large part in these functions, especially in the formative years. Therefore it was inevitably an authoritarian and paternal form of administration, without much opportunity for local discussion or initiative.

Developments in Buganda

The 1900 Agreement had apparently granted the Baganda a large measure of self-government. What is perhaps more important is that it encouraged them to feel that their's was a 'state within a state'. While it was true that they retained their Kabaka, Lukiko, Ministers and Chiefs, in practice the British officials tended to deal directly with the chiefs as in other parts of the Protectorate, and by-passed both the Kabaka and the Lukiko. This arose partly from the fact of the Kabaka's youth in the early years of the twentieth century when he played no direct part in public affairs. In 1914 Daudi Chwa came of age and the Regency came to an end, although Apolo Kagwa still retained the important office of Katikiro. But increasingly the Kabaka wished to take his rightful place in the government of his kingdom. He found, however, that Kagwa was reluctant to give way and that during the Regency the Lukiko and Bakungu chiefs had got used to having their own way. In addition his relationship with the Protectorate government was not at all easy, as we shall see. Three particular issues during this period will serve to highlight some of these problems.

1. The Bataka land claim

The Bataka were the clan heads, the trustees and guardians of their people, and as such an even older and more fundamental part of Baganda society than the Kabakaship itself. In the political changes of the late nineteenth and early twentieth centuries they had lost power to the new order of chiefs, the Bakungu. This had culminated in the distribution of 'mailo' land following the signing of the 1900 Agreement, which almost entirely ignored the rights and interests of the Bataka. In 1921 they formed the Bataka Association and appealed to the Kabaka to redress their grievances. He sympathised with them but was unable to persuade the Lukiko to make any concessions. The Bataka then asked the Protectorate government to intervene. A commission of enquiry was set up to investigate and recommended that land which had been unjustly taken should be returned to the rightful owners. However, when the matter was referred to the Colonial Secretary, L. S. Amery he decided that this would involve too many complications and the difficulty of compensation. The 'mailo' system had been in operation for twenty-five years already. Thus the losers were the Bataka and, indirectly, the Kabaka.

2. The fall of Apolo Kagwa

We have seen in Chapter 14 how Kagwa rose to power in Buganda as Regent and Katikiro, retaining his influence into the 1920s. He stood for the privileges and powers of the Bakungu who had done so well out of the Buganda Agreement. Thus he came directly into conflict with the Bataka over their land claim. He also found himself at odds with the Kabaka, for reasons already mentioned. But more seriously he began to disagree with the way in which the British officials dealt directly with the chiefs, claiming that in all matters apart from taxation the chiefs should work through the Kabaka and his Ministers. This tension came to a head in 1925 over a relatively minor issue, the granting of beer licenses in the 'Kibuga', which is the area around the Kabaka's palace. The Kibuga chief claimed that this was *his* duty and appealed to the Provincial Commissioner for support. Kagwa was extremely angry at this, but when the matter was referred to the Governor the authority of the Commissioner was upheld and Kagwa was humiliated. He promptly resigned. The significance of his fall from power was that it demonstrated how far Buganda was controlled by the Protectorate government, and how directly this authority could be exercised when necessary.

3. Taxation in Buganda

With the expansion of cotton and coffee cultivation Buganda's revenue and wealth grew steadily greater. This became a matter of increasing concern to the Protectorate government, first because of reported mismanagement and corruption within the Buganda Treasury, and secondly because it wished to increase its own share of the revenue from taxation. The Kabaka was persuaded to appoint a commission to look into the matter. In addition, the Governor was concerned about the Lukiko's attempts to raise additional revenue from taxation within the kingdom. According to the 1900 Agreement they were permitted to raise only two local taxes, the 'busulu' and the 'envujo'. The former originated in labour service that had in many cases been commuted for a payment of ten shillings; the latter was tribute in the form of food and beer. The Lukiko chiefs now wished to tax the cash crops being grown by their peasants, and introduced measures to do so on two occasions, in 1920 and 1926. The Governor rejected both attempts, using his power of veto. So here again we note the way in which the Protectorate Government could and did override the wishes of the Buganda Lukiko, in this case because it felt that it had to stand up for the interests of the peasant farmers who were not, of course, represented on the Lukiko. The outcome can also be seen as a setback for the Bakungu aristocracy of Buganda and a step towards greater independence for the peasantry.

Thus the political development of Buganda in this period illustrates the growing tensions between the various social classes and political groups, as well as those between the Buganda and Protectorate Governments. In 1935 the new Governor, Mitchell, reminded the Kabaka that he must act within the policies of the Protectorate Government and that in the last resort the latter must always prevail. On the other hand Mitchell was anxious to restore as much responsibility as possible to chiefs and councils throughout the Protectorate. In Buganda this led to

British officials being instructed by the Governor that they were to act in an advisory capacity as far as possible. As a token of this change the Provincial Commissioner for Buganda was renamed Resident, implying that his principal function was advice rather than administration. The policy was continued by Dundas, the next Governor.

The growth of African political opinion

African opinion was not roused into action by opposition to immigrant communities in the same way as in Kenya. Nevertheless matters involving the distribution of land often stirred up strong feelings and led to the formation of special groups, such as the Bataka Association. Traditional systems of land tenure were not based on individual ownership; land was the property of the community and could not be sold. However, land granted on the 'mailo' system was freehold, which meant that the owner could do what he liked with it. The difference between the two was all the more significant at a time when the value of land was increasing rapidly as a result of cash crops like cotton and coffee. The chiefs and ruling families in the other kingdoms tried to get the mailo system extended to their areas but without success. This created much bitterness, especially among the Busoga chiefs who had at first been offered a small concession.

Political opinion in Buganda was divided between the young educated men who felt that the Lukiko and system of land-ownership should be reformed, and those representing the Bakungu interests. But the Young Baganda Association was soon split by religious differences. A Luganda newspaper *Sekanyolya*, published in Nairobi, expressed strong criticism of the landed chiefs. Another occasion that revealed the sharp divisions within Buganda society was the remarriage of the Kabaka's widow in 1941. According to Baganda tradition the Queen Mother or 'Namasole' should never re-marry, and since the Katikiro, Nsibirwa, had assisted her to do so his resignation was demanded by the Lukiko. The Governor refused to intervene on behalf of the Katikiro and agreed to appoint whoever the chiefs chose to replace him. This policy of non-intervention appeared to many to be a failure, because it did not reform the political and social structure of Buganda. After 1945, however, the next Governor, Sir John Hall was to reverse this trend.

Economic development

In spite of the recommendations of a Development Commission report in 1920, described by one

Fig. 17.2 Boys handling cotton in Uganda.

historian as a 'Planters' Charter', and the pro-settler views of the Governor of that time, Sir Robert Coryndon, Uganda's agricultural economy continued to be based on peasant cultivation. Cotton and coffee were the basic cash crops grown by Africans and they continued to head the list of exports. The world depression of the early 1920s may have played a part in discouraging settler participation in Uganda but there were others prepared to try out new ideas.

Sugar was first produced on a commercial scale in the 1920s by an Indian, Nanji Kalidas Mehta, who acquired 2 000 hectares (5 000 acres) of land around Lugazi in east Buganda in 1924. The following year he built a sugar factory capable of producing refined sugar and, as a by-product, industrial alcohol. By 1926 he was producing about 4 000 tonnes per season. Another sugar estate and factory was opened up at Kakira in Busoga by Muljibhai Madhvani. The great advantage of growing sugar was that it found a ready local market and was not therefore subject to the fluctuations of the world price.

Tea and tobacco were also started in the 1930s, the first by Asians, with a limited area in order to comply with international arrangements; the second largely by Africans in Bunyoro, Kigezi and the West Nile. By 1945 tobacco had become the third major export crop. Much of the success for these and other products was due to the research and investigation carried out by the Department of Agriculture. Its scientific and technical staff experimented with new strains, traced the causes of disease and analysed soil samples in such a way as to increase both the quality and quantity of the country's natural resources.

Further improvements in transport and communications continued, so that by 1932 there were 2 900 kilometres (1 800 miles) of good main road in Uganda, linking the main towns and market centres. In 1931 the railway was extended to Kampala, crossing the Nile at Jinja. The processing and marketing of agricultural produce remained in the hands of Asian and European firms. Thus the African producer was often at the mercy of those who bought his raw cotton or coffee, and needed the protection of a cooperative organisation. However, little government encouragement was given at this time to African participation in trade or marketing.

Kenya: growth of political movements

In 1920 the British Government changed the name of its East African Protectorate to Kenya Colony. Although this was in one sense a mere formality it did reflect the increasingly important part that the European community was coming to play in public affairs. This had become evident during the First World War, when the settlers made a significant contribution to the war effort. Col. Grogan, one of their leaders, had taken the initiative in setting up the War Council to coordinate the country's resources and manpower. The government recognised this and was prepared to give the settlers a greater share of responsibility. Since 1907 they had been represented on the Legislative Council; they were promised elected representatives in 1920, and in 1918 they were given seats on the Executive Council. In its policies on land and labour the Government appeared to be doing all it could to satisfy the demands of the settlers. In fact, it appeared in 1920 as though the settlers were going to have everything their own way.

However, the British Government was faced with a dilemma. On the one hand it had encouraged Europeans to settle and make their home here, on the other hand it was becoming increasingly aware of its position as the trustee or guardian of the African inhabitants. There was much discussion and thought at this time about the policy of trusteeship; it had been stressed in the League of Nations and proclaimed by men such as Lord Lugard. It led to a new awareness of the functions of colonial powers, and an increase in the provision of medical, educational and other social services. As far as Kenya was concerned the Government found itself confronted with the demands of political organisations representing the three races—African, Asian and European. To reconcile these was not an easy task for the Governors appointed to Kenya between the wars. Some tended to favour the settlers, others tried to be impartial. But the interaction of the racial communities played a major part in the development of political movements and leaders in Kenya. We shall examine these groups in this chapter and show how the Government reacted to this situation.

The growth of political opinion in Kenya

1. European

This was dominated by the interests of the settlers and led by such aggressive characters as Col. Grogan and Lord Delamere. The Europeans were the first to organise themselves into a political group. Earlier attempts had led to the setting up of the Convention of Associations in 1911 and this became the main platform for their views. In 1920 they were granted the right to elect eleven members to the Legislative Council, an advantage that neither of the other communities yet enjoyed. Their principal aims were simply to make Kenya into a self-governing dominion within the Empire under white control, and to retain the Highlands for their own exclusive occupation. This would mean increasing their role and influence in government and excluding other races from similar participation. They therefore opposed the Asian demands for 'parity' in political as well as other matters. They argued that Asian immigration ought to be restricted, and that schools and hospitals should be racially segregated. They also opposed the encouragement of African cultivation of cash crops, believing that it would lower the quality of Kenya's produce and, more significant, draw off their supplies of labour. All these views were summed up in the two words 'separate development', a policy that would recognise and protect the civilisation that they had brought to East Africa and which the other communities could learn from and follow. Two particular issues, land and labour, illustrate the attitude and assumptions of the settlers and we shall refer to these later in the chapter.

2. Asian

Compelled of necessity to live in the towns the Asian community developed their own social and cultural organisations in these centres. In the East African Indian National Congress they combined to present their grievances to the Government, and were often able to secure the active support of the British Government in India. Among their leaders in Kenya was A. M. Jeevanjee. Their complaints were aimed principally at the European settler community whom they far outnumbered, and with whom they demanded parity, or equality, in matters of politics and economic opportunity. They felt particularly strongly about their exclusion from the Highlands, and also about the various forms of segregation. On the whole they did not find common cause with African groups, although individuals such as Makhan Singh did much for the early Trade Union movement.

3. African

African opinion did not begin to make itself felt until the 1920s when, as a result of the war and closer contact with European culture and life, various groups formed to press for their own needs.

At first they were inevitably local and tribal, moderate rather than extreme in their aims. In 1920 the Kikuyu Association was formed, consisting of a number of chiefs and headmen, led by Chief Koinange. Not content with this the younger Kikuyu, under Harry Thuku, formed the more militant Young Kikuyu Association the following year. They demanded the withdrawal of the 'Kipande' or identity card that Africans were obliged by law to carry with them, a cut in the Poll Tax, better labour conditions and the return of Kikuyu land. Thuku was arrested and deported to Kismayu in 1922 but the movement continued under the name of The Kikuyu Central Association. In 1922 a group of young men, 'graduates' of the C.M.S. school at Maseno, formed the Young Kavirondo Association. They too had worries about the security of their land, fearing that part of it might be alienated. They were resentful about the system of taxation and the Kipande. But after 1923, when it was reorganised by Archdeacon Owen as the Kavirondo Taxpayers Welfare Association, the movement lost its militancy.

In 1928 the Scottish Mission's attempt to stamp out the custom of female circumcision among the Kikuyu aroused great resentment. The K.C.A. was provoked into action, defending Kikuyu traditional life and culture against the alien attitude of Europeans. Prominent in this controversy was Jomo Kenyatta, first editor of the official K.C.A. publication *Muigwithania* and General Secretary of the Association. One of the consequences of this clash with the Missions was the starting of the Independent Schools Movement by the Kikuyu. From these schools were to come some of the most outspoken critics of the Europeans and of colonial rule. It will be noted that much of the political activity among Africans at this time was centred around the Kikuyu. This is hardly surprising, since they were the ones most directly involved with the Europeans over the issue of land and closest to the heart and centre of European influence, Nairobi.

The 1930s saw the formation of various other African organisations, intended largely to protest about particular issues. Thus the North Kavirondo Association was the Baluhya response to the alienation of their land at Kakamega, following the discovery of gold in 1931. The Ukamba Members Association objected to the Government's methods of reducing the number of their cattle in an attempt to prevent over grazing. These were local and limited, but there began to be more contact and exchange between the leaders of these groups. They often differed in age, background and outlook but were beginning to share a common nationalist ambition and hope. In 1944 Eliud Mathu was nominated the first African member of Legislative Council and in order to provide him with the widest possible support the Kenya African Union was founded that year, with Thuku as its first President.

The Devonshire White Paper, 1923

The rivalry between the Asian and European communities over the issues of land and political representation led to the summoning of a conference in London by the Colonial Secretary, the Duke of Devonshire, in 1923. Afterwards a White Paper, a statement of Government policy, was issued, setting out the Government's intentions and attitudes towards the three racial groups.

1. It declared that Kenya was primarily an African territory and that the interests of the Africans must remain paramount. The British Government had a trust and responsibility to protect and ensure the welfare of these people.
2. It recognised the contribution made by the European community to Kenya's development, but made it clear that there could be no further advance towards self-government under European rule alone. All races must eventually participate. However, it did accept that the Highlands were to be reserved for European occupation.
3. The Asians were to be granted five elected seats on the Legislative Council, and elected representatives on municipal councils. But these were to be arranged on a communal rather than a common electoral roll. In other words, each race would elect separate representatives, so that the Asians would not be able to out-vote the Europeans. There was to be no restriction on Indian immigration and no segregation in residential areas. On the other hand, Asians were still not permitted to acquire land in the Highlands.

This was a turning point in the Colony's development. It pleased neither the Europeans nor the Asians. The former saw that they would never be able to achieve their goal of self-government, something that their compatriots in Rhodesia were to achieve in that same year. The Asians were bitterly disappointed at their failure to acquire 'parity' with the Europeans and refused to take up their seats on the Legislative Council until 1933. The Africans, who had not been represented at the conference, were in a sense the main beneficiaries. Although not granted a voice in Government, except through a nominated European (Dr Arthur) from 1924, their

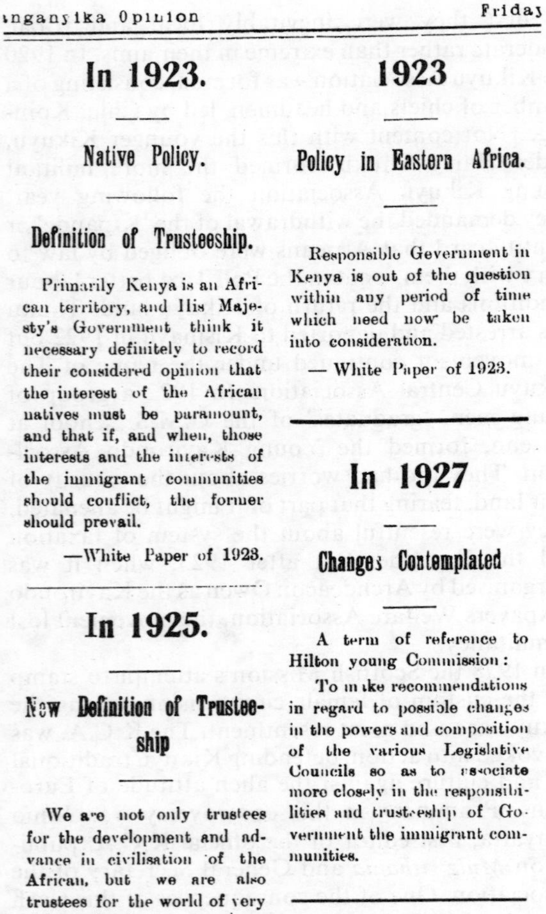
nganyika Opinion — Friday

In 1923.

Native Policy.

Definition of Trusteeship.

Primarily Kenya is an African territory, and His Majesty's Government think it necessary definitely to record their considered opinion that the interest of the African natives must be paramount, and that if, and when, those interests and the interests of the immigrant communities should conflict, the former should prevail.

—White Paper of 1923.

In 1925.

New Definition of Trusteeship

We are not only trustees for the development and advance in civilisation of the African, but we are also trustees for the world of very rich territories.

In fact the development of the community sense is one of its paramount tasks.

—Ormsby Gore Commission Report.

In 1929.

Trusteeship Exploded.

There is an obligation to the natives, and there is also an obligation to the immigrant Communities, neither of which can be ignored.

-- Hilton Young Commission Report.

1923

Policy in Eastern Africa.

Responsible Government in Kenya is out of the question within any period of time which need now be taken into consideration.

— White Paper of 1923.

In 1927

Changes Contemplated

A term of reference to Hilton young Commission:

To make recommendations in regard to possible changes in the powers and composition of the various Legislative Councils so as to associate more closely in the responsibilities and trusteeship of Government the immigrant communities.

In 1929

Changes Advised

In my opinion such a form of Government (self-govt.), and an elected majority, for Kenya, or for any one of the local Governments, is perfectly reconcilable with our general scheme for the constitution of the Eastern African territories.

— Sir Hilton young. Chairman of Closer Union Commission.

Fig. 17.3 Newspaper extracts which reflect some of the views of the time.

leaders were given a guarantee of future intentions and a foundation for their hopes and claims in the years ahead. But it did not resolve either of their two major grievances, labour and land.

The issue of labour

The basic regulations covering the recruitment of African labour for public works and work on European farms had been laid down in the Master and Servant Ordinance of 1906. But the chief difficulty lay in encouraging sufficient men to volunteer for such work. So long as his livelihood was based on a subsistence economy the African saw no purpose or gain in leaving his home. This was one of the Government's motives in introducing the Poll Tax, to make the Africans earn money in order to pay their taxes. The general transition to a cash economy also induced Africans to seek additional ways of earning money. Nor were the opportunities for earning money in the Reserves sufficiently attractive. Thus the only alternatives were to migrate and become a squatter on European farms, or work for a period away from home every year.

Fig. 17.4 A Wagogo labourer in Tanzania carries a work card in his ear.

It was the pressures that settlers and certain officials brought to bear on Africans that caused much hardship and suffering. Two further regulations made this even worse. In 1919 the new Governor, General Northey, instructed his Chief Native Commissioner to issue a circular to all government officials stressing the urgent need to increase the labour force by all possible lawful means. This 'Northey Circular' was framed in such a way as to put strong pressure on chiefs and other officials to produce their quota of recruits. The circular aroused much criticism among missionaries, and in Britain. Even more controversial was the enforcement in 1920 of the regulation that all male Africans over sixteen must carry a Kipande, an identity card contained in a metal box. Failure to produce it was a punishable offence. The idea behind this was to make it more difficult for labourers to desert their employer. One advantage for the bearer was that when he had completed his work this would be recorded on his card, thus protecting him from unscrupulous chiefs and recruiting agents. However, to most Africans the Kipande became a badge of servitude, and a major cause of discontent.

Land

Ever since land had first been alienated for European settlement in Kenya it had been a cause of tension and division between the races. Africans felt that they had been deprived of their birth-right, while Asians were bitter about discrimination in favour of the settlers. To make matters worse there was much misunderstanding over the basic issues of land tenure and land use. To Africans land was traditionally owned by the tribe or clan and could not be disposed of without their general consent; to the European land was a matter of individual ownership, with the right to sell or dispose as he pleased. And again, African land-use, whether nomadic pastoralism or shifting agriculture, meant that there would be periods when parts of their land were left unoccupied or uncultivated; to the European this appeared to be vacant and empty land. These differences were made worse by government regulations concerning land.

Land had first been divided into racial and tribal areas, the 'White' Highlands and the African Reserves, with much of the best land going to the Europeans. The 1915 Crown Lands Ordinance had increased African insecurity by making the Reserves Crown land and the inhabitants tenants-at-will who could, therefore, be evicted. At the same time it pleased the settlers by extending their leases to nine hundred and ninety-nine year periods. In response to African unrest it was agreed in 1926 to define the boundaries of the Reserves and to declare that such land could only be alienated by consent of the local authority and the Colonial Secretary in London. However this did not appear to mean much, for in 1931 when gold was discovered at Kakamega the law was hastily amended to enable the Government to alienate land in Reserves where minerals were found.

Meanwhile the increasing pressure of population growth within the Reserves indicated that land available for African use would soon be totally inadequate. In 1932 a Land Commission under Sir William Morris Carter was appointed to investigate African grievances and to define the limits of European settlement areas. Two years later it submitted its report. As a result the Reserves were extended by more than 6 760 sq. kilometres (2 600 sq. miles) and declared Native Land under the control of a Native Lands Trust Board. The area of the 'White Highlands' was extended from 28 890 (10 345) to 43 420 kilometres (16 700 sq. miles) of which 10 400 kilometres (4 000 miles) was forest reserve. This might have appeared satisfactory for the settlers and officials but it was far from answering the African demands. It meant that the Reserves could do little more than produce subsistence crops, and so offered no incentive for progressive and enterprising development. Many Africans were doomed to remain as squatters and labourers on European farms. Thus the seeds of discontent remained and grew.

Economic development

In spite of the set-backs caused by the economic crises of the 1920s and 1930s agricultural production increased during the inter-war years. Much of the emphasis on research and development was directed towards the European areas, and Africans were correspondingly neglected. Coffee and sisal became the main plantation crops by 1929, accounting for 51 % of the total exports. Increasing reliance was placed upon maize, since there was a ready local demand and thus it did not suffer from the fluctuations in world prices. It was also becoming a staple food crop for Africans, who were at last allowed to grow coffee on a small scale in the Meru and Kisii areas. Cotton production in Nyanza increased steadily. On European farms beef and dairy cattle opened up new markets and local industries. This growing diversity in agriculture was increased further by the introduction, in the 1930s,

of tea and pyrethrum in the highlands. Much of the marketing of these crops was in the hands of Europeans, the Kenya Farmers Association playing a prominent role.

A loan of thirteen and a half million pounds from the British Government enabled new branch lines and extensions to be made to the railway system. Nanyuki, Nyahururu (Thomsons Falls), Solai, Kitale and Butere were all linked to the main line, while the extension from Nakuru to Jinja in Uganda was completed between 1921 and 1928. Roads were also improved and extended. The greater part of this improvement in communications was intended primarily for the European areas of settlement. This bias towards European production and development was pointed out and criticised in a financial report made by Lord Moyne at the request of the Government in 1932. He recommended greater emphasis on and encouragement for African agriculture, with better services and amenities in the Reserves. He pointed out that the African population contributed $37\frac{1}{2}\%$ of the colony's total revenue in direct taxation, while the non-Africans were paying less than their share. In addition, the African was getting far less for his money in the form of services than the European and Asian. The Moyne Report was not liked by the settlers but it did lead the Colonial Office to recognise the need for some form of direct taxation on non-Africans.

Education

By the 1920s the need for education was becoming evident to many Africans. Not only was it the gateway to material rewards and benefits, but it provided the means of presenting their grievances and challenging the political ambitions of the other communities. The only way of acquiring education in the early years was to attend a mission school, and this explains why so many of the first generation of modern African leaders shared a common background. Mission education tended to stress the superiority of academic over practical training and was, of course, strongly European in content. An important step towards defining the needs for a more African type of education was taken when the Government in Britain set up the Phelps-Stokes Commission in 1924. In its report it stressed the need for agricultural and practical courses with relevance for rural life. One result of this was the establishment of the Jeanes School at Kabete in 1925, intended to train supervisors for local schools. Africans, however, saw the need for more than this and pressed for further academic education. In 1926 the main Protestant Missions combined to found The Alliance High School which became the first secondary school for Africans in the country. Similar schools developed at Kabaa (Holy Ghost Fathers) and at Maseno (C.M.S.). Thus a start had been made, although for many years African education lagged behind the European and Asian schools in numbers and facilities.

Questions

1. Explain why Uganda did not become a 'White Man's Country'.
2. Why were the relations between the Buganda and Protectorate Governments so strained between 1920 and 1939?
3. Compare the contributions made by Africans to the economic development of Kenya and Uganda between the two World Wars.
4. Trace the growth of African political movements in Kenya from 1920 to 1944; how far did they succeed?
5. Show the significance of *either* the Devonshire White Paper *or* The Carter Land Commission in the development of Kenya.

Activities

1. Find out all you can about the development of one major cash crop in your area (where and when it was first introduced, who by, how it was grown, marketed and exported).
2. Describe the conduct of a typical 'baraza' by a local chief in your area in the 1920s or '30s. What problems would have been raised and what topics would have been discussed?

Chapter 18
Closer union in East Africa

Introduction

Ever since 1898 it had been suggested that closer union within East Africa was both practicable and desirable. When Johnston went to Uganda in 1899 he had been told to bear in mind the possibility of merging the two British Protectorates. After his retirement in 1905 Sir Charles Eliot had pointed out the advisability of doing so as soon as possible, 'for the longer they remain apart the more they tend to become different in administrative systems and regulations'. The truth of this statement was to be borne out in the years ahead. But the British Government hesitated and delayed, and with each passing year the development of its East African territories became more divergent. However, the idea was revived with the acquisition of Tanganyika after the First World War. Winston Churchill, when Colonial Secretary in 1922, declared that he looked forward to the day when 'a great East African Federation, almost an empire' would be established. The idea was enthusiastically followed up by his successor, L. S. Amery, in 1924.

In that year a Commission under the chairmanship of the Hon. W. Ormsby-Gore was sent out from Britain to study and report on the possibility of closer union and coordination in East Africa. It found a general dislike of closer union from most sections of the population and recommended that while political union was not possible for the time being there should be, through the medium of regular Governors Conferences, a move towards cooperation in matters of common interest. These included railways and harbours, posts and telegraphs, agriculture and health. It emphasised that any moves towards federation must come from within East Africa and should not be imposed from without. What, then, were the feelings of the various East African communities?

The attitudes of East Africans towards closer union
1. Uganda

The feeling here was expressed largely by the leaders in Buganda. They were opposed to it from the start, fearing that it would threaten the special status and security they enjoyed as a result of the 1900 Agreement. Africans in Uganda were generally apprehensive of any move that might place them under the dominance of the settlers in Kenya. So sensitive were the Baganda about anything to do with federation that when many years later, in 1953, the Colonial Secretary made a reference to the possibility of an East African Federation, there was an immediate outcry that culminated in the deportation of the Kabaka.

2. Tanganyika

Here the most outspoken critic of federation was the Governor, Sir Donald Cameron. He was particularly annoyed at the attempt made by the Governors of Kenya and Uganda in 1926 to stop the building of a rail link between Tabora and Mwanza, which would inevitably take away some of the trade and traffic that went through Uganda and Kenya. Cameron even threatened to resign if the suggestion was put into effect. The British Government realised that its mandate in Tanganyika made it responsible to the League of Nations, and there could well be strong condemnation of any move seen to threaten the well-being of the African population. For these reasons opinion in Tanganyika was not in favour of closer union.

3. Kenya

At first most people opposed the scheme, including

the settlers. African leaders feared that it would interfere with their demands for representation on the Legislative Council. However, European feeling began to change, particularly after Lord Delamere had convened a meeting at Tukuyu in southern Tanganyika of settler representatives from East and Central Africa. It was realised that there might be much to gain from the federation, provided they had a major voice in government and in its policies. The Kenya settlers became keen supporters of the idea, and were encouraged by the appointment of Sir Edward Grigg as Governor. He had been instructed by the British Government to prepare plans for a federal union. In 1927 his committee on closer union reported that the scheme could be implemented, pointing out that the boundaries between the three territories were in any case artificial and that there would be much to gain by coordinating the resources of East Africa.

A change of policy towards economic cooperation rather than federation

In spite of doubts and opposition from many quarters within East Africa the British Government pressed ahead with its ideas. In 1928 yet another survey was made, by the Hilton Young Commission; it came to the conclusion that while a complete political federation was not possible a High Commissioner for East Africa should be appointed with power to control the policies affecting the African population and to issue directives on certain matters to the three Governors. But this came to nothing and was not supported by the settlers.

After a number of further investigations and reports the idea of federation was finally dropped in the 1930s. However, it had been made clear that there was scope for much closer coordination in economic and social affairs, and it was along these lines that the Governors conferences developed. From 1930 they met annually. Already in 1920 an East African Currency Board had been set up, and by 1930 railways, customs, defence, posts and telegraphs were shared, at least between Kenya and Uganda. All three territories came to adopt a common system of tariffs and there was a move towards standardising policies on African taxation, elementary education, communications and industry. All these matters were dealt with by Govern-

ment officials from the three territories, so that there was, as yet, little communication between unofficials. During the Second World War there was a Joint Economic Council for East and Central Africa, with its own secretariat, to share the resources available and contribute to the war effort. A number of other bodies were also set up to deal with supplies, research and development and refugees. Although this lasted only for the duration of the war it did give greater encouragement to the idea of some form of union.

The formation of the East African High Commission

In 1945 the Colonial Secretary, Mr Creech-Jones, put forward proposals for the establishment of an East African High Commission. It was to have limited and defined powers and its functions would bring together all the services already shared in common. There was strong feeling in East Africa about the racial composition of any legislative body that might be set up as part of the organisation, and this affected the final proposals. It was emphasised that this would not lead to a federation and that each territory would retain its existing forms of government. The East African High Commission came into being in 1948, with its headquarters in Nairobi.

The Commission consisted of the three Governors, together with an executive organisation headed by the Commissioner, and a legislative body with powers to make laws affecting the matters over which it had control. The members of the legislature were to be chosen by the three countries on a racial basis, some being elected while others were nominated. The powers of the High Commission were limited. It had no direct source of revenue and depended for its income on grants from each member state. It had no police force of its own, and no courts or power to enforce laws of its own, apart from the regulations mentioned above. Moreover its activities would depend on the unanimous support of the three Governors, any one of whom could exercise the power of veto.

In spite of these limitations the High Commission proved to be an effective and useful body, combining and coordinating a wide range of functions. These included:
East African Railways and Harbours
East African Posts and Telegraphs
East African Customs and Excise

East African Income Tax department
Defence: Army and Navy
Civil Aviation Directorate
Research institutions: Medical, Veterinary, Agricultural, etc.
East African Literature Bureau.
Higher Education: Makerere College.

Questions

1. Why was the British Government reluctant to establish an East African Federation during the period 1900 to 1939?
2. Compare the attitudes of the European settlers in Kenya and the African rulers in Uganda towards the issue of Federation between 1920 and 1960.
3. What steps were taken after 1945 to bring the East African territories closer together; how far had this been taken by 1960?

Activities

1. Arrange a class debate on the topic of closer union in East Africa, comparing the present-day reasons for and against with those used in the 1929–40 period.
2. Make a list of the principal benefits produced as a result of the establishment of the East African High Commission.

Chapter 19
The struggle for Independence, 1945–1963

Introduction: The outcome of the second world war

The Second World War started as a European struggle between Germany and Italy on the one hand and Britain and France on the other. But it soon involved other major powers including the U.S.A., Russia and Japan. The fighting took place in Europe, North Africa, Ethiopia and Somaliland, Burma and South East Asia and in the Pacific. It lasted from 1939 to 1945. East Africa was not invaded or attacked, although the Italian occupation of Ethiopia and Somaliland did threaten the northern frontier in the early period. Troops from South Africa joined African and British soldiers in Kenya under the command of General Cunningham who launched an offensive against the Italians in 1941 and drove them out of Ethiopia. African troops also served in Madagascar and Burma.

These African soldiers learnt a great deal from the war. By travelling to other continents and countries, by fighting alongside soldiers from India, Australia, South and West Africa, they acquired a new confidence and awareness of their position in the world. They were told that this was a war against oppression and dictatorship, to secure freedom and independence for all. It was hardly surprising, therefore, that they should carry these ideas back with them and apply them to their own situation. Many of them learnt, or already knew, how to read. Their return to East Africa after the war gave fresh impetus and force to African political movements.

The close of the war brought another important change, reflected in the aims and ideals of the newly formed United Nations Organisation. This was the body that took the place of the League of Nations and took over the latter's responsibility for the mandated territories. There was a strong anti-colonial sentiment among many member states, including the new super-powers Russia and the U.S.A. The United Nations Charter stated that all peoples of the world had the right to choose their own form of government. This was now seen to apply to all countries, including colonies. Consequently pressure was brought to bear on those powers with overseas possessions, notably Britain and France.

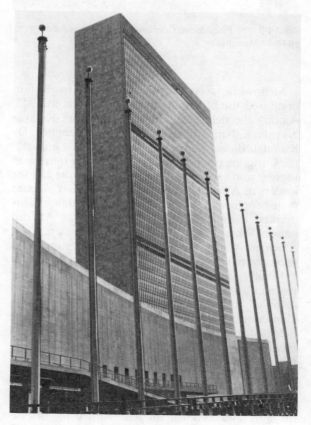

Fig. 19.1 The United Nations Building, New York.

163

Fig. 19.2 The Pan African Conference, 10th November 1945, in Manchester.

Meanwhile certain African leaders in Britain organised the fifth Pan African Congress in 1945. Among the delegates who attended were Kwame Nkrumah, Nnamdi Azikiwe, Leopold Senghor, Dr Kamuzu Banda and Jomo Kenyatta. Not only did the Congress provide an opportunity for these men to meet and exchange ideas but it led to the call for leaders of African opinion to organise and prepare their people for the struggle for independence. This marked a new phase in the growth of African nationalism; it was the first serious attempt by educated African patriots to rally mass support in their campaign.

Finally there were significant changes taking place in Britain itself that were to affect the African colonies. In the General Election of 1945 the Conservative party leader, Winston Churchill, was defeated and a Socialist government, led by Clement Attlee, took over. The Socialists were committed to the decolonisation of the British Empire, and by 1947 they had already granted independence to India and Pakistan. Then there was the economic and financial crisis facing the country, exhausted by the war. Thus, even if she had wanted to, Britain would not have been able to maintain her Empire

and role as a major world power. All these forces, political and economic, external and internal, led to the disintegration of the Empire and the achievement of self-government by the colonies. The first to do so in East Africa was Tanganyika.

The preparation of Tanganyika for self-government

Under the new United Nations Organisation Tanganyika became the responsibility of the Trusteeship Council. While Britain continued as the administering power the Council took a much more positive and active interest in this and the other former mandate territories. At regular intervals missions were sent out to check on progress and listen to grievances. Their reports were used to bring pressure on Britain to hasten political and constitutional change. The Council's activities also gave much publicity to the situation and needs of the territory. Thus Britain was being constantly urged to prepare the people of Tanganyika for eventual self-government, and this was one of the reasons why it was the first of the East African states to achieve independence.

First steps towards self-government

The march towards independence took two main stages, the first in the decade after 1945. The British officials still believed that change could best come through the development of traditional authorities. This was supported by a U.N.O. declaration in 1947 that the consolidation of tribal constitutional authority was the first essential step in the process of development towards self-government. Sir Edward Twining, who became Governor in 1949, decided that the people of Tanganyika should be trained in stages, moving from one to the next only when the British Government considered they were ready. In 1949 he set up a committee to examine and recommend what constitutional advance should be made. It reported in 1951, stating that while self-government must be the ultimate goal this should come gradually. Africans were not considered ready for full participation in the work of government, nor were they even ready for elections, and therefore the Governor should continue to nominate their representatives to Legislative Council. The committee went on to suggest that the Legislative

Council should retain its official majority but that the unofficial seats should be divided equally between the three races. This did not satisfy the Tanganyika African Association which had been pressing for either an African majority of unofficials, or at least a number equal to all other races combined. The idea of equal racial representation was reaffirmed by Professor Mackenzie who had been asked by the Government in 1953 to re-examine the situation. Although he did not consider Africans were ready he recommended that the Government ought to aim at having elections for unofficial members on a common roll basis. He also proposed that each constituency should have three members, one for each race. These proposals came into effect in 1955 with the new Legislative Council containing thirty-one official and thirty unofficial members. Two more Africans were nominated to the Executive Council, bringing their total to three.

The scheme for gradual development was doomed to failure. Not only had the traditional authorities lost much of their local respect and influence but the younger generation of educated leaders opposed them and showed, to the surprise of the British authorities, an ability to understand the issues involved and to organise themselves effectively. The Government failed to recognise the significance of these men and treated them merely as troublemakers. But by 1954 they had to face the fact that they must come to terms with these new political leaders and abandon their old policies.

Fig. 19.3 Julius Nyerere.

The birth of T.A.N.U.

The background to the emergence of the Tanganyika African Association has been mentioned in Chapter 16. Soon after his return from university in Britain in 1953 Julius Nyerere was elected President of T.A.A. Nyerere was one of the new men in African politics. As the son of a chief he had been sent to Tabora school to be educated and had then gone on to Makerere College in Uganda where he secured a scholarship to Edinburgh University. On becoming President of T.A.A. he was determined to turn it into a country-wide political party with which to fight for independence. At a meeting in Dar es Salaam on July 7, 1954 the Association's name was changed to Tanganyika African National Union, emphasising the task of uniting the country behind the nationalist movement. To mark this important anniversary Tanzania now observes July 7 (Saba Saba) as a National holiday.

The size of the country and the lack of adequate transport made the work of the T.A.N.U. leaders extremely difficult. It took time and effort to tour the country, establish branches and coordinate the support of their followers. Their clear call for independence upset the Government's plans for a more cautious advance to self-government and therefore aroused its hostility. Some T.A.N.U. members even went as far as denouncing government schemes for agricultural improvement and pest control. This discredited the Party and led to some of its meetings being banned. But Nyerere's policy was quite straightforward and did not include support for such senseless acts. He declared that T.A.N.U. would not follow a racialist policy, and that Europeans and Asians would not suffer after independence. However, he made it clear that Tanganyika was primarily African, although multi-racial, and must therefore have an African majority government. It was largely due to the leadership and example of Julius Nyerere and Oscar Kambona that T.A.N.U. flourished as a truly national party. Kambona became the party's Secretary General, a post he held until he left the country in 1967. The movement grew in strength and popularity.

The U.N. visiting mission that came in 1954 was impressed by the enthusiasm and determination of

Fig. 19.4 Oscar Kambona.

The 1958–59 elections and responsible government

Now that political parties were established the Government accepted the fact that elections should be held for the Legislative Council. They were to take place in two stages, in 1958 and 1959, this being considered more convenient and manageable. They were based on the earlier recommendation that each constituency should have three members, one for each race. T.A.N.U. put up three candidates of different races for each seat and urged its members to vote for the non-African candidates as well. In this way it not only won a landslide victory over its opponents but showed that it was a truly national and non-racial party. The African National Congress, formed by a breakaway group from T.A.N.U., and the U.T.P. could not compete in the face of such success and before long had disbanded. This early victory by a strong national party saved Tanganyika from the divisions and differences that held up the political movements in Kenya and Uganda.

Another factor that quickened Tanganyika's advance to independence was the appointment of Sir Richard Turnbull as Governor in July 1958. He had served as Chief Secretary in Kenya during the Emergency and appreciated that slow progress towards self-government could create violence. He saw no reason why this should happen in Tanganyika and took rapid action to reassure the African leaders that he meant what he said. He was the first Governor to declare publicly that the Africans would be predominant in a self-governing Tanganyika. In May 1959 he introduced a Council of Ministers five of whom were elected members of Legislative Council. A committee under Sir Richard Ramage was then set up to plan the next constitutional advance. It recommended an enlarged Legislative Council with seventy-one elected members and a smaller number of nominated members, ten seats being reserved for Europeans, eleven for Asians and fifty open to all. It also proposed that the Executive Council should be replaced by a Council of Ministers, a majority of whom should be elected. The franchise should be extended to all literate adults or those with an average annual income of at least £75. It was felt by T.A.N.U. that this might, in areas where illiteracy was high, disqualify too large a number of people. They preferred universal adult suffrage which means 'one man one vote'. But Nyerere persuaded his followers to accept these proposals as a step forward. The Governor announced at the end of 1959 that

the party leaders who presented their case. In its report the mission proposed a planned constitutional advance towards independence over the next twenty to twenty-five years. In fact, independence was to come within seven years, with a speed that must have taken even Nyerere by surprise. He visited the United Nations in New York in 1955 and on several other occasions to explain his aims and press for support. He won much sympathy and respect.

In 1956 a new party emerged to challenge T.A.N.U. This was the United Tanganyika Party, claiming to follow a genuinely multi-racial policy and supported by many non-Africans in public life. But T.A.N.U.'s size and popularity were by now almost overwhelming. In 1957 when Nyerere was first appointed to Legislative Council the party demanded independence within two years. Nyerere resigned his seat when his demand for 'one man one vote' was rejected.

responsible government would be achieved in 1960.

This meant that although the country would not yet be fully independent the elected representatives of the people would effectively control most of the functions of government. It was the final stage before independence. In the 1960 elections T.A.N.U. won seventy of the seventy-one seats. Nyerere then became the First Minister and chose nine members of his party to join him on the Council of Ministers, three Europeans being nominated in addition. Nyerere called for independence in 1961, undertook to Africanise the civil service introducing a special training scheme to accelerate the changeover, and repeated his declaration that people of other races were welcome to remain provided they accepted the new government and played their part in nation building.

The attainment of Independence

In March 1961 the Colonial Secretary, Ian Macleod, attended a conference in Dar es Salaam to work out the final timetable for independence. On May 1st full internal self-government was achieved, so that only foreign affairs, defence and the police force remained in the hands of the British authorities. Now the Legislative Council assumed its new name of National Assembly, the Council of Ministers becoming the Cabinet and the Chief Minister was now Prime Minister. Among the outstanding problems to be resolved before the final date for independence was Tanganyika's relationship with the other East African states, and particularly the East African High Commission. It was decided that the latter should be re-formed as the Common Services Organisation, the three Governors being replaced by the Chief Ministers of the three states. Nyerere also made a statesman-like offer to delay Tanganyika's independence if this would help the cause of East African unity. But it did not succeed and so, on December 9th 1961 the Duke of Edinburgh on behalf of the Queen handed over the reins of power to the elected leaders of the people in a colourful midnight ceremony.

To assist in the immediate task of overcoming the problems of poverty, ignorance and disease the country needed aid. Britain, the U.S.A., European states and U.N.O. agencies gave promises of assistance. Tanganyika remained within the Commonwealth, though only after it had made clear that it would not sit alongside South Africa. The latter withdrew from the Commonwealth shortly afterwards. In its foreign policy Tanganyika stood as a non-aligned member of the United Nations.

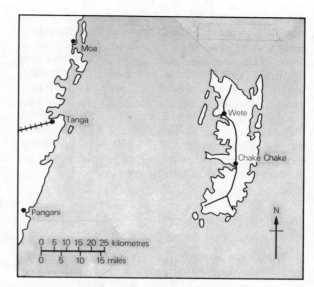

Map 43 Pemba Island

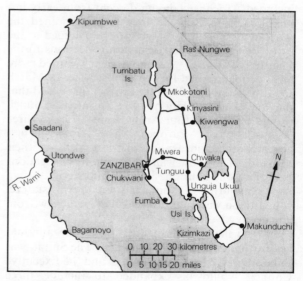

Map 44 Zanzibar Island

Constitutional development in Zanzibar

Throughout the colonial period the British regarded the Arabs as traditional rulers of the island. In contrast to the mainland, life on Zanzibar and Pemba appeared quiet and placid, at least on the surface. No doubt the system of indirect rule suited both the British and the Sultan, Khalifa II. As A. J. Hughes describes the situation, 'For over half a century this amiable ruler enjoyed the pomp and

167

circumstance of his position, while the British representative exercised the power.' There had been little formal change in the pattern of government since 1925, when the Protectorate Council had been abolished and Executive and Legislative Councils set up. These were, of course, composed mainly of British officials, and of the six unofficials three were Arabs, two Indians and one European. The first African was appointed in 1946 and a second added in 1947. There appeared to be little need for change and little demand for it. But during the 1950's the first signs of political unrest appeared.

Political parties and constitutional development

Political parties developed along racial lines, the Arab Association, the Indian and Muslim Associations (representing Hindu and Muslim groups respectively), and the Shirazi Association which included Africans claiming descent from early immigrants from Persia. Other Africans joined the African Association. These groups emerged in the early 1950s, the Arabs demanding elections to the Legislative Council while the Africans wanted more local people trained for the civil service. In March 1954 the Resident, Sir John Rankin, proposed that the racial composition of Legislative Council should be fixed at four Arabs, four Africans, three Asians and one European. The Arabs at first accepted these ideas but then stepped up their demands. They now wanted common roll elections based on 'one man one vote', a ministerial system and a majority of unofficials on the legislature. When these were not granted they withdrew from all part in government.

In 1955 the new Resident, H. S. Potter, announced further constitutional changes. The Sultan was to be advised by a Privy Council, and the Executive Council would be expanded to include three unofficial members, African, Asian and Arab, each of whom would take a special interest in a particular government department. This was intended to prepare for a full ministerial system. The Legislative Council was to have twelve unofficials and thirteen officials. Walter Coutts was asked to visit Zanzibar and recommend the best method of electing the unofficials. He suggested that six seats should be chosen on the basis of common roll elections, with a limited franchise. The other six would continue to be nominated. Preparations went ahead for elections in 1957, and the Arabs agreed to drop their boycott.

Elections and responsible government

In order to contest the elections there was a certain reorganisation among the racial groups mentioned above. In 1955 the Zanzibar Nationalist Party (Z.N.P.) had been formed, led by the more progressive Arabs who were radical in outlook and in touch with Arab and Pan-African movements elsewhere on the continent. By 1957 they were well organised and the dominant party on the island, although strongly racialist in their membership. Their chief rival was the Afro-Shirazi Party, formed in 1957, suspected by the Z.N.P. of being Government supported, but led by Sheikh Abeid Karume. Racial tension rose during the election campaign and there were several violent clashes. The outcome was victory for the A.S.P. with 60% of the vote, only 21% going to the Z.N.P. Following the election African and Asian communities continued to be hostile to each other. An attempt at reconciliation between the parties led to the setting up of a joint Freedom Committee, which drew up a programme for the attainment of independence, but the co-operation did not last long.

Further Government measures were announced in 1959 to make the Legislative and Executive Councils more representative. Both party leaders, Ali Muhsin and Karume, were demanding rapid advance to self-government. In 1960 Sir Hilary Blood was appointed Constitutional Commissioner, with the task of recommending the next stage in political development after consulting local leaders. All presented their views, including the newly formed Zanzibar and Pemba People's Party which had broken away from the A.S.P. and contained 'Shirazi' Africans and many from Pemba. Its leader was Sheikh Mohammed Shamte. Sir Hilary proposed that the numbers of officials on both Executive and Legislative Councils should be reduced to three and that the number of elected members on the latter should be twenty-one, chosen from single member constituencies, with up to five nominated unofficials as well. The Resident's place as chairman should be taken by a Speaker, although the resident would remain as chairman of Executive Council. The leader of the majority party in the legislature would then become Chief Minister. This would advance Zanzibar to the stage of responsible government. An additional seat was added for Zanzibar town, making the total twenty-two.

The first elections in 1961 resulted in deadlock. The A.S.P. won ten seats, Z.N.P. nine and the Z.P.P.P. three. The latter split and joined the other two, so that both had eleven seats. Further elections had to be held and in the run up to these sixty-eight people died in the violence and many were injured. A state of emergency was declared and troops had to be flown over from the mainland. In the second election A.S.P. and Z.N.P. both won ten seats, and the Z.P.P.P. three. On the assumption that a coalition between Z.N.P. and Z.P.P.P. was more likely the Resident called upon Ali Muhsin to form a government. It was agreed that Mohammed Shamte should become Chief Minister, while Ali Muhsin would become Minister of Education. The A.S.P. decided to boycott all government activities for a month.

The attainment of independence and the revolution

In the conference called to plan the final stage to independence the A.S.P. demanded further elections but the Z.N.P. and Z.P.P.P. refused, considering that this would only cause further bloodshed, violence and delay. Perhaps of more significance was their reluctance to risk losing power themselves. In June 1963 full internal self-government was achieved and final elections took place the following month to contest the thirty-one elected seats on the enlarged National Assembly. The A.S.P. won thirteen, Z.N.P. twelve, and Z.P.P.P. six. Thus although the A.S.P. was the largest single party in the Assembly the coalition of Z.N.P. and Z.P.P.P. continued in power. African bitterness and resentment was further increased by this. In December the British handed over power to this coalition govern-

ment, under the sovereignty of the Sultan. But to the African population this was no more than 'Uhuru ya Waarabu', Arab Independence, and seemed to perpetuate the age-old dominance of Arabs over the coastal people.

On the morning of January 12, 1964 a surprise attack took the new government and the Sultan completely by surprise. A small group of well-armed men led by John Okello had captured the Police armoury at Ziwani, then the radio station and other government focal points. The Sultan escaped in his yacht to Mombasa but many members of the Shamte Government were taken prisoner or killed. Okello himself came from Lango in Uganda and had come to Zanzibar in 1959, becoming secretary of the A.S.P. Youth Wing in Pemba two years later. He became involved in the underground movement planning the revolution and played an important part in carrying it out. But political leadership now passed to Karume and his A.S.P. comrades, aided by Abdulrahman Babu's U.M.M.A. group. They set up a Revolutionary Council to govern the new Republic. Before long negotiations had started with President Nyerere of Tanganyika and on April 22 the union of the two

Fig. 19.5 President Nyerere and Vice President Kawawa.

Fig. 19.6 Abeid Karume.

169

states under the new name of the Republic of Tanzania was proclaimed. Nyerere became its President, while Karume and Kawawa were to be First and Second Vice Presidents respectively.

The attainment of independence in Rwanda/Urundi

The handing over of power

So long as the Belgian authorities continued to rely on the Tutsi monarchies the old caste system and social divisions remained, with the Hutu majority being kept out of any share in administration. Until the 1950s this policy remained unchanged; the Belgians did not consider that the time had yet come for a move towards representative and responsible government. Why then did they change so abruptly and suddenly in the mid-1950s? The answer is probably to be found in the post-war events. Pressure from the newly formed United Nations Organisation and their own decline had forced both Britain and France into the realisation that they would have to relinquish their overseas colonies. They began to make preparations for the transfer of power to locally elected governments. At the same time nationalist movements were becoming increasingly effective in East and West Africa, with the emergence of political parties and popular leaders. However much the Belgians might try to ignore these factors they could not hope to isolate the Congo or Rwanda-Urundi from them. The attainment of independence by Ghana in 1957, the historic visit of De Gaulle to Brazzaville in 1958 and the All Africa Conference at Accra in the same year prompted the first demands for self-government in the Congo. And so it was that Belgian colonial policy switched suddenly, and with little or no preparation, to the handing over of power. They had been under considerable pressure from visiting United Nations missions to introduce reforms in Rwanda-Urundi. In 1956 the first elections had been held, to set up advisory councils in the capital, Usumbura. As Belgian plans for democratically elected governments became clear so the tribal divisions and resentments intensified. The Hutu would obviously be able to win a majority of seats on the new councils, while the Tutsi saw themselves as betrayed and deserted, even though many of them were aware of the need for change and cooperation. As early as 1953 Mwami Mutara had abolished the traditional 'ubuhake' system, so

that the Hutu were able to become cattle owners. But the divisions and resentments went so deep and were so embedded in history that it was hard to see how anyone could prevent political rivalry from erupting into tribal violence. Thus the announcement by the Belgians in November 1959 of plans for independence in Rwanda-Urundi was followed by the first fore-taste of civil war.

A visiting United Nations mission in 1960 urged that Rwanda-Urundi should remain united when independence was granted. But this was decisively rejected by the people in the first national elections held the following year. Already separate political parties had been formed in each kingdom, none of which was willing to give up the prospect of attaining power. The Tutsi who had hitherto taken political authority for granted were now faced with the need to appeal to a largely hostile electorate for support. In Rwanda they formed the National Rwanda Society (U.N.A.R.) which opposed the granting of independence on a fully democratic basis. In order to counter the sympathy and support shown by the Belgian administration and church leaders for their Hutu rivals they sent a delegation to the United Nations. Here they succeeded in winning the sympathy of a number of nations, especially those more critical of Belgian colonial policy. In Urundi (shortly to become Burundi) the tribal tensions were not as acute, as the Tutsi-controlled U.P.R.O.N.A. Party, led by the Mwami's son, Louis Rwagasori, had some Hutu supporters. It was based on Usumbura. The rivals to these largely Tutsi organisations were, in Rwanda, Parmehutu (the Democratic Republican Party) led by Gregoire Kayibanda, a former inspector of schools and editor of a Catholic newspaper, and in Urundi the Parti Democrate Chretien (P.D.C.) led by Ntindereza, son of the powerful chief Baranyanka.

The obvious preference for the Hutu parties shown by the Belgians did nothing to ease the tribal tension that built up in the months before independence. This was a particularly difficult time for the Mwamis of both kingdoms and their families who, after years of support and encouragement by the Belgian administration, now suddenly found themselves discarded and threatened. The death of Mwami Mutara of Rwanda in July 1959 and the accession of the young and inexperienced Kigeri V (who shortly afterwards was deposed and went into exile) helped to provoke the conflict that broke out in the same year, leading to heavy loss of life, destruction of property and the flight of many Tutsi refugees into neighbouring territories. This sealed

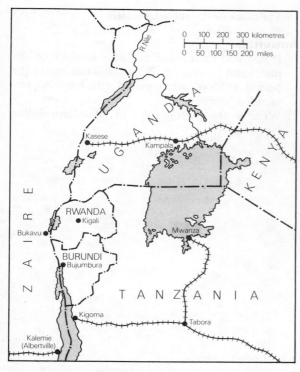

Map 45 Rwanda and Burundi today

Fig. 19.7 President Gregoire Kayibanda.

the fate of the monarchy in Rwanda. In 1961 the people voted for a republic and Kayibanda was duly elected President. In Burundi the monarchy survived, with limited powers, for a few years until the deposition of Ntare V in 1966 and his subsequent death on return from exile in 1972.

Both countries became independent on July 1st, 1962 after a brief transitional period of internal self-government. The capital of Burundi was renamed Bujumbura, while Rwanda's capital remained Kigali. A customs and economic union between them lasted until 1964. Both remain largely dependant on agriculture for their revenue and livelihood, coffee being the principal export. Attempts have been made to make up for the lack of trained and educated manpower, a problem shared by the Congo (Zaire). But educational progress and economic development have alike been hampered by the continuing unrest and upheaval in both states. Both have suffered further periods of violence and tribal fighting since independence, the most recent being the bloodshed in Burundi in 1972 (in which Ntare V was killed). Large numbers of Tutsi have either died or fled into exile. Following the overthrow of the monarchies both states are

now republics ruled by Presidents through one-party systems. Kayibanda, having assumed office in 1962, was re-elected in 1965 and 1969, Parmehutu winning all the seats in the Rwanda National Assembly. Following the deposition of the king in 1966 General Micombero Michel assumed office as President of Burundi and rules with the aid of his Cabinet through the U.P.R.O.N.A. party structure. For purposes of local government Burundi was divided into eight provinces under military governors, while Rwanda has ten Prefectures.

Thus the withdrawal of colonial power has brought fundamental changes to these two states. The dominance of the Tutsi aristocracy has ended and with it the monarchies that founded and established the kingdoms of Rwanda and Rundi. But the new Hutu leaders are faced with even greater social and economic challenges if their two nations are to survive as independent units in twentieth century Africa.

Questions

1. Why is 1945 considered to be an important turning point in the development of African nationalism?
2. What were the reasons that led Tanganyika to achieve independence before the other East African states?
3. Describe how first responsible government and

171

then self-government were brought about in Tanganyika between 1958 and 1960.

4. What internal problems did Zanzibar face in the change from colonial rule to self-government?
5. What do you think the inhabitants of East Africa gained and what did they lose by being under British rule?
6. Describe the main problems that had to be overcome in the attainment of independence in Tanzania or Rwanda-Urundi.

Activities

1. If you had been asked to find a solution to the racial and political problems of Zanzibar in the period 1950–60 what would you have recommended?
2. Write a short biography of Mwalimu Julius Nyerere.

Chapter 20
The struggle for Independence in Uganda and Kenya, 1945–1963

Introduction

For many years the British authorities in Uganda did not face the challenge of African nationalist movements that confronted the Governments of Kenya and Tanganyika. There were a number of reasons for this. In the first place Uganda had never been a settled colony like Kenya, so that popular African grievances such as those involving settlers over land and labour did not exist. Secondly, the existence of recognised and established authorities in the kingdoms gave Africans in those areas the political and administrative openings that they required. For most Africans these local authorities were their own governments and they felt little need for any other form of government. Political groups such as the Bataka in Buganda existed within these kingdoms, their interests and concerns being largely confined to local affairs. Thus there was little sign before the 1950s of any truly national movement.

Political reform and change in Uganda

The 1949 riots and some early reforms

In 1949 the grievances of the cotton growers once again led to violence. As in the 1945 disturbances the main cause of dissatisfaction was over the way the sale and marketing of cotton was handled by the Government, the growers being paid a fixed price over which they had no control. The African Farmers Union was supported by the Bataka Party, a movement of young educated Baganda who wanted to make their government more representative. They added their own demands to those of the farmers: that chiefs be elected by their own people, that the Lukiko should have sixty elected members, and that the present Buganda Ministers

should resign. They also resented and feared the newly established East Africa High Commission.

Thus the riots were aimed at both the Buganda and the Protectorate Governments. The leaders were arrested and imprisoned. The authorities did not consider their complaints were justified. The Governor, Sir John Hall, believed that his predecessor had allowed too much freedom in Buganda, and therefore reinforced the old policy of closer supervision. But he did not realise that there were new forces at work that would make the reliance on traditional chiefs irrelevant. As far as central government was concerned the Baganda authorities had finally, after much persuasion and reassurance, agreed to nominate a representative to the Legislative Council. Two other Africans were also appointed in 1945, from Eastern and Western provinces. When the Governor proposed to increase African representation to eight in 1949, including two from Buganda, the fears and suspicions of the Lukiko were aroused once again. They refused to comply, so that in the end the Kabaka had to nominate both. In 1952 a new Governor, Sir Andrew Cohen, was appointed. He was a man with radical and dynamic views, and was determined to accelerate the reforms started by his predecessor. In 1953 he planned a further expansion of Legislative Council with twenty-eight on each side, both official and unofficial. Fourteen of the latter were to be African, three of them from Buganda. Then there were to be eleven unofficial 'cross bench' members, who were to be free to vote for either side except where a major issue was at stake. To correspond with these changes at the centre reforms in local government were also introduced, with elected councils in each district outside Buganda. As a result of consultations between the Governor and Kabaka similar changes were applied within Buganda. The Kabaka's Government was to take control of primary and junior secondary schools, rural health services, agricultural and veterinary services. The Kabaka was to appoint three more Ministers to his government and the Lukiko was to approve all such ministerial appointments in future. To make it more democratic, the Lukiko was to have sixty of its eighty-nine members elected.

The deportation of the Kabaka and the 1955 Buganda Agreement

Although Sir Andrew Cohen had managed to persuade the Kabaka and Lukiko to accept these reforms it was an uneasy compromise. It was not long before fresh sources of disagreement emerged. The Baganda leaders condemned and discouraged support for the Uganda National Congress, the first truly national movement in Uganda, formed in 1952 by Ignatius Musazi. Cohen's suggestion for a further increase in the size of Legislative Council alarmed them still further. But the immediate cause of the crisis that broke out in 1953 was a casual reference to the possibility of an East African Federation in a speech made by the Colonial Secretary, Oliver Lyttelton, in London. This caused uproar among African leaders in East Africa, and particularly in Buganda. Such remarks, coming shortly after the formation of the Central African Federation, created very genuine fears.

The Kabaka and Lukiko retaliated by demanding that Buganda be handed back to the Foreign Office, with the object of achieving independence separately from the rest of the Protectorate. In spite of an assurance that the issue of federation would not be raised so long as local opinion was against it the Kabaka and his Ministers would not withdraw their demand for secession. Complete deadlock was reached, and finally the Governor withdrew British recognition for the Kabaka as ruler of Buganda, and on November 30th had him flown to exile in Britain. This action had the opposite effect to that intended. It made the Kabaka a hero in the eyes of his people, and united Buganda opinion solidly behind the demand for his return. But neither side would give way, so that finally it was agreed that a mediator, Sir Keith Hancock, a constitutional historian, should discuss possible alternative solutions with both the Buganda and Protectorate Governments. After months of negotiation a solution was found and an Agreement was signed which modified and replaced the 1900 Buganda Agreement. The Kabaka was to become a constitutional monarch, in other words he should in future govern through and with the consent of his Ministers. The Ministers were to be appointed by the Lukiko and approved by the Governor. The Lukiko itself was to have a majority of its members elected by the 'Saza' or County Councils. Buganda would remain within the Protectorate and would send representatives to the Legislative Council. For their part the British promised that federation would not be imposed on the people of East Africa without their consent, and they agreed to allow the return of the Kabaka. Mutesa II came back in October 1955 and was received with acclamation.

The development of political parties and the first elections

In 1952, as mentioned above, the Uganda National Congress was formed by Ignatius Musazi, a former leader of the Farmers' Union. He called for all Uganda people to unite and strive for independence together. The Congress stressed that the future of Uganda must be in African hands, although like T.A.N.U. it followed a non-racial policy. From the start it faced strong hostility from the Buganda authorities, who saw it as an attempt to undermine the influence of the kingdoms. Only when it campaigned for the Kabaka's return from exile did it win much sympathy within Buganda. Nevertheless it was the first truly national African political party.

In 1956 Matayo Mugwanya formed the Democratic Party in Buganda, with a largely Catholic following. Two years later Benedicto Kiwanuka took over the leadership and made efforts to increase and widen the membership to make it a truly national movement. Like the U.N.C. the D.P. aimed at independence for the whole Protectorate and openly opposed Buganda's isolationist tendency. It was not long before these parties had their first opportunity to test their strength. Elections were planned for 1958. The vote was to be given to adult men and women who either owned property worth £400 or had an annual income of £100.

However, Buganda and Bugisu decided to boycott the elections altogether, while Ankole preferred to choose its representatives indirectly. There was obviously strong resistance to democratic ideas and methods among many of the leaders in the kingdoms. In the event elections took place in only ten of the eighteen constituencies. U.N.C. won four seats, D.P. one and Independent candidates four. Following the election several U.N.C. and Independent members combined to form the Uganda People's Congress, a largely non-Buganda group including the member for Lango, Milton Obote. It was a reaction to the pride and assertiveness of the Baganda and united all the anti-Baganda feeling in the Protectorate. It grew in strength at the expense of the U.N.C., now severely weakened and shortly to disappear from active politics.

The Wild Report of 1959 and the 1961 election

A constitutional committee under the chairmanship of Mr J. V. Wild was set up in November 1958 to draw up plans for the next elections in 1961. The committee was asked to bear in mind the need for 'reserved seats' for minorities. The Lukiko refused to participate but other political groups were represented. Direct elections on a common roll were recommended for the whole country, based on universal suffrage or 'one man one vote', with an enlarged Council, but no reserved seats. It was suggested that the party that won the election should form a government.

Before the election was held the question of the future status and position of the kingdoms within a self-governing Uganda was raised. The rulers asked for the postponement of the election until this had been settled. This was refused and Buganda's Lukiko then announced it would not take part in the election. Meanwhile in 1960 the U.P.U. and Obote's group merged to form the Uganda People's Congress, pledged to unite the country and lead the fight for independence. In the election, however, the D.P. won forty-three seats, U.P.C. thirty-five, the U.N.C. only one, and Independents two. The D.P.'s advantage lay in Buganda where it was the only major party, the Lukiko having taken no part. Kiwanuka was then invited to form a government and become the country's first Chief Minister, while Obote and the U.P.C. formed the official Opposition.

The Munster Report and the attainment of independence

The anxiety shown by the kingdoms led to the appointment of a special committee to consider the future relationship of these authorities to the government of independent Uganda. It was presided over by the Earl of Munster, and issued its report in July 1961. It recommended that Buganda should remain part of Uganda but in a federal relationship with the central government. Representatives, whether directly or indirectly elected, would be sent from Buganda to the National Assembly. The relationship with the other three kingdoms was to be semi-federal. Elsewhere in the country the central government would have direct

control. This report, reflecting much that was in the original 1900 Buganda Agreement, became the basis of the new constitution. This was confirmed at a constitutional conference in London in September 1961. Buganda was not only to be able to choose her own way of selecting her twenty-one representatives for the National Assembly but was to have control over her own internal security, judiciary, education, health, veterinary and agricultural services. Uganda's National Assembly was to consist of eighty-two members, and nine others specially elected by the National Assembly. A two-thirds majority would be required for any constitutional amendment, while no kingdom's constitution was to be altered without its own consent. A Cabinet of Ministers, headed by a Prime Minister, would form the executive and would be answerable to the National Assembly.

Self government was achieved on March 1st 1962, and Kiwanuka became the first Prime Minister of Uganda. But there was still one more election to come before full independence. The two national parties, the D.P. and U.P.C. were joined by a third, the Kabaka Yekka or 'King Alone', which stood for the traditional authority and influence of the Kabaka within Buganda. It aimed at destroying the D.P.'s influence in Buganda, and formed an alliance with the U.P.C. Between them they won a clear majority of seats in the National Assembly, so that it was Obote, not Kiwanuka, who led Uganda into Independence on October 9th, 1962. The following year Kabaka Mutesa II was installed as Uganda's first President.

Political unrest and constitutional development in Kenya

In 1944 Sir Philip Mitchell had been appointed Governor of Kenya. He aimed at building a multi-racial society in Kenya, in which all races would eventually participate on equal terms. But he saw this as a long-term prospect, one that would take many years to achieve. Meanwhile he expected the European community to continue to play a leading role. This was reassuring for the settlers, who looked upon Kenya as their home and were determined to maintain their dominant position. The war had given a considerable boost to the production of cash crops so that the post-war years

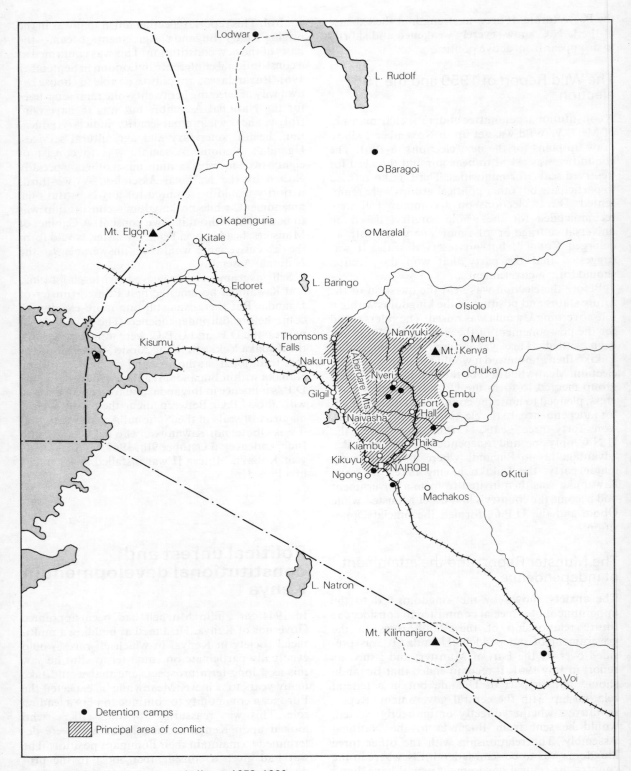

Lodwar
L. Rudolf
Baragoi
Maralal
Kapenguria
Mt. Elgon ▲
Kitale
Isiolo
L. Baringo
Eldoret
Nanyuki
Meru
Thomsons Falls
Mt. Kenya ▲
Kisumu
Nakuru
Nyeri
Chuka
Aberdare Mts.
Gilgil
Embu
Fort Hall
Naivasha
Kiambu
Thika
Kikuyu
NAIROBI
Kitui
Ngong
Machakos
L. Natron
Mt. Kilimanjaro ▲
Voi

● Detention camps

▨ Principal area of conflict

Map 46 The Mau Mau emergency in Kenya, 1952–1960

were a time of growing prosperity for the settlers. African farmers, on the other hand, continued to suffer many disadvantages in the marketing of their crops, while the restrictions imposed on the growing of cash crops within the Reserves made them even more dependant on employment in the towns or on European farms. Nairobi and Mombasa were expanding rapidly, but work was not always easy to find, while wages were low and housing inadequate.

It was at this time and because of these conditions that the Trade Union movement began to grow. The first major industrial strike occurred in Mombasa in 1947. The situation was made more critical by the return of soldiers from the war. They were soon embittered by what they found, the contrast between the prosperity of the Europeans and Asians and the poverty of most Africans.

K.A.U. and the return of Kenyatta

In October 1944 the Kenya African Union had been formed, the first national movement among Africans. Its primary aim was to set up a country-wide organisation through which Eliud Mathu, the newly appointed member of Legislative Council, could consult local opinion. Harry Thuku was the first chairman, but handed over the leadership to James Gichuru in 1945. The following year Jomo Kenyatta returned to Kenya, having been in Britain for fifteen years. Throughout this period he had kept in touch with local leaders and their activities so that he was soon accepted as the obvious leader, and in 1947 was elected President of K.A.U. In the same year he took over the Githunguri Training College and started to consolidate the independent schools movement in Central Province. Kenyatta realised the need for a strong national party, backed by popular support, throughout the country. But even though Africans from other tribes occupied a number of important posts within K.A.U. it remained a predominantly Kikuyu movement, and failed to make much headway outside Central Province.

Among the problems facing Kenyatta and his followers were the open hostility of the European community towards his political activities, amounting at one point to a demand for his deportation, and the difficulty of arousing political consciousness among the masses, many of whom were illiterate. For those who could read there were several newspapers expressing African opinions: *Sauti ya Mwafrika* (K.A.U.'s own paper), the *Nyanza Times, Mumenyeri* and the Coast *African Express*.

Constitutional developments, 1945–1948

In 1946 a second African, B. A. Ohanga, was appointed to Legislative Council, and in 1948 the total was raised to four. By 1948 the unofficials on that body outnumbered the officials. The eleven European and five Asian members were elected by their own communities, while the four Africans and two Arabs were appointed by the Governor. At this time the Governor introduced the membership system, whereby certain members of the Executive Council were given responsibility for particular government departments. This marked a step towards the Ministerial system.

The British Government's colonial policy at this time, as was briefly noted at the beginning of Chapter 19, was the gradual advance towards self-government along carefully planned lines. It was left to the Governor of each individual territory to decide how best to implement this programme, and some moved faster than others. But few had yet begun to think in terms of independence and least of all the authorities in Kenya. Thus the demands of the African leaders were turned down, while it was pointed out to them that Africans would still require the guidance and protection of the colonial authority for some time. The Government feared that rapid political change would only lead to chaos; little did they realise that chaos would shortly come as the result of moving too slowly.

Mau Mau and the emergency

By 1950 extremists among the African leaders were becoming impatient at the slow progress of constitutional change. It was obvious that the settlers had much to do with this. In 1950 a prominent settler announced, 'We are here to stay and the other races must accept that fact with all that it implies.' But African nationalists were not prepared to accept it. In 1951 K.A.U. asked for greater African representation on Legislative Council and there were even calls for direct elections on a common roll. One party member, Fred Kubai, demanded independence within three years. Tension between the races increased and the Government proposed a conference in 1953 to discuss these matters.

However, events were moving fast in another direction. Since 1946 a group of extremists within K.A.U. including a number of ex-soldiers had formed an underground movement in the Nairobi

Fig. 20.2 Mau Mau detainees in a camp.

Fig. 20.3 'General China' in court just after he had been sentenced to death.

Fig. 20.4 An extract from a newspaper of the time.

area. They made plans for direct action, using the traditional oathing practices to extend their organisation and maintain secrecy. They were prepared to use violence to achieve their ends, while moderates in K.A.U. like Mbotela were not. Many others decided to go along with the Freedom Fighters, who also called themselves the Kenya Land Freedom Army. But the name by which they became best known was Mau Mau. By 1950 acts of violence had roused the fears of the settlers, who called for Government action. In 1951 Mau Mau was declared an unlawful society. Its leaders moved into the forests, chiefly in the Aberdare and Mount Kenya areas, and continued their activities. In October 1952 Senior Chief Waruhiu was murdered for his loyalty to the Government. The gravity of the situation was at last realised and the new Governor, Sir Evelyn Baring, declared a state of emergency. Kenyatta and many other K.A.U. leaders were arrested, charged with organising and supporting the wave of violence. The armed forces were brought into action and reinforcements flown out from Britain.

In April 1953 Kenyatta and his colleagues were tried at Kapenguria and convicted, being sentenced to seven years imprisonment at Lodwar, near Lake Rudolf. In June 1953 K.A.U. was banned. But for four years fighting continued and many lives were lost. Mass arrests of Kikuyu were carried out and all suspects were herded into protected villages and their movements controlled. (See Map 46.) By 1956 the resistance of the Mau Mau fighters was broken. Many of their leaders, including Waruhiu Itote, known as 'General China', and Dedan Kimathi, had been captured, while disagreements among their groups had further weakened their cause. The emergency was not finally lifted until 1960.

It had been a costly war. The approximate numbers of lives lost included fifty-eight Europeans and Asians, two thousand Kikuyu civilians, and one thousand Government troops; while the Freedom Fighters are believed to have lost about ten thousand men. Life was made both difficult and dangerous for those living in Central Province where most of the fighting took place. The numerous emergency regulations were an added inconvenience, particularly for those living in Nairobi or Central Province. It had been a costly operation for the British Government in terms of manpower and resources. They also felt the criticism of those who had always opposed colonialism. The effect, therefore, was to accelerate the pace of change, or as Professor Ogot puts it, 'The shock of Mau Mau had created the right atmosphere in that the Imperial Power was now willing to talk with the African leaders.'

The Lyttlelton and Lennox-Boyd proposals

As a result of the visit of the Colonial Secretary, Oliver Lyttlelton, in 1954, further constitutional reforms were introduced. The object was still to produce a multi-racial form of government, and as a step in this direction a Council of Ministers containing six unofficial Ministers in addition to the official members was set up. Among the unofficials was the first African to hold a Ministerial post, B. A. Ohanga. There were criticisms of the 'Lyttlelton' constitution from both sides. Extreme Europeans led by Gp. Capt. Briggs would not accept multi-racial government on any conditions, while among many Africans was the feeling that it simply perpetuated European domination.

In 1955 the ban on African political organisations was lifted to permit them to function at a local level. At the same time plans were made for elections and voting qualifications for Africans. The vote was restricted to those with certain income, property or educational qualifications, with additional votes for those who satisfied more than one of these conditions. In March 1957 the first African elections were held, in eight constituencies. The newly elected members demanded fifteen more seats and common roll elections based on universal franchise. They refused to accept Ministerial appointments until these demands were met.

The new Colonial Secretary, Allan Lennox-Boyd, made fresh proposals in 1958, including six additional African seats and twelve Specially Elected Members, four from each racial group, who would be chosen by the Legislative Council itself. Although rejected by the Africans these were put into effect. The demands of the African politicians were now becoming more far-reaching, and this was due largely to two very able leaders, Tom Mboya and Oginga Odinga. Mboya had first shown his talent and skill when he became Secretary General of the Kenya Federation of Labour in 1953. Under his leadership the K.F.L. had done much for the rights and welfare of African workers, particularly at a time when they had no political organisation to defend their interests. Mboya had also established useful links overseas in the Labour movement and in the U.S.A. Odinga was of an older generation but he too had done much to encourage a national spirit among Africans, and in 1958 came out boldly with a call for Kenyatta's release from detention. It was this timely action of Odinga's that was largely responsible for Kenyatta's return to prominence as the undisputed leader and centre of negotiations.

Political parties and policies

Although divided by the Lyttleton reforms into two camps, the Europeans continued to take an active interest in events throughout the 1950s. It was not until after the famous 'Wind of Change' speech made by the British Prime Minister, MacMillan, while on a tour of African countries in 1960, that the settlers realised that Kenya was no longer to remain a White Man's country. In 1959 Michael Blundell resigned as Minister of Agriculture to form the New Kenya Group, an attempt at a multi-racial party. But no elected African members joined him, partly because he failed to support their demands for a common electoral roll and the opening up of the White Highlands to all races. The more extreme Europeans formed the United Party, led by Briggs. They called for the abolition of Legislative Council and its replacement by a series of Regional Assemblies, one of which would cover the area of the White Highlands and would be reserved for them.

African political groups had been small and lacking in unity, partly because of Government regulations, and partly because of Kenyatta's absence in detention. But after the constitutional conference in London in 1960 two parties were formed; the Kenya African National Union (K.A.N.U.) and the Kenya African Democratic Union (K.A.D.U.). Both aimed at uniting the country in the final campaign for independence, but were divided over the form of constitution that they wanted. Gichuru, Odinga and Mboya were among the leaders of K.A.N.U. at its formation. They represented between them the two largest ethnic groups in the country, the Kikuyu and the Luo. They wanted a strong unitary constitution to bind the country together. K.A.D.U. on the other hand, led by Ngala, Muliro and Moi, feared domination by the Kikuyu-Luo group and wanted a federal form of constitution that would protect the interests of the smaller tribes. Thus rivalry between the two African parties assumed tribal proportions, although even within the parties there were clashes between tribes and personalities. Undoubtedly these divisions and differences delayed constitutional progress in Kenya.

The constitutional conferences, 1960 and 1962

We have seen how Kenya's constitution was affected by the proposals of two Colonial Secretaries in the 1950s; and two more were to play a crucial part in the final stages. In 1960 Ian Macleod called a Conference in London, attended by all members of the Legislative Council. This was the last occasion at which European and Asian groups were represented and tried to safeguard their own particular interests. But much the most important part was played by the African group with its demands for responsible government and for the release of Jomo Kenyatta. To the Africans Kenyatta was now their accepted leader and indispensable to their cause. To the Europeans he represented a threat to security and a barrier to any further agreement. Macleod's solution had to balance all these views and find a compromise acceptable to the majority. He announced that the legislature would consist of fifty-three elected members and twelve National members (chosen by the elected members). Twenty of the elected seats were reserved for the minority races. The new Council of Ministers was to have four Africans, three Europeans and an Asian. The Highlands were to be open to all races.

Fig. 20.5 Jomo Kenyatta arrives in London (November 1961) to ask for an immediate constitutional conference. He is met by Tom Mboya.

If these proposals were to lead rapidly to self-government it was vital for the African leaders to work together. But shortly after the formation of K.A.N.U. fears of tribal dominance led to the formation of K.A.D.U. Rivalry between them increased as the 1961 elections approached. Nineteen of the open seats were won by K.A.N.U. and eleven by K.A.D.U. But K.A.N.U. refused to form a government without Kenyatta, a demand that brought a sharp reaction from the extreme settler group, now led by Cavendish-Bentinck. The outcome was a coalition government between K.A.D.U. and Blundell's group, with Ngala as Leader of Government Business in Legislative Council. Kenyatta was eventually released in August 1961, but the hopes that he would be able to unite the two African parties were not to be. He decided to become the leader of K.A.N.U., and in this capacity led his party to the second constitutional conference in London the following year.

This conference, presided over by Reginald Maudling as Colonial Secretary, was intended to work out the final steps to independence and the form of constitution that Kenya was to have. K.A.D.U.'s plan was for 'Majimbo', or a federation of regions each with specific powers. K.A.N.U. pressed for strong unitary government. The outcome was a federal form of constitution, with six regions each retaining considerable powers. The central government was to consist of a two chamber National Assembly with a Prime Minister and Cabinet formed from the party with a majority of seats. Careful safeguards were inserted to protect the regional assemblies and their powers, and the interests of the minorities. But a number of details were left to be decided upon by the K.A.D.U./K.A.N.U. coalition government that was to be formed. Already there were threats of secession from the coast Arabs living within the 16 kilometre (10 mile) strip that Britain had leased from the Sultan of Zanzibar, as well as from the Somalis in the Northern Frontier district. K.A.N.U. had only accepted the new constitutional

In the midst of joy comes a call to build the nation

'UHURU NA KAZI' SAYS PREMIER
Pledge to the future by stadium crowd

KENYA yesterday celebrated its first day as a free and sovereign State. The formal ceremony conferring Independence took place at the Uhuru Stadium in Nairobi in the morning when the Duke of Edinburgh handed to Mr. Kenyatta the Statutory Instruments completing the severance of colonial ties.

In a speech after the ceremony, Mr. Kenyatta warned that the people of Kenya must now work hard to give meaning to Independence and renewed his call for nation-building in the spirit of harambee.

The Governor-General, Mr. MacDonald, and the Prime Minister were sworn in, followed by members of the Cabinet. There were no changes in the list of Ministers from those in the self-government administration. It is understood that no appointment as Foreign Minister has so far been made.

As congratulatory messages poured in for Mr. Kenyatta from all over the world, festivities continued throughout Kenya.

Lively scenes in arena

There were lively scenes at the Uhuru Stadium, with more tribal dancing accompanying the Independence ceremony, followed in the afternoon by a Youth Rally attended by the Duke, the Governor-General, the Prime Minister and other Cabinet Ministers.

Last night Mr. Kenyatta was host at a glittering State Ball attended by the Duke, the Governor-General and Mrs. MacDonald and hundreds of other guests including heads of State and notabilities from many lands.

Among the messages of goodwill to the new nation was one last night from the Secretary for Commonwealth Relations, Mr. Duncan Sandys (Report Page 13). Mr. Sandys said that the end of the colonial phase marked the beginning of a new relationship between Britain and

and Angola as examples of places where this situation existed.

"It is our duty to see that we set them free—we should fight in any way, using all means to give them freedom."

A united Africa was import-

Setting the seal on Kenya's Sovereignty, Mr. Kenyatta waves aloft to a cheering crowd the official instruments of Independence which he has just received from the Duke of Edinburgh at the Uhuru Stadium. With them on the platform are the Lord Chief Justice, Sir John Ainley, and Mrs. Kenyatta.

Fig. 20.6 Headlines from the day after Independence.

arrangements reluctantly, and counted on winning sufficient seats in the 1963 elections to be able to change the constitution in its own favour.

1963 election and independence

The period leading up to the elections in May 1963 was not an easy one for the African leaders. Officially Ministers with equal status in a coalition government, both Ngala and Kenyatta were busy preparing their parties for the coming contest. The outcome was a victory for K.A.N.U.:

	House of Reps.	*Senate*
K.A.N.U.	73	18
K.A.D.U.	31	16
A.P.P.	8	–
Indep.	8	2

(*A.P.P. stands for African People's Party.*)

In June 1963 Kenya achieved self-government, 'Madaraka', and Kenyatta became Prime Minister, presiding over a Cabinet of K.A.N.U. Ministers. Ngala and his party formed the Opposition. Then on December 12th that year 'Uhuru' was finally attained, while K.A.N.U.'s strength increased with the addition of various Independents and others. The following year Kenya became a Republic, with Kenyatta as its first President.

Questions

1. Explain the reasons for the delay in the formation of African political movements in Uganda.
2. Why was the Kabaka deported in 1953 and what was the outcome of the negotiations that followed this event?
3. Compare the constitutions drawn up for Uganda and Kenya when they attained independence.
4. Explain the factors that led to the Mau Mau revolt in Kenya; what effect did it have on Kenya's development?
5. Give an account of the life and career of any one East African leader and show how he contributed to his country's achievement of independence.

Activities

1. What do the following initials stand for:
   U.N.C.   U.P.C.   K.A.D.U.   K.F.L.
   D.P.   K.A.U.   A.P.P.   K.Y.
2. In both Kenya and Uganda there were arguments for and against federal forms of government at this time. Discuss the advantages and disadvantages of Federal and Unitary systems of government.

Chapter 21
East Africa since Independence

Introduction

The achievement of independence marked the end of the struggle against colonial rule. The East African states had gained their political freedom, and with it the self-respect and dignity that they had so long striven for. But the end of one stage marked the beginning of the next, that of nation-building. The new leaders needed strong and stable governments if they were to carry out all the social and economic plans they had prepared. The problems they inherited were complex, but with the new vitality and enthusiasm of a free people they faced them with confidence.

The first crisis came in January 1964 when a series of mutinies broke out in the armies of all three mainland states, challenging the authority of the new governments. It has not been established whether there was a link between them, but in each case there were demands for better pay and promotion and the threat of action if the authorities did not give way. However, with the aid of British troops flown out to restore order, the mutinies were quickly contained and security restored. The ringleaders were arrested and brought to trial. The governments were able to turn their attention once again to their long-term plans for development. There were certain changes that could be implemented quickly, while others of necessity took longer. We can perhaps best consider these by looking at constitutional and political changes, economic and social changes, and then at East African unity and foreign affairs.

Long term plans for development

Constitutional and political changes

All three states had inherited constitutions based upon the so-called 'Westminster' pattern. In many ways this was found unsuitable for African people and their ideals. In the first place the practice of having a Head of State (the monarch) separate and distinct from the Head of Government (the Prime Minister), was not in accordance with African traditions. Thus each nation became a Republic within a year of independence, with a President who was also head of the government and leader of the major political party. The situation in Uganda was slightly different, in that the Kabaka became President without these accompanying powers in 1963, but this itself was part of the reason for his eventual downfall three years later.

The trend towards a strong central government also became more noticeable. Both Kenya and Uganda abandoned their federal constitutions and the regional assemblies in Kenya, and the traditional Kingdoms in Uganda, were abolished. It was felt more important to foster unity than to permit local autonomy at this stage in building new nations. This idea was also behind the move towards one-party systems. Within a few years T.A.N.U., U.P.C. and K.A.N.U. had become the dominant political units in their countries. In Tanzania there was in fact only one party from the start of independence, and this was formally confirmed in the constitution. Thus the party and the civil service in Tanzania are virtually one and the same thing, government officials being also party officials. But in Kenya and Uganda the move towards the one-party system has been moulded by events rather than by laws. In Kenya K.A.D.U. voluntarily disbanded itself in 1964 and joined K.A.N.U. In 1966 some of the more radical members of K.A.N.U., led by Odinga, broke away and formed the Kenya Peoples Union, demanding more socialist measures and policies. In 1969, following a disturbance in Kisumu, the party was banned and its leaders put in detention. Kenya has since remained a one-party state. In Uganda Obote's

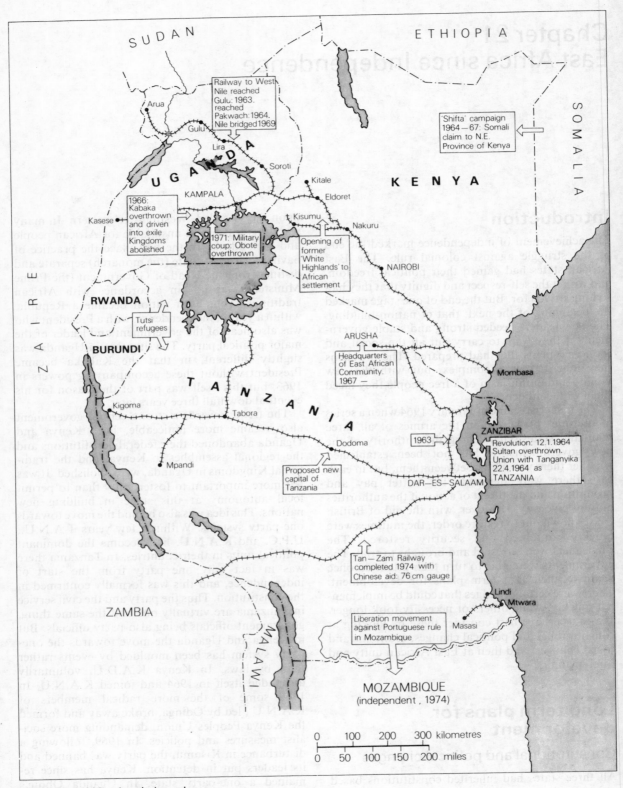

SUDAN

ETHIOPIA

SOMALIA

KENYA

UGANDA

Arua

Gulu

Lira

Soroti

Kitale

Eldoret

KAMPALA

Kasese

Kisumu

Nakuru

NAIROBI

Railway to West
Nile reached
Gulu: 1963.
reached
Pakwach: 1964.
Nile bridged 1969

'Shifta' campaign
1964–67: Somali
claim to N.E.
Province of Kenya

1966:
Kabaka
overthrown
and driven
into exile
Kingdoms
abolished

1971: Military
coup: Obote
overthrown

Opening of
former
'White
Highlands' to
African
settlement

RWANDA

BURUNDI

Tutsi
refugees

ZAIRE

Kigoma

Tabora

TANZANIA

ARUSHA

Headquarters
of East African
Community.
1967 –

Mombasa

Dodoma

1963

ZANZIBAR

Revolution: 12.1.1964
Sultan overthrown.
Union with Tanganyika
22.4.1964 as
TANZANIA

Proposed new
capital of
Tanzania

DAR–ES–SALAAM

Mpandi

ZAMBIA

MALAWI

Tan–Zam Railway
completed 1974 with
Chinese aid: 76 cm gauge

Lindi

Mtwara

Liberation movement
against Portuguese rule
in Mozambique

Masasi

MOZAMBIQUE
(independent, 1974)

0   100   200   300 kilometres
0   50   100   150   200 miles

Map 47 East Africa since Independence

U.P.C. quickly absorbed many of the D.P. and Kabaka Yekka members who 'crossed the floor', thus becoming virtually a one-party state. But there were divisions within the U.P.C. and in 1966 Obote arrested five of his own Ministers and suspended the constitution. This threatened the position of the Kabaka as President of Uganda. When the Lukiko passed a resolution more or less expelling the central government from Buganda the crisis broke into violence. The Kabaka's palace was stormed by armed troops but the Kabaka himself escaped and fled into exile. A new constitution was brought into force, with Obote as President of a unitary state, the kingdoms and their rulers having been abolished.

All three East African states declared their belief in the principles of African socialism, although their methods of expressing it differed. Tanzania's ideas were embodied in The Arusha Declaration of 1967, Kenya's in 'Sessional Paper no. 10 on African Socialism', and Uganda's in The Common Man's Charter of 1970. Of these the Arusha Declaration was perhaps the most explicit and has become the theme of Tanzania's development plans. It stresses in particular:

1. Self-reliance: the need to use local resources wherever possible, and the avoidance of too much reliance on foreign aid.

2. Ujamaa: The building of a socialist society based on the African traditions of 'family-hood' which stressed the participation of each member for the good of all. (Tanzanians, particularly the youth, are therefore called upon to do national service and to sacrifice in the cause of nation building).

3. The removal of all distinctions based upon class, wealth, status, etc. and the recognition of human equality.

4. Control by the people of all major sources and means of production: i.e. nationalisation.

Economic and social development

The spirit and enthusiasm expressed in the ideals of 'Harambee' in Kenya and 'Ujamaa' in Tanzania led to great activity, especially in the rural areas, on projects such as the building of schools, roads and dispensaries. The setting up of National Youth Services also reflected the same purpose of self-help and service to the community. In the fields of business, trade and central and local government an intensive programme of Africanisation was launched, to replace many of the Europeans and Asians in these positions. Special training schemes such as at the Kenya Institute of Administration helped to prepare Africans for greater responsibility. At the

Fig. 21.1 Moshi Airport, Tanzania and an East African Airways plane.

Fig. 21.2 Makerere University, Kampala.

same time it was made clear that the East African states would continue to need professional and technical assistants from overseas for some time. As far as the ownership of industries and business was concerned different attitudes were adopted. Tanzania preferred outright nationalisation, whereas Kenya and Uganda sought to combine both private and state ownership and recognised the need to attract foreign investment. While agriculture remained the main source of income for all three states, there were moves towards greater industrialisation. It was realised that the colonial era had made East Africa's economy too dependent on certain cash crops, and that efforts must be made to diversify their products, by developing new forms of agriculture and alternative sources of income, such as tourism. One of the most important changes in economic growth has been the extension of trade and financial relations with other countries, including Japan, Western Europe and the U.S.A. International agencies such as the United Nations and World Bank have assisted in the granting of loans. Important and costly projects have been planned and financed in conjunction with foreign nations; Chinese participation in the building of the Tanzania-Zambia railway being one example.

As far as social services are concerned, perhaps the most striking advances have been those in education, from the local village primary school to the three universities of Makerere, Nairobi and Dar

es Salaam. Not only have the numbers of those attending schools and colleges increased out of all proportion to those being educated during the colonial period, but much has been done to adapt the content of education to the new needs of nation building. Great sacrifices were made in the setting up of 'Harambee Schools' in Kenya, the result of local enthusiasm and initiative. It was realised that education provided the key to advancement and self-improvement even more than it had done before independence.

The East African community

The hope that independence might bring about closer union between the East African states has not been realised. In the years leading up to independence bodies such as P.A.F.M.E.C.A. (the Pan African Freedom Movement for East and Central Africa) kept the idea alive, and in 1963 the three East African leaders issued a joint statement showing their desire for closer union. But although many of the obstacles to federation had been removed, notably the fear of domination by the Kenya settlers, there was still certain suspicion of Kenya's economic predominance. However it was agreed that a commission should be set up to review the position and suggest ways and means of strengthening links between the states to the mutual advantage of all. Professor Philip was appointed to lead the enquiry in 1965, and his report formed the basis of the Treaty of Economic Cooperation that was signed in June 1967.

This established the East African Community, with its headquarters in Arusha. It took the place of the East African Common Services Organisation and was thus continuing many of the functions and duties of the original East African High Commission. But it was intended that the new organisation should do more than operate the existing common services such as railways, harbours, posts and telegraphs. It was to encourage the development of inter-territorial trade on a common market basis, i.e. the gradual removal of all tariffs and other official restrictions. It was also to attract foreign trade and investment on a much larger scale than could have been achieved by each member state individually. It was hoped that eventually other neighbouring states might join the Community, such as Somalia, Ethiopia and Zambia.

These were the aims. The achievements in the first ten years after independence were not as great. The continuing predominance of Kenya's economy over the other two caused friction and reluctance to lower the barriers to free trade. There have also been growing differences in policy between the three, and this has also hampered the harmonisation of trade and commerce in East Africa. Thirdly, the political upheaval in Uganda following President Obote's fall from power in 1971 has caused the Community to fall apart. However, there is much that remains in common between the three states, and many of the services have continued to operate under the Community, as indicated below.

The services that come under the control of the East African Community are:

Service	Headquarters
E.A. Railways Corporation	Nairobi
E.A. Harbours Corporation	Dar es Salaam
E.A. Post and Telecommunications	Kampala
E.A. Customs and Excise	Mombasa
E.A. Development Bank	Kampala
E.A. Income Tax Dept.	Nairobi
Medical Research Centre	Mwanza
The Amani Institute (scientific research)	Amani, Tanzania
Agriculture, Veterinary and Forestry research	Muguga Kenya
Fisheries Research	Jinja
E.A. Literature Bureau	Nairobi
E.A. Meteorological Dept.	Nairobi
E.A. Civil Aviation Directorate	Nairobi
E.A. Marine Fisheries	Zanzibar
Court of Appeal for East Africa	Nairobi
E.A. Industrial Research	Nairobi
E.A. Tropical Pesticides	Arusha

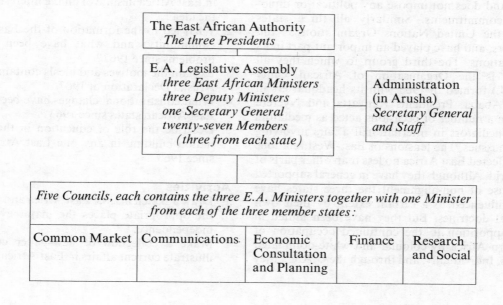

The East African Authority
The three Presidents

E.A. Legislative Assembly
three East African Ministers
three Deputy Ministers
one Secretary General
twenty-seven Members
(three from each state)

Administration
(in Arusha)
Secretary General
and Staff

Five Councils, each contains the three E.A. Ministers together with one Minister from each of the three member states:

Common Market	Communications	Economic Consultation and Planning	Finance	Research and Social

Fig. 21.3 The Tan Zam Railway.

Foreign policies

All three East African states decided to remain within the Commonwealth on attaining independence, although Tanzania made it plain that she would not do so if South Africa remained a member. Commonwealth membership has provided certain financial, economic and technical advantages, and does not impose any political or diplomatic commitments. Similarly all three states joined the United Nations Organisation as full members, and have played an important part in its deliberations. The third group to which they all belong is the Organisation of African Unity (O.A.U.) formed in 1963 with its headquarters in Addis Ababa. Presidents Kenyatta and Nyerere have on a number of occasions acted as mediators and conciliators in international affairs involving African issues. The tensions of East-West relations have affected East Africa no less than other parts of the world. Although they have in general supported the cause of non-alignment the three states have been influenced to a certain extent by their own political doctrines. But they have been united in their opposition to the continued occupation of southern Africa by colonial and white-dominated powers. Individually, and through the O.A.U., they

have given material and moral support to the liberation movements in Mozambique, Angola and Rhodesia.

Questions

1. Why has political federation not been achieved in East Africa in spite of all the interest shown in the idea?
2. What led to the formation of the East African Community; and what have been its main problems since 1967?
3. Explain the motives and ideals contained in The Arusha Declaration of 1967.
4. What constitutional changes have been made in East African states since 1963?
5. Describe the role of education in the work of nation-building in any one East African state since 1963.

Activities

1. Draw a sketch map of East Africa and mark on it the appropriate places the major events since independence.
2. Make a collection of newspaper cuttings to illustrate current affairs in East Africa.

Index